1980

THE BRADFORD BOOK OF COLLECTOR'S PLATES

RAND McNALLY

1980
THE BRADFORD BOOK OF
COLLECTOR'S PLATES

THE OFFICIAL GUIDE TO ALL EDITIONS
TRADED ON THE WORLD'S LARGEST EXCHANGE

EDITED BY

Beverly Amato

Scott Bryant

Harriet Dalaskey

Gerald Eckert

Marianne Fink

Lisa Hill

Patricia Kral

Thomas Legge

Mary Metrow

Livingston Platt

Lynn Pollack

Mary Ryan

Gary Tillery

Paul Traiber

Nancy Wortman

Photographs by Gerald Hoos
Art Direction by Robert Bowman, Richard Hustad

RAND McNALLY

Chicago   New York   San Francisco

THE BRADFORD EXCHANGE
NILES CHICAGO, ILLINOIS 60648

Library of Congress Catalog Card No. 77-77526

ISBN 528-88137-X

ISSN 0161-2794

CONTENTS

INTRODUCTION

BRADEX-LISTED PLATES

OVER-THE-COUNTER PLATES

APPENDIXES

THE WORLD'S MOST TRADED ART

By J. Roderick MacArthur
Director of the Board of Governors
of the Bradford Exchange

Revised, expanded and updated for 1980, this is the fifth edition of what has been considered the "bible" of plate collecting since it first appeared — the *Bradford Book of Collector's Plates*, initially published by McGraw Hill and since by Rand McNally.

If you regard limited-edition collector's plates as an art form like oils, lithographs and etchings, then their vastly expanded market in recent years — estimated at 21,700 transactions per day in 1979 among distributors, dealers and individual collectors around the world — has made them both the art form most widely collected in America and the most traded art in the world.

And this *Bradford Book* is the official directory of this most traded art for North American collectors.

Best estimates at the end of 1979 placed the number of plate collectors in the United States at more than 3,900,000. Included in this figure are an estimated 400,000 who have entered the market in the past year alone. The total number does not include hundreds of thousands more who casually own collector's plates but do not yet think of themselves as "collectors."

As you leaf through the miniature gallery of plate art in this book, you'll find a full-color illustration of every major collector's plate now traded in the American market — from the 1895 Bing & Grøndahl *Christmas* **(14-B.36-1.1)** up to the 1980 first issue in the D'Arceau-Limoges *City of Paris Collection* **(18-D.15-5.1)** pictured on the inside front cover.

J. Roderick MacArthur

This 1980 *Bradford Book* includes 111 new issues, seven new series, and one maker who is newly listed on the Exchange. It provides a comprehensive index to plate makers and sponsors, and another index of series,

GROWTH OF COLLECTOR'S PLATE MARKET FROM 1960 THROUGH 1979

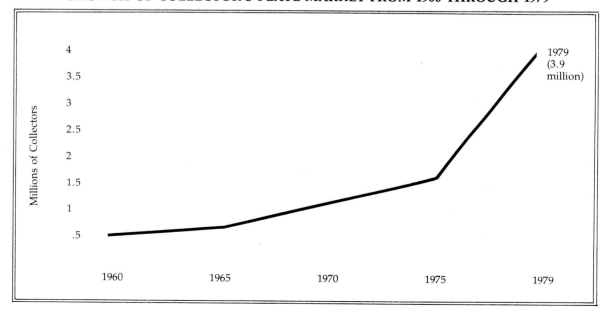

titles and subjects. It contains some new details about makers and expanded information about the artists represented by the plates. Also, for the first time, it includes an appendix of over-the-counter plates; that is, true collector's plates which have been generally available on the market but without sufficient trading activity to merit Bradex listing.

In short, the book is the definitive reference work for the current market in limited-edition collector's plates, a resource book needed more acutely than ever as the number of collectors continues to grow.

The greatest identifiable concentration of collectors — more than 1,000,000 in the United States and 21 other countries — is that served by the Bradford Exchange, the largest trading organization in collector's plates in the world. Last year, transactions on the Exchange totalled 1,461,000 — up 28% from 1978.

The Bradford Museum houses the world's first permanent exhibit of all 1,112 limited-edition plates now listed on the Bradex and valued at more than a quarter million dollars.

OFFICIAL IDENTIFICATION

The Bradford Book is organized to give you the official identification of the maker, artist, edition limit, series, issue price, and year of each of the world's 1,112 most actively traded plates. The indexing by Bradex number permits quick, precise identification. The Bradex number is a plate's code on the Exchange and immediately identifies it by country of origin, maker, series, and plate number. (e.g. "Behind the Frozen Window," the 1895 Bing & Grondahl *Christmas* plate, is identified as **14-B.36-1.1**; or **14**-Denmark, **B.36**-Bing & Grondahl, **1** first series from the maker, **.1** first issue in the series. For a more complete explanation, see page 41).

1895 Bing & Grøndahl *Christmas*
(14-B.36-1.1)
Issue Price: $ .50
Price at January 1, 1980: $4,000.00

Over the past decade, the "hobby" of plate collecting has not only expanded greatly in North America and Europe, but even reached such distant lands as Australia, Japan and South Africa. No other form of art has shown such dramatic market expansion and appreciation.

Stories of huge profits are commonplace. People who bought the Lalique *Annual* **(18-L.3-1.1)** in 1965, for example, or the Goebel *Hummel Annual* **(22-G.54-1.1)** in 1971, or the Rockwell Society *Heritage* **(84-R.70-3.1)** in 1977, have seen their plates rise in value from 934% to

7400%. And scores of other plates have at least doubled in price. Last year the entire Market Bradex, the "Dow-Jones" index of plate prices, hit a new all-time high of 344. (The Market Bradex is a reflection of overall market performance determined by the current quote-price/issue-price ratio of the 12 most significant plate series.)

Back in 1972, when the market in collector's plates was not advancing — was, in fact, experiencing a recession — analysts here at the Exchange reached two conclusions. First, despite the setback, the market was fundamentally strong and growing stronger. Second,

1965 Lalique *Annual*
(18-L.3-1.1)
Issue Price: $25.00
Price at January 1, 1980: $1,850.00

1977 Rockwell Society *Heritage*
(84-R.70-3.1)
Issue Price: $14.50
Price at January 1, 1980: $150.00

1971 Goebel *Hummel Annual*
(22-G.54-1.1)
Issue Price: $25.00
Price at January 1, 1980: $1,000.00

nowhere was there an authoritative directory that collectors could rely on for complete, factual information on the hundreds of plates that were already being traded.

There were a few "guides," but none of them contained straightforward information backed up by facts. Instead, they were filled with descriptions of "lovely" and "priceless" plates and cluttered with "personal favorites" that were rarely actually traded. They gave "current market prices" that were hopelessly out of date even before the book came off the press.

That was when we decided to compile an authoritative book ourselves — the annual *Bradford Book of Collector's Plates* — which finally became the official standard of reference.

NO "PERSONAL FAVORITES"

We laid down some rules: One, there would be no "lovely" plates. The beauty of a plate's design would be in the eye of the collector.

Two, there would be no "priceless" plates. If a plate is traded, it has a price.

Three, there would be no personal favorites. If a plate is a favorite with collectors, that too will be reflected in the market trading, the only true reason for listing.

Finally, there would be no attempt to give current market prices. The market moves so quickly that to remain current you must consult a dealer or the Exchange quotations published six times a year.

So the *Bradford Book* contains only issue prices. You won't find a plate called "lovely" or "priceless" anywhere in its pages. You won't find someone's "favorite" plate that was once quickly promoted and just as quickly forgotten. You won't find a plate issued to commemorate the anniversary of your bank, your school, or your state (and there have been many). You won't even find more than six of the scores of plate series that were issued for the American Bicentennial; only these six are regularly traded in the market.

NO "SUPERMARKET" OR "COTERIE" PLATES

And you won't find Bradex listings for any of the plates known as "supermarket plates" and "coterie plates."

As the name implies, supermarket plates are sold in supermarkets, discount stores, or chain stores, or are given away as premiums by fast-food franchises or banks, for example. Supermarket plates are limited only by the manufacturer's idea of how many can be sold. They imitate collector's plates but are not at all the same.

Coterie plates, on the other hand, can be true collector's plates, but they are made in such small or obscure editions that in today's vastly expanded market they remain unknown except to a small coterie of collectors. (They may, however, be listed as "over the counter.")

A plate is listed on the Exchange itself, and pictured in this book, *because of the volume of continued trading —* either past or expected *— NOT by whether or not it will increase in market price.* A new plate that continues a series already traded is listed before trading begins. And a new series from a maker whose other series are widely traded may be listed if demand is expected to carry over to the new series.

DIRECTORY TO THE "HEART" OF THE MARKET

The 1,112 Bradex-listed plates which are illustrated in the directory portion of this book comprise the "heart" of the collector's plate market. They are the most actively traded among collectors and consequently are the most volatile. But there are thousands more plates which are still true limited editions which are considered "over the counter" issues and included as an appendix to this 1980 edition of the *Bradford Book.*

A SINGLE SHAPE... A REMARKABLE VARIETY

1978 Arabia *Annual*
(16-A.69-1.3)
One of the very rare squared plates
listed on the Exchange

In case you're new to the subject, collector's plates bear pictures or sculpture and are made in a dozen countries in various sizes but mainly in only one shape — round. A few plates have been introduced in squared shapes, but so far only three — the Rörstrand *Christmas* series **(76-R.54-1)**, the Royal Doulton *Christmas* series **(26-R.62-1)** and Arabia's *Annual* series **(16-A.69-1)** — have "made the Bradex," that is, have been listed on the Exchange.

1971 Belleek *Christmas*
(26-B.18-1.2)
(Parian China)

Nearly all listed plates can be considered hand-made (although some are more so than others) and many are completely hand painted.

They can be made in wafer-thin china like the Belleek **(26-B.18-1)** or in heavy sculptured stone like those by Studio Dante di Volteradici of Italy **(38-V.90-2)** and Incolay Studios of California **(84-I.31-1)**. They can be metal (silver, silverplate, copper, and pewter), crystal like Lalique **(18-L.3-1)**, even wood like the Anri **(38-A.54-0)**. But most are made of ceramic, from simple terra cotta to true hard-fire porcelain.

1979 Anri *Christmas*
(38-A.54-1.9)
(Wood)

1980 Studio Dante di Volteradici
Living Madonnas
(38-V.90-2.3)
(Ivory Alabaster)

You'll find them hanging on the walls of museums or displayed in homes with great pride on plate rails or in shadow boxes, in small stands or display cases on side tables. They are sold in department stores, gift shops, antique stores, and in shops specializing in limited-edition collectibles — a recent development which underscores the rising interest in collector's plates over the past decade. A very few can be imported only from abroad one at a time by individual private collectors.

1979 Incolay Studios *Romantic Poets*
(84-I.31-1.3)
(Incolay Stone)

1976 D'Arceau-Limoges
Women of the Century
(18-D.15-3.1)
Series originally available only by
subscription directly from France

And always you find them moving with their changing prices on and off the floor of the Exchange. Here, however, they are represented merely by thousands of pieces of paper called "buy-orders" and "sell-orders" which change hands without an actual plate in sight.

**The Bradford Exchange
(Trading Floor)**

The action is fast, and the rewards can be great. (But don't be too tempted to speculate until you have heard what happened to some pretty smart speculators eight years ago.)

EDITION LIMITS AND MARKET VALUE

One thing all collector's plates have in common, of course, is that they are "limited editions."

There has been much debate as to what this means. Some manufacturers give the precise number of their editions; others, particularly those with the widest following, like Bing & Grøndahl **(14-B.36-0)**, insist that the edition size be kept a deep, dark secret.

But there is one thing you can be sure of: with only a single exception,* *no plate in the Bradford Book (or listed on the Exchange) has ever been reissued once the edition closed.*

The range among the limited edition sizes is vast. The smallest *announced* edition limit listed in the *Bradford Book* is 500 for three issues from two Veneto Flair series **(38-V.22-1)** and **(38-V.22-9)**; the largest is 30,000 for the Haviland *Christmas* **(18-H.6-1)**. But the *undisclosed* editions are by far the largest, ranging from less than one thousand for the earliest into the hundreds of thousands for the later ones.

1979 Pickard *Children of Renoir*
(84-P.29-4.3)
A limited edition of only 5,000 plates

There was a time, when the market was small, that a new plate series in an edition of 2,000 or less could become established and sometimes trade up in price to dizzying heights. Today, with the market so vastly expanded, this is very unlikely. With the rare exception of a series like the *Children of Renoir* **(84-P.29-4)** from Pickard (with 5,000-plate editions), an unknown new series launched with an edition of less than 10,000 would probably remain unknown except as a coterie plate.

So don't be discouraged from adding an obscure plate you really like to your collection — *but don't expect it to go up in market value just because the edition is small* — the market value of a plate is *never* determined by the size of the edition alone. Rather, it is determined by the *ratio* of supply to demand, and a very small edition can't create much demand.

Most plates are produced in series — either "closed-end" in a predetermined number of editions, or "open-end" to continue indefinitely. The Edwin M. Knowles *Wizard of Oz Collection* **(84-K.41-1)** is a closed-end series of eight issues — one in 1977, three in 1978, three in 1979 and one in 1980. The Bing & Grøndahl *Christmas* series **(14-B.36-1)** is open-end, with one new issue each year. Most collectors specialize in one or more of these series. (In fact, they *must* specialize in something; there are 1,112 listed plates in this book and the only complete collection anywhere is in the Bradford Museum.)

*The one exception is the Rosenthal *Traditional Christmas* series **(22-R.55-1)**. Editions from 1910 to 1957 in this series were reopened briefly between 1969 and 1971, with all re-issues identified on the back by year of manufacture. These plates are now Bradex-listed on the firm assurance by the maker that the practice ceased forever in 1971. Thus, they are limited editions at last, and current trading prices reflect all plates in the editions regardless of when they were made.

1977 Knowles *Wizard of Oz*
(84-K.41-1.1)
First in a closed-end series of eight plates

1980 Bing & Grøndahl *Christmas*
(14-B.36-1.86)
Eighty-sixth plate in an open-end series

1980 Knowles *Wizard of Oz*
(84-K.41-1.8)
Eighth in a closed-end series of eight plates

The first plate in a series is usually — but not always — the most wanted, since collectors traditionally seek out the new or unusual. Some collectors used to refer to these plates as "first editions," but this was a misnomer. Practically all plates listed are first editions since an edition is normally never reopened; the first in a series is properly called a "first issue."

THE UNEXPLAINED PHENOMENON

Because these plates have gradually become the most widely collected form of art and prices for the prized editions have outstripped the most glamorous stocks and bonds, it was probably inevitable that amateur sociologists would try to explain the phenomenon. At any rate, we have not lacked for "explanations" that compare plate collecting to other fields — but always with a certain strained logic.

Bing & Grøndahl — the very oldest manufacturer of collector's plates and therefore presumably an authority on the subject — says that collector's plates are "closely connected with the traditions of interior decorating." While plates certainly do decorate an interior, to suggest that this is their primary function is to lose sight of the joy of acquisition, the searching, bidding, and trading that collectors delight in — to lose, in fact, the very idea of collecting.

Others call collector's plates "giftware" and bring us no closer to an answer. Of course, collector's plates make fine gifts — that's what they were originally intended for, before they became collector's plates. But again, we are not *collecting* merely by giving or receiving a gift.

What is more confusing — and most widespread — is the comparison of collector's plates with antiques. A surprising number of dealers, manufacturers, and collectors — all of whom should know better — have suggested that plates can somehow become "instant antiques." It is easy to see how some people might prefer them to real antiques because they are so easily identified. The plate itself usually carries its own identification. And the danger of copies and counterfeits is close to nonexistent. (Only one counterfeit has ever reached the Exchange, a copy made in Portugal of the famous 1962 Royal Copenhagen "The Little Mermaid at Wintertime" **14-R.59-1.55**.)

But not even the earliest collector's plates are yet a century old and so can't be considered antiques by generally accepted definition. And the fast-moving market in plates can hardly compare with the slow, involved trading of antiques.

Still others compare plate collecting with stamp collecting and coin collecting — and there are comfortable similarities: a defined national market, for instance, with fast-changing prices and occasional wild speculation. But there are important differences as well. No plate collector would compare the art of his plate with the art that appears on a stamp or a coin. Both stamps and coins are generally hidden away in albums, while collector's plates are intended for display. And there is another, most vital difference — no stamp or coin is normally issued as a limited edition. It becomes so only after it is discontinued.

Comparisons with other forms of art are little better. There is not the same uniform, codified market in other art as there is in collector's plates, and no concerted trading other than the occasional spectacular auction.

So that leads us to compare the continuous trading in plates with that of stocks and bonds. Of course, many plates are collected as investments, but unlike stocks and bonds they are not collected *only* as investments. To do so would be to ignore their aesthetic appeal entirely.

Plates cannot generally be compared with stocks and bonds. The activity of stocks is rarely reflected in the plate market. When stocks fall, plates tend to go up. In fact, after some disagreement with the U.S. Securities and Exchange Commission back in 1973, the official view of the Bradford Exchange has been that, if collector's plates are to be considered investments, they should be defined as commodities, not securities, preferably art commodities, and modern art at that.

THE STANDARD YARDSTICK

There is no denying that many plate editions have proved to be spectacular investments. But how can you know which plates will succeed and which will fall by the wayside?

No one knows with absolute certainty. However, in 1972 analysts at the Bradford Exchange compiled what ultimately became known as the Eight-Point Checklist for evaluation of any plate. Since then, with minor evolutionary modification, this checklist has become something of a standard yardstick.

1. *Maker*: Is the maker known for its standards of fine workmanship and continuity of other plate series?
2. *Artistry*: Is it original art created especially for this plate by an artist of note? Is the subject one of broad, but not trite, appeal?

3. *Edition Size*: Is the edition clearly limited but not too limited to create a market? If the edition is closed, are dealers bidding in the secondary market?
4. *Collectibility*: Is it one, preferably the first, of a collectible periodic series or merely a single issue?
5. *Time of Acquisition*: Can you get it at the right time — at issue or while the price is still rising?
6. *Sponsorship*: Is it issued in association with a government or a prestigious institution?
7. *Commemorative Importance*: Does it commemorate a seasonal event or a historic event? If so, does it bring new insight to the event? Or is it an event in the history of the artist or of the maker?
8. *Material*: If made of ceramic, is it true hard-paste (or "hard-fire") porcelain, bone china or fine china? If made of metal, is it solid gold or silver? If made of glass, is it genuine 24% lead crystal?

These points are intended to be listed in order of importance, but for purposes of investment, point five — *Time of Acquisition* — is crucial. If you pay too much for a plate, it may take years to break even. Yet even at a high aftermarket price, a plate can be a bargain if it is still going up.

FROM QUAINT DANISH CHRISTMAS CUSTOM — TO WORLD'S MOST TRADED ART FORM

Every history ever written about collector's plates agrees that they originated in Denmark 85 years ago with a small blue-and-white plate issued by Bing & Grøndahl. Two semi-official histories say the idea was inspired by an old Danish custom of presenting gifts of food on beautifully decorated wooden plates to the common folk at Christmastime. After the food was eaten, the plate remained to remind the people of the spirit of Christmas giving throughout the year. This is a pretty story, but apparently no one has ever seen one of these wooden plates that supposedly represented such a widespread custom.

Officials at Bing & Grøndahl have said that the custom more likely had its beginnings in the Renaissance, when an honored guest was given the plates from which he had eaten his meal.

Other authorities have suggested even earlier precursors: armorial plates commissioned by city officials, guilds or wealthy patrons to be created in the Orient and imported. In Renaissance Italy, young lovers presented their beloveds with *piatti di pampa*, display plates adorned with historical or other figure compositions, sometimes an idealized portrait of the intended recipient.

In addition to these decorative plates, another family of wares, generally called "commemorative plates," has been suggested as an ancestor. According to historian Arlene Palmer in the *Oxford Companion to the De-*

corative Arts, "the first recognizable European landscape scene of Chinese (export) porcelain commemorates the Rotterdam riots of 1690," — which would put the birth of the commemorative plate genre at about 1700. One of the best known of these early commemoratives is the six-plate "South Sea Bubble" set. Created in the Orient circa 1720 for Dutch import, the set was a memento of the scandal involving the South Sea Company (an English firm whose main business was slave trading) in which fortunes were made and lost through wild speculation in company stock as it soared and crashed in 1720.

Villeroy & Boch's
"Snow White and the Seven Dwarfs"
Produced from 1890 to 1900

The actual development of collector's plates marked an evolutionary step in European porcelain making. Many of the characteristics of the first true limited-edition collector's plate existed prior to its creation by Bing & Grøndahl in 1895.

Meissen, Königliche Porzellan-Manufaktur Berlin (KPM) and the French house of Sevres were established in the 1700s and began to issue small editions of commemorative plates in honor of renowned generals, successful military campaigns, coronations and the like.

In the latter half of the nineteenth century, particularly in Italy, plate sets became popular. They were decorated with thematically-related scenes such as the months, signs of the Zodiac, seasons and biblical events. These plate sets and commemorative plates provided a background for the yet-to-be-developed notion of the collector's plate series. Yet, as close as they may seem to collector's plates, these were not limited editions as we understand them today. The maker would willingly produce additional issues if sufficient demand were demonstrated, and some plates actually did remain in a manufacturer's product line for years.

An example of this was Villeroy & Boch's "Snow White and the Seven Dwarfs" by Heinrich Schlitt, produced from 1890 to 1900 to meet continuing demand.

1888 Royal Copenhagen plate
by Arnold Krog

In 1888, Arnold Krog, art director for Royal Copenhagen Manufactory, devised a process by which intermediate tones of a single color could be applied to a bas-relief design and fused under the glaze into the plate body. This development made possible very subtle use of light and shadow and opened up a new dimension to plate artists. The resulting creations — predominantly in shades of cobalt blue — came to be known as "Copenhagen blue on whites." Royal Copenhagen's first such plate featured the maker's hallmark. It was specially made for the Great Scandinavian Fair of 1888 held in Copenhagen and was among the ware awarded the Grand Prix at the Paris World's Fair a year later.

The stage was now set for the first true collector's plate. All of the technical and aesthetic elements had been introduced. It remained for one maker to combine them in a limited-edition plate which would be the first in a continuing series on the same theme.

That maker was Bing & Grøndahl, another Copenhagen house which had been established in 1853 by M. H. and J. H. Bing & Frederick Vilhelm Grøndahl. The plate, created for Christmas 1895 with a design by F. A. Hallin, was entitled "Behind the Frozen Window" **(14-B.36-1.1)**. It was the first commemorative plate to feature the key information — in script and permanently fired into the plate — of the date and occasion of issuance. It was also in the "Copenhagen blue on white" style that Arnold Krog had introduced seven years earlier. Finally, it was a true "limited edition," although it is doubtful that Mr. Harald Bing, son of one

Harald Bing

of the firm's founders and the man responsible for the now-famous issue, thought of it as such. But when he "closed out" availability at year's end, breaking the mold, and followed his 1895 Christmas plate the next year with a new plate dated "Christmas 1896," the collector's plate was born.

Bing & Grøndahl claims to have kept secret the number of plates produced, but knowledgeable estimates suggest that about 400 of the historic 1895 plates were made. It is believed that the majority of these still exist, many as part of complete collections of the Bing & Grøndahl *Christmas* series, and most now in the United States. The plate, which originally sold for about 50 cents, traded in 1979 at as high as $4,000.00 on the U.S. Exchange.

In her book, *Modern Porcelain* (Harper and Row, 1962), Alberta Tremble tells us this first collector's plate was issued to commemorate the reorganization of the Bing & Grøndahl company and the opening of its new, greatly enlarged plant. According to Ms. Tremble, "The plates caught on like wildfire. Potters everywhere copied the idea."

In fact, very few copied the idea, and for the most part those who did met with short-lived success. Nonetheless, plate collecting gained wide recognition in Denmark by the turn of the century and spread to Sweden and Norway shortly thereafter.

Aluminia, a majolica factory in Copenhagen (later acquired by Royal Copenhagen), introduced its *Children's Day Christmas* series of plates in 1904 and continued to produce an annual issue until 1939. Rörstrand of Sweden also began a series in 1904 and hung on until 1926 before giving up, and the Norwegian house of Porsgrund offered a Christmas plate in 1909, but never followed it up. Both Rörstrand **(76-R.54-0)** and Porsgrund **(54-P.62-0)** failed to resume production until 1968 — and only then because the new American market had begun to develop.

In 1908, Royal Copenhagen began its *Christmas* series **(14-R.59-1)**, and that series, like Bing & Grøndahl's, has continued despite wars and economic crises, making it the second-oldest continuously produced series.

1908 Royal Copenhagen *Christmas*
(14-R.59-1.1)

As early as 1905, the German manufacturer Rosenthal apparently contracted with an enterprising Copenhagen department store, Buck & Nissen, to do a series of porcelain Christmas plates for the Danish market. As interest in collector's plates spread from Denmark to the provinces of northern Germany, Rosenthal

1910 Rosenthal *Traditional Christmas*
(22-R.55-1.1)

began to promote the series under its own hallmark to German collectors. This dual edition — with identical artwork — continued from 1907 through 1909. In 1910, Rosenthal severed the relationship with Buck & Nissen and issued its own proprietary plate, "Winter Peace," **(22-R.55-1.1)**, the first in its *Traditional Christmas* series, which continued through 1974.

Two other German makers began series of Christmas plates prior to World War I. The Hutschenreuther *Christmas* series (OTC) ended in 1935, and the Königliche Porzellan-Manufaktur Berlin (KPM) series (OTC) managed to survive only until the mid 1920s.

During the 1920s and 1930s, few if any manufacturers produced new collector's plate series, and many series and makers dropped out of the market entirely. The vast dislocations caused by a massive economic depression and World War II produced a generation with little interest in limited-edition plates, which were widely perceived as little more than curios. During the war years of the 1940s, shortages of raw materials led to the scaling down of edition sizes, which later resulted in increased prices for plates of that era.

THE MODERN MARKET

Although the early Christmas plates are true collector's plates as we understand them, they were not collected at their time of issue as they are today. Danish families collected them but never suspected that one edition might be more valuable than another, and little thought was given to the idea of acquiring a complete collection. As Danes emigrated to the United States, they brought collector's plates with them. But until the late 1940s, the plates were virtually unknown to Americans except in a few antique shops in Scandinavian neighborhoods. Only two importers, the U.S. representatives of the Georg Jensen Company and the Stanley Corcoran Company, were bringing in plates by Bing & Grøndahl and Royal Copenhagen. The collector's plate began to be seen, but no clamor for acquisition was yet heard.

The first American dealers entered the market with no idea of what they were starting.

"If you had told me in 1947 that someday there would be millions of plate collectors, I just wouldn't have believed you," says Chicago antique dealer William Freudenberg, Jr. Yet in 1947, he became the very first to recognize the possibilities of Danish plates when he began reselling them to other antique dealers.

"I simply found them at an auction house," he says, "and took a few to see what I could do." Freuden-

berg's asking price for the oldest Bing & Grøndahl at that time was only $4.50 (the same plate that was quoted at $4,000.00 in the market in 1979).

William Freudenberg, Jr.

In 1949 Pat Owen of Viking Imports in Fort Lauderdale, Florida, became a collector's plate dealer through a fluke. An American company wanted to sell cash registers in Denmark, but exporting Danish currency was prohibited. To get around this, the purchasing company used Danish kroner to buy collector's plates from young Danes who had no interest in their families' collections. These were then resold for U.S. dollars to Mrs. Owen, and she became the first American dealer to sell plates to gift shops and department stores.

Pat Owen

That same year Rev. Elias Rasmussen, a Norwegian-born pastor from Minneapolis, was traveling in Denmark when he met an elderly lady who was trying to sell her plates. As he told it, no one in Denmark wanted them at any price. So Rev. Rasmussen brought them back to America to see if he could sell them for her. Within a few years he was reselling plates by the thousands. After Rev. Rasmussen's death, his son continued the business.

Elias Rasmussen

In 1950, Dane Jon Nielsen settled in Dearborn, Michigan and began importing Danish plates along with antiques from the old country. He sold them all for about $3.50 apiece regardless of the year of issue.

Jon Nielsen

"Not until 1953 did dealers want any current plates," he remembers. "The next year I raised my prices to $3.75, and you should have heard them complain that I was charging too much."

But the event that really moved collector's plates out of the realm of antiques and giftware took place in 1951. Another transplanted Dane, Svend Jensen in Rye, New York, had begun importing Danish plates the year before. He was the first to charge different prices for various back issues. In 1951 he printed and circulated the first back-issue price list based on his estimates of the rarity of each edition. With this simple act, the modern American market in collector's plates was born.

Svend Jensen

Antique dealers and gift shops around the country were soon quoting Svend Jensen's prices, and other price lists began to appear. Collectors with recently issued plates tried to complete their collections with earlier plates. Prices were bid up well beyond those of Svend Jensen's early lists; yet as late as 1955 the historic Bing & Grøndahl plate from 1895 could still be bought for only $75.00.

In the early 1950s foreign demand began to be recognized by the Danish manufacturers. In 1953, Royal Copenhagen, in an effort to appeal to a wider spectrum of international collectors, eliminated the word "Jul" from the front of their plate to avoid a language barrier and began to offer universal winter scenes instead of designs which emphasized the Christmas holiday and its religious aspects.

Two "winners" on the early plate market were the 1945 Royal Copenhagen *Christmas* issue, "A Peaceful Motif" **(14-R.59-1.38)**, and the 1951 Royal Copenhagen *Christmas* issue "Christmas Angel" **(14-R.59-1.44)**. Both plates were designed by artist Richard Bocher, and

1945 Royal Copenhagen *Christmas*
(14-R.59-1.38)

1962 Royal Copenhagen *Christmas*
(14-R.59-1.55)

many collectors found his sentimental portrayals of youthful angels a refreshing departure from the customary landmarks, cathedrals and Danish countryside scenes featured in the series. The plates, which were issued in Denmark at prices equivalent to $4.00 and $5.00, respectively, traded widely throughout the early 1950s, and by 1953 both were trading as high as $300.00 in the U.S.

By 1960, with the supply of antiques dwindling and more and more plate collectors asking for current editions of the Danish Christmas plates, antique dealers started to add the new editions to their lines even though they were hardly antiques. As the new editions also began to appear in specialty gift shops, new customers began looking for still earlier issues, and a circular trading pattern developed from one kind of dealer to another.

Some enterprising dealers found they could still bypass American distributors and go directly to Denmark for plates. As late as 1960, Earl Falack of Edward's 5th Avenue, Ltd., New York, found some Danish dealers still blithely unaware of the boom occurring across the Atlantic. He recalls that Royal Copenhagen back issues of random years could still be purchased in lots of 1,000 or even 2,000 at from only $2.00 to $5.00 per plate.

In 1962, the steadily escalating American demand for European plates combined with demand from both European collectors and noncollectors — Germans and Danes in particular — who were enamored of the tales of Hans Christian Andersen to create a sensational sellout of the 1962 Royal Copenhagen *Christmas* plate, "Little Mermaid" **(14-R.59-1.55)**. Issued at about $11.00, it immediately began to rise in market price, appreciating also partly because the mold broke before the edition could be completed. By spring 1963, the plate had shot up to about $30.00 in Denmark and was trading at $50.00 in the U.S. (In 1979, "Little Mermaid" brought as much as $250.00 in Denmark and $212.00 in the U.S.)

One result of the price rise of the "Little Mermaid" was a general increase in prices for earlier editions. Another result was the transformation of legions of memento collectors into avid investment seekers — in Denmark as well as the U.S. The plate's success increased public awareness of plate collecting as a lucrative pastime and paved the way for one of the pivotal events in the history of limited-edition plates.

CRYSTAL SHATTERS MARKET

In 1965 Lalique of France, whose crystalware was selling in shops where Danish plates were unheard of, brought out an etched crystal plate of two entwined birds. The plate, *"Deux Oiseaux"* **(18-L.3-1.1)** — now legendary among collectors for its rise from $25.00 to over $1,700.00 in little more than a decade — shattered the previously accepted boundaries of plate collecting; it was not porcelain, not Danish, not blue-and-white, not even a Christmas plate. It was simply called an "annual" (the series closed in 1976), and its issue finally established limited-edition plates as true "collector's items."

The impact of *"Deux Oiseaux"* was delayed in Europe, since the plate was distributed only in North America, but the news in Europe about its precedent-shattering reception eventually caused both makers and collectors to take notice of the enormous profit potential in limited-edition plates.

Two years later, in 1967, Bareuther in Germany introduced a *Christmas* series to commemorate its 100th anniversary **(22-B.7-1.1)**. In 1968 it began a Danish Church *Christmas* series **(22-D.5-1)** for the Danish market. And in 1969 it started a *Father's Day* series **(22-B.7-2)**. KPM, after a hiatus of some 45 years, re-entered the market in 1969 — also with a *Christmas* series **(OTC)**.

Rörstrand of Sweden **(76-R.54-1)** and Porsgrund of Norway **(54-P.62-1)** both re-entered the market in 1968 with *Christmas* series that were successful in their native countries as well as the United States.

Despite the growing success of collector's plates, Bing & Grøndahl issued the first Mother's Day plate, "Dog and Puppies" **(14-B.36-3.1)** in 1969 with a certain degree of caution. Expanded edition sizes of Danish blue-and-white issues in the mid-1960s in response to the post- "Little Mermaid" boom had softened the Danish market. "Dog and Puppies" was thus given a modest production schedule. American collectors, however, were becoming increasingly aware of the high prices commanded by back-issue Bing & Grøndahl plates. Given the opportunity to acquire a first-issue plate from the world's most prominent limited-edition plate manufacturer, they scrambled to buy it at the U.S. issue price of $9.75. Their hunches paid off when the U.S. allocation sold out within weeks and the price jumped to $25.00. By Christmas the figure was $65.00, and in 1979 "Dog and Puppies" traded at $500.00.

1969 Bing & Grøndahl *Mother's Day*
(14-B.36-3.1)

The maker's concern about the soft Danish market proved well-founded, however, as Danish dealers had little immediate interest in the first Mother's Day plate. In spring of 1969, Jon Nielsen, returning from a Danish buying trip, purchased 18 plates at the gift shop in the Copenhagen airport for $3.50 each. The manager said he had 125 more if Nielsen wanted them. Nielsen did.

Other American dealers joined Nielsen in buying the issue in bulk and reselling the plates to U.S. collectors. The effect was to make "Dog and Puppies" virtually unobtainable in Europe. This scarcity has continued to the present day and explains why the plate's current market price in, for example, Germany, is more than 70% greater than in the United States.

Danish indifference to "Dog and Puppies" didn't last long. The severity of the local shortage soon became evident, and the price rose sharply. By late summer of 1969 it brought the equivalent of $30.00, and by Christmas $50.00. The plate has continued to rise throughout the 1970s and late in 1979 brought up to 3000 kroner (about $560.00).

Late in 1969, Wedgwood in England issued its first *Christmas* plate, "Windsor Castle" **(26-W.90-1.1)**. It was intended for export to the North American market, and the response there was quick and enthusiastic. The entire allocation sold out immediately, and within a year the plate was trading at twice its $25.00 U.S. issue

1969 Wedgwood *Christmas*
(26-W.90-1.1)

price. Wedgwood cancelled 40% of its U.K. orders to divert the plates to meet this sudden demand, then learned to its surprise that "Windsor Castle" was just as well received on the home market. Many British dealers who were able to get the plate sold it to customers at 20% above its L4.20p ($10.00) U.K issue price. By Christmas the figure had jumped to L20.00 ($48.00), nearly five times the issue price. British collectors, who had long purchased Bing & Grøndahl, Royal Copenhagen and Rosenthal collector's plates for strictly aesthetic purposes, began to recognize their investment potential. Speculation pushed the price of "Windsor Castle"

up to L100.00 ($240.00) by spring and L130.00 by the end of 1970.

On the strength of the glittering success of this one plate, the U.K. limited-edition plate market was born. British collectors were soon purchasing other first-issue plates from British makers, hopeful that each would match the success of "Windsor Castle." The 1970 Spode *Christmas* issue **(26-S.63-1.1)** was one of the first to benefit from this wave of interest.

With rising demand for limited-edition plates on both sides of the Atlantic, it was only natural that more and more manufacturers began to design and produce editions specifically to meet it. In 1970 Kaiser, Haviland, Belleek, Berlin Design, Lenox, Santa Clara, Pickard, Reed and Barton, and Orrefors started making collector's plates. All were successful. Franklin Mint made history by issuing the first silver collector's plate, "Bringing Home the Tree" **(84-F.64-1.1)** by Norman Rockwell, and it too was a runaway success — doubling in market price in a year. Prices increased as soon as editions closed, bid up by ever more, and more avid, collectors.

The excitement spilled over into Canada where thousands of new collectors vied with U.S. collectors for the most popular issues. Wedgwood's 1969 "Windsor Castle," was the first big winner. Spurred by U.S. trading, the 1969 Royal Copenhagen *Christmas* plate **(14-R.59-1.62)** inspired delayed but extraordinary demand in Canada. By late 1970 it traded at triple its $14.00 issue price.

The thousands of new Canadian collectors also served to stimulate the growing "boom" in collector's plates on the U.S. side of the border. In 1971, still more makers like Furstenberg, Gorham and Lladró entered the U.S. market. Haviland Parlon began a unique and successful series based on medieval tapestries **(18-H.8-1)**. Veneto Flair **(38-V.22-0)** began a series of handmade plates from Italy. Older makers such as Royal Copenhagen and Wedgwood introduced Mother's Day series **(14-R.59-2 and 26-W.90-2)**. Rosenthal began a new Christmas series **(22-R.55-2)** designed by Danish artist Bjørn Wiinblad, which was initially overlooked by German collectors but did quite well on the Danish and U.S. markets.

Also in 1971, both Goebel **(22-G.54-1)** and Schmid Bros. **(22-S.12-1)** introduced series with first issues which carried the same design by Sister M. I. Hummel. Both series were successful and have continued to the present, although the coincidence sparked lawsuits which continued for years.

Even this new surge in supply could not keep up with demand. As the number of collectors and dealers increased, prices continued to rise. News of the boom began to appear in the U.S. press. In December 1971, the *Wall Street Journal* ran an article under the headline "While You Were Going Under, Granny Got In At $100, Got Out At $450." The article was based on the

1971 Rosenthal *Wiinblad Christmas*
(22-R.55-2.1)

spectacular price rise of the first Franklin Mint *Christmas* plate. Reporter Scott R. Schmedel also singled out the 1969 Wedgwood *Christmas* plate which was then selling for about $200.00 — 800% of issue price. To show this could be momentary inflation, Mr. Schmedel quoted a serious Wedgwood collector as predicting its value would fall back and stabilize at around $80.00. Instead, it held its price ever since and traded at $270.00 at the end of 1979. The *Wall Street Journal* article and others like it were widely reprinted and set the stage for 1972 as the year of the speculator.

THE CRASH OF 1972

In 1972 still more makers entered the market. Perhaps it was inevitable that some of them should be less than reputable. Plates of poor design and quality were rushed into production. Thousands of new dealers and collectors began speculating with little or no knowledge of plates or of the market. New "mints" sprang up to mass-produce silver plates on the heels of Franklin Mint's success.

One such new mint advertised its silver "Collie and Pups" **(OTC)** with pictures of an acid-etched plate and sold thousands before the plate was produced. Prices rose dramatically, but the actual plate was stamped, not etched, and many collectors were sadly disillusioned as the price of the issue plummeted. Another new mint introduced six new silver plates at once.

Suddenly dealers all over the country found themselves overstocked and prices for silver plates fell below issue. All other plates began to fall on the heels of the silver crash. Dealers panicked, and the speculator-collectors, many of whom had gone into part-time business as "bedroom dealers," saw their visions of quick riches vanish.

1972 "Collie and Pups"
The plate that set off the
"crash of '72"

1973 D'Arceau-Limoges
Lafayette Legacy
(18-D.15-1.1)

1973 Royal Doulton
Mother and Child
(26-R.62-2.1)

After the "crash of '72," the following year became the year of the "shakeout." Several "mints" closed their doors. Some 100,000 fewer silver plates were issued in 1973 than in 1972, and thousands of those in existence were melted back into silver. Established makers cut back production dramatically, and the bedroom dealers disappeared.

The effect of the U.S. "crash of '72" spread to Denmark. There, overproduction of traditional lines by Bing & Grøndahl and Royal Copenhagen, coupled with a host of new issues from competitors, glutted the market. With little appreciation possible on their purchases, many collectors stayed out of the market, and dealers found themselves hopelessly overstocked.

The Canadian, German and United Kingdom markets were relatively untouched by the "crash" except as it affected makers who had to contend with less U.S. demand for their products. And even that proved to be a short-term interruption. In the midst of the bear market of 1973, American interest was rekindled by two new series from Europe. A French series for the American Bicentennial, the *Lafayette Legacy Collection* from D'Arceau-Limoges **(18-D.15-1)** was unavailable to U.S. dealers. But the plates were imported by enough individual collectors directly from France to become the most sought after of all U.S. Bicentennial issues. The first issue traded at 324% of its $14.82 issue price in late 1979. "Colette and Child" **(26-R.62-2.1)** from Royal Doulton was the first plate by artist Edna Hibel and led the field toward recovery, selling out immediately and shooting up to 888% of its $40.00 issue price within two years of its appearance. Although marginal plates disappeared from trading, established plates regained their market strength.

As if to underscore the confidence during this period in the Canadian market — which was relatively unscathed by the U.S. crash — Charles Sorvin for Hutschenreuther introduced in 1973 a series specifically for Canadian collectors. The Hutschenreuther *Canada Christmas* **(OTC)** — produced in West Germany exclusively for Canadian distribution — was well received and rose moderately in aftermarket trading.

1973 Hutschenreuther
Canada Christmas
(OTC)

1974 Gorham *Rockwell Christmas*
(84-G.58-3.1)

It was at about this time — in the mid-1970s — that the growing demand of European collectors and dealers was first felt in the American market. As news of the American plate collecting boom slowly spread abroad, plates that originated in Europe but had languished in the market there — issues such as the Rörstrand *Christmas* series **(76-R.54-1)** — were bid up even higher in the American market as European dealers and their agents bought them up for resale back in Europe. Another example of this was the Rosenthal *Wiinblad Christmas* series **(22-R.55-2)**, which had gone relatively unnoticed when it was introduced on the German market in 1971. "Maria mit Kind" **(22-R.55-2.1)**, the first issue, was sought after in the U.S. and Denmark as a radical departure in plate art. As news of the issue's mounting success began to reach the German market via magazine articles in 1973 and 1974, a brisk aftermarket developed. Dealers and individual collectors bought plates abroad at appreciated prices and resold them to German collectors who were willing to bid even higher prices to obtain the scarce first issue. This in turn caused a scarcity on the U.S. market and drove the price up there. In December of 1979, "Maria mit Kind" was quoted in the U.S. at 1590% of its $100.00 issue price; in Germany at 2683% of its DM 145.00 ($44.00) issue price.

THE MARKET MATURES

The U.S. market gradually began to strengthen in the mid-1970s as it became apparent that even a dramatic crash couldn't permanently stifle collector demand and speculator optimism. In 1974 both Gorham **(84-G.58-3)** and The Rockwell Society of America **(84-R.70-1)** introduced series for Christmas with the artwork of Norman Rockwell. Within a year, each first issue had doubled in market price.

1974 Rockwell Society *Christmas*
(84-R.70-1.1)

In 1975, D'Arceau-Limoges came out with its *Noel Vitrail Christmas* series **(18-D.15-2)** which looked like stained glass on translucent Limoges porcelain. It, too, sold out quickly and within a year had doubled in market price.

1975 D'Arceau-Limoges *Christmas*
(18-D.15-2.1)

In contrast, the Danish market continued to be sluggish as makers were slow to cut back on edition sizes in reaction to the glut of plates issued in 1972-1973.

In the United Kingdom "Victorian Boy and Girl" **(22-R.62-7.1)**, the 1976 first issue in Royal Doulton's *Valentine's Day* series, proved to be a market catalyst reminiscent of Wedgwood's "Windsor Castle" seven years earlier, selling out within days of its announcement and more than doubling in price during its first year on the market.

1976 Royal Doulton
Valentine's Day
(26-R.62-7.1)

In the Canadian market the first plate to generate exceptional excitement following the 1973 Hutschenreuther *Canada Christmas* was the 1977 first issue in the Wedgwood *Blossoming of Suzanne* series **(26-W.90-4.1)**, entitled "Innocence" and by Romantic painter Mary Vickers. The plate sold out in Canada in less than a month. Issued at $60.00, it shot up to $225.00 in some areas as dealers scrambled to meet the sharp demand. As much as six months later, dealers were still purchasing plates on the U.S. market for resale in Canada. This in turn drove up the price of "Innocence" on the U.S. market where it traded at triple the issue price by mid-summer of 1978. The Canadian price finally leveled off in the same range.

1977 Wedgwood
Blossoming of Suzanne
(26-W.90-4.1)

On the German market in 1974, Rosenthal introduced a daring new Annual series in crystal **(OTC)**. A 3,000-plate edition segmented into three 1,000-plate groups — platinum-, gold- and clear-etched — was well received, and the three averaged approximately 50% above issue in late 1979. Another landmark plate was "Madonna mit dem Kind" **(OTC)** — a distinctively Japanese portrayal of Mary and the infant Jesus — issued in 1975 by Noritake. The 3,000-plate edition sold out within eight days, and the price rose dramatically on the secondary market. By the end of 1979 the plate traded on the German Bradford Exchange at more than nine times its issue price.

1975 Noritake *Christmas*
(OTC)

1977 Studio Dante di Volteradici
Grand Opera
(38-V.90-1.1)

New materials began to appear. "Rigoletto" **(38-V.90-1.1)** was issued in 1976; the first *Grand Opera* plate from Italy's Studio Dante di Volteradici and the first plate in ivory alabaster. It almost tripled within a year and ended 1979 at 429% of its $35.00 issue price. "Brown's Lincoln" **(84-R.69-1.1)** was also issued in 1976, the first *Famous Americans* plate from RiverShore and the first copper collector's plate. Demolishing the "crash"-inspired myth that metal plates were losers, it soared on the secondary market, ending 1979 at 1038%

The late 1970s also brought us closer to a "world market" with issues of various national origins traded simultaneously on several foreign markets. Thus, the U.S.-made 1978 Rockwell Society *Heritage* issue, "The Cobbler" **(84-R.70-3.2)** ended 1979 quoted in the U.S. at $74.00 — or 379% of issue price; in Canada at Can. $75.00 — or 254%; in Germany at DM 138.00 (U.S. $80.00) — or 207%; and in the U.K. at L35.00 (U.S.$77.50) — or 282%. The German-made 1978 Goebel *Hummel Annual*, "Happy Pastime" **(22-**

1977 Incolay Studios
Romantic Poets
(84-I.31-1.1)

1978 Rockwell Society *Heritage*
(84-R.70-3.2)

of its $40.00 issue price. "She Walks in Beauty" **(84-I.31-1.1)** was issued in 1977, the first *Romantic Poets* plate from Incolay Studios of California and the first cameo collector's plate. It traded in December 1979 at 413% of its $60.00 issue price.

G.54-1.8) ended 1979 quoted in the U.S. at $150.00 — or 231% of issue price; in Canada at Can. $200.00 — or 252%; in Germany at DM 220.00 (U.S.$127.50) — or 205%; and in the U.K. at L68.00 (U.S.$150.50 — or 172%. The Finnish-made 1978 Arabia *Annual*, "Lem-

1978 Goebel *Hummel Annual*
(22-G.54-1.8)

minkainen's Chase" **(16-A.69-1.3)** ended 1979 quoted in the U.S. at $70.00 — or 179% of issue price; in Germany at DM 132.00 (U.S.$76.50) — or 140%; in the U.K. at L30.00 (U.S. $66.00) — or 154%; but was never traded in Canada actively enough to warrant Bradex listing there.

The "world market" was also evident in reports of increasing interest from countries previously considered beyond the realm of plate collecting. This was due in part to the aggressive marketing by Bing & Grøndahl and Royal Copenhagen in scores of countries around the world as well as to magazine and newspaper articles describing the phenomenal growth of plate collecting in North America over the past decade.

THE 1980s — DECADE OF PROMISE

As the decade of the 1970s ended, there was some cause for concern about the health of the U.S. market. A sharp increase in the number of new issues in 1979 and an unprecedented six-month-long decline in the U.S. Market Bradex over the second half of the year were reminiscent of the turmoil in 1972. A few market watchers saw the prelude to a possible collapse.

But others noted that the slide came off a two-year bull market, that despite it the Bradex had registered a net nine-point gain on the year, and that there were already signs that collectors — far from panicking — were quietly filling out their collections at bargain prices in anticipation of a resurgent market and continuing monetary inflation.

The 1972 crash, being unprecedented, had shaken the market to its foundations and caused many to predict it would never recover. The very fact of its resurgence in the 1970s showed makers, dealers and col-

lectors alike that even a sharp downturn would be only transitory. The vastly expanded market of 1980 — estimated at 5,000,000 collectors in a score of countries around the world — seems proof enough of resilience to reassure even the most bearish trader.

With the market expanding by hundreds of thousands more people every year and plate collecting catching on in an ever-growing number of countries, the decade of the 1980s seems to hold promise indeed... particularly when all those new people start looking for the closed editions we can still get today.

1979—THE YEAR IN REVIEW

Compiled by the Staff of the Bradford Exchange Trading Floor

Seldom has the plate market traversed such a profoundly contradictory year. Nineteen-seventy-nine rewarded both bulls and bears as its first half saw the Market Bradex reach a record high of 344 on the heaviest trading in history and the second half brought a market slump which placed unprepared traders in a near-panic frame of mind reminiscent of the "crash of '72."

The bear side reflected a steady decline in trading activity from the all-time high it reached in February; the disappointing performance of most new issues "softened" the market for major manufacturers and caused a reported 16 makers (notably Lincoln Mint and Metal Arts Co. — which were not Bradex listed) to cease all production in collector's plates; and an unprecedented six month decline in the Market Bradex totalled seven points.

But there were also bull signals: the Bradex registered a net gain of nine points over the year, holding at an all-time high of 344 for four months; the number of reported transactions on the Exchange rose 28% from 1978 to a record 1,461,000; the number of individual traders was up 41%; and Exchange trading volume exceeded that of 1978 in 10 out of the 12 months.

CHART OF BRADEX

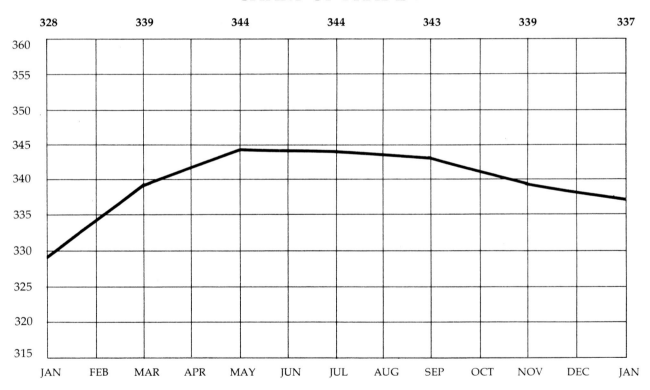

| | 328 | 339 | 344 | 344 | 343 | 339 | 337 |

Market trading started sluggishly in 1979, mainly because of cancellations caused by late delivery of several new issues, severe weather conditions in the northern half of the country, and dealer caution due to a predicted nationwide recession. However, continuing speculation in Rockwell issues — a carry-over trend from the fourth quarter 1978 market — drove up both trading volume and prices throughout February; and as March closed, Exchange records had been set in both total quarterly trading volume (458,968 transactions) and single-week dollar volume ($1,275,467).

The heated trading in back-issue Rockwells was exemplified by the first four four-plate issues in Gorham's *Rockwell Four Seasons* series **(84-G.58-1.1 through 84-G.58-1.4)**, which gained an average of 113.75 points between January 1 and April 30 as the bull market pushed the Bradex to an all-time record 344. There were still hot issues in May and June — such as the 1976 Fairmont *Famous Clowns* **(84-F.4-2.1)**, up 50 points — but disturbing signs of market "softening" set in. Prices for back-issue Goebel *Hummel Annuals* **(22-G.54-1)**, a key indicator series, fell a collective 7.7%; and Rockwell volume, while still significant, dropped 31% from the April level.

July and August trading was uncharacteristically high — 49% above the same period in 1978; but the large

1976 Fairmont *Famous Clowns*
(84-F.4-2.1)

1973 Gorham *Rockwell Four Seasons*
(84-G.58-1.3)

number of new issues diluted collector demand by some 40 to 50 percent more than at the same point in 1978. Many prices suffered as declines outnumbered advances for the first time in the year (204 to 148) and August ended with the Bradex down one point — the first drop registered since February 1976.

The fear that the prolonged bull market might be followed by a downturn of equal scope caused many dealers to overreact to the "softening." Price-cutting to get rid of inventory spread dramatically, especially during the last four months of the year as dealers made room for new Christmas issues. Hardest hit were the Goebel *Hummel Annuals* **(22-G.54-1)**, down an average of 15.2 points over the final two months alone.

Nineteen-seventy-nine ended with the market in broad retreat. November and December trading saw 6 of the 12 key indicator series post losses, and the Bradex drop two more points to end the year at 337. Declines outnumbered advances 129 to 100. Back-issue volume was 54% above the same period in 1978 as bargain hunters took advantage of reduced prices.

NEW ISSUES FLOOD THE MARKET

The proliferation of new issues — 377 in all — was unquestionably the most significant characteristic of 1979. "Amateur" makers and dealers, who had made only minimal impact on the market since the "crash of '72" and the "shakeout of '73," were back in full force, responding to the two-year bull market and the "boom" conditions which prevailed following Norman Rockwell's death. A vast array of new issues from both established and new "amateur" makers (there were an estimated 40 new Rockwells alone) flooded the market and — compounded by large edition sizes — caused turmoil at the dealer level. Errors in judgment over which plates to order and stock, or worse still, reckless

attempts to order some of everything so that all customers could be accommodated, left many dealers with bloated inventories of non-sellers in the summer months. To maintain cash-flow and make room for even newer issues, they discounted slow movers — depressing the market and branding some plates as "losers" which in other seasons might have fared quite well. A host of new Christmas first-issues exacerbated the problem, and by year's end the Bradex had registered an unprecedented six straight months of decline.

"ROCKWELLMANIA"

The year also witnessed a continuation of the phenomenal demand for Norman Rockwell issues which had begun within hours of the artist's passing on the morning of November 9 the year before. This demand revived the sluggish market, played a key part in the sharp 15-point gain registered by the Bradex in the final two months of 1978, and continued well into the first half of 1979.

The impact of "Rockwellmania" can best be tracked by comparing the percentage of trading in Rockwell issues to the total trading volume — a figure which normally ran at about 19% prior to the artist's death. In November and December of 1978, the figure jumped to 52%; in January and February 1979, it was at 30%; and even in April, it stood at 28%.

Prices of Rockwell issues also advanced broadly. Within six months of the artist's death, more than four out of five Bradex-listed Rockwell plates rose in trading price — at an average of 58%. Not until mid-1979 did average prices level off and volume return to normal.

Spurred by this apparently insatiable demand, makers introduced dozens of new reproductions and special tributes to the artist himself. Among them:

NORMAN ROCKWELL
(1894-1978)

1979 Brantwood Collection
"Tribute to Rockwell"
(OTC)

Gorham's "Triple Self-Portrait," issued at $37.50; the Norman Rockwell Museum's "Norman Rockwell Remembered," issued at $45.00; and the Brantwood Collection's "Tribute to Rockwell," issued at $50.00. (All of these special tributes, however, were non-Bradex-listed, over-the-counter [OTC] issues, and all failed to trade up in the market.)

ROCKWELL BOOM SPARKS LAWSUITS

Perhaps inevitably, given the potential for quick profits in a hectic bull market, the Rockwell boom also produced lawsuits. Curtis Publishing Company, owners of the *Saturday Evening Post*, sued the Norman Rockwell Museum, Inc. of Lincolnwood, Illinois, and Philadelphia for copyright infringement. The Museum was also sued jointly by the Rockwell Society of America and Edwin M. Knowles China Company for deceptive trade practices.

Curtis Publishing Company sued on two Museum plates, "Norman Rockwell Remembered" **(OTC)** and "Santa's Children", stating in the complaint that the Museum "... does not have the right to offer authentic Norman Rockwell collectibles ... and is not authorized, sponsored or in any way associated with or approved

1979 Gorham
"Triple Self-Portrait"
(OTC)

1979 Norman Rockwell Museum
"Santa's Children"

by the Estate of Norman Rockwell." The Museum agreed to stop selling "Santa's Children."

According to the complaint, the Rockwell Society and Knowles charged the Museum with ". . . fraudulently attempting to palm off their forgeries as works of Norman Rockwell authenticated and certified by the Society." Knowles claimed the Museum had "pirated" the artwork of the Society's first three Rockwell *Heritage* plates **(84-R.70-3.1 to 84-R.70-3.3)** in figurines under the name "Heirloom Collection," in imitation of the Society's "Heritage Collection." An agreed order issued by the court specified that the Museum could not sell the figurines as the "Heirloom Collection," nor sell them as a group, and further required the Museum to place corrective advertising.

Afterward, a minor sensation was caused when a transcript of testimony from the trial was passed to the press which gave presumably secret "rough figures" on edition sizes of the Knowles plates. Many market observers were surprised to learn that the edition size of "The Toy Maker" **(84-R.70-3.1)**, a plate which had appreciated more than ten-fold in price in three years, was said to be approximately 280,000 plates. The editions of "The Cobbler" **(84-R.70-3.2)** and "Bedtime" **(84-R.70-2.3)**, also exceptional performers in the market, reportedly numbered 300,000 and 130,000, respectively. Knowles officials subsequently would neither confirm nor deny the figures, but this was apparently the first time that any allegedly authentic production figures had ever been revealed for any of the large, important, "undisclosed" editions (such as the Hummels) since Bing & Grøndahl began keeping their secrets 85 years ago.

If any further evidence were needed, the figures proved again that large edition sizes do not prevent after-market appreciation.

1978 Rockwell Society *Heritage*
(84-R.70-3.2)

The Rockwell Society also filed suit against Trein's of Dixon, Illinois, for plates and figurines made under the name "First International" which the complaint said "were pirated from illustrations by Norman Rockwell appearing on a Society-sponsored collector's plate." It charged that Trein's "conspired and schemed to deceive the public into believing that their plates and figurines were sponsored or backed by the Rockwell Society . . .". At year's end the suit was still pending in federal court.

GOEBEL HUMMEL ANNUALS SUFFER

While Rockwell issues were enjoying a record year, another big-edition mainstay of the plate market suffered sharp reverses. The Goebel *Hummel Annual* series **(22-G.54-1)** — one of the 12 key indicators which comprise the Market Bradex — dropped 21.2% overall during the year despite exceptional performance by the 1979 issue, "Singing Lesson" **(22-G.54-1.9)**.

1979 Goebel *Hummel Annual*
(22-G.54-1.9)

After remaining relatively stable at record highs for the first four months, prices of back issues in the series began to tumble in May. The sharpest decline was posted by "Globe Trotter" **(22-G.54-1.3)**, a '73 issue which dropped 117 points, or 36% over May and June. Collector uncertainty and "profit-taking" sales caused further broad declines in subsequent months. "Singing Lesson" nevertheless went up in market price for much of the year thanks to dealer and collector speculation based on the experience of the 1978 issue — which had tripled in price in the uncertain climate caused by year-long delivery problems. Goebel's reassurances that the delivery problem would not recur failed to check this widespread speculation. But when the plate arrived at dealer's shops on schedule, speculation ended abruptly and "Singing Lesson" joined the downward trend. Issued at $90.00, it had traded as high as $214.00 but closed the year at $171.00, and was even being discounted as low as $65.00 — $25.00 below issue — in some areas by bewildered and cash-poor dealers.

1979 Viletta *Zolan's Children*
"Sabina in the Grass"
(84-V.36-1.2)

1979 PLATE OF THE YEAR

The Plate of the Year competition — to recognize the highest yearly gain in the market among the year's new releases — was unusually intense in 1979 and proved the closest race in history. The surprise winner was "Sabina in the Grass" **(84-V.36-1.2)**, by Donald Zolan, second issue in Viletta's *Zolan's Children* series. Goebel's aforementioned "Singing Lesson," was the early frontrunner, posting a 67% gain to $150.00 by the end of February. In June, "Leapfrog" **(42-G.74-1.1)**, the first Dave Grossman Designs *Annual*, entered the race, advancing 42% from its $60.00 issue price to $85.00. "Singing Lesson" added another 43% on the August 31 Bradex Quotations, where it peaked at $214.00 — 138% of issue. "Michio" **(22-R.55-8.4)**, the 1979 Rosenthal

1979 Rosenthal *Oriental Gold*
(22-R.55-8.4)

Oriental Gold issue by Edna Hibel, also briefly joined the race. Issued at $325.00, it advanced $100.00 on the same Quotations — up 31% to $425.00. But the plate lost 25 points in the next two months and remained at 23% above issue price until year's end.

A slow-starter, "Sabina" didn't enter the race until August, when it advanced $6.00 — up 27% to $28.00 from the issue price of $22.00. Another nine-point gain in October brought it up 32% to $37.00. Entering the final two months of the year, the contenders came down the home stretch with "Singing Lesson" down $12.00 to $202.00, but still leading at 124% above issue price; "Sabina" at 68%; "Leapfrog" still at 42% over issue; and "Michio" at 23%. As the holiday season began, many traders were wondering if "Singing Lesson" would win the race, even while losing market strength, and why the plate generally acknowledged as the market favorite, "Mary, Mary" **(84-R.17-2.1)**, the 1979 *McClelland's Mother Goose* issue by Reco, had not posted a gain. Although outselling all the others by a wide margin, "Mary, Mary" had apparently not sold out completely before year's end.

1979 Reco International
McClelland's Mother Goose
"Mary, Mary"
(84-R.17-2.1)

Not until the final analysis of trades in the last days of 1979 did the winner emerge. "Singing Lesson" fell $31.00, bringing it down to $171.00 — 90% over issue price; "Leapfrog" lost $5.00, bringing it down to 33% over issue, and "Sabina" made a respectable jump of 14%, bringing it up to $42.00 — 90.9% over issue, and barely edging out "Singing Lesson" to claim the title.

"Sabina in the Grass" broke an established precedent. As the successor to "Erik and Dandelion" **(84-V.36-1.1)** in Villeta's *Zolan's Children* series it was the first non-first-issue to become Plate of the Year.

BACK-ISSUES EXCEL

The second-half slump notwithstanding, 1979 was still a year in which a collector could watch a previously well-chosen "portfolio" of plates appreciate far more rapidly than the rate of inflation. The special character of the market — a diluted demand for new issues because of the sharp increase in their number — left many "fast-buck" speculators disappointed but favored many collectors who had hung onto back issues.

Indeed, only 3 of the year's top 25 gainers were 1979 issues: "Sabina in the Grass"; "Singing Lesson"; and Pickard's "Girl with Hoop" **(84-P.29-4.3)**, third in the *Children of Renoir* series. Selling out at the $55.00 issue price in late summer, "Girl with Hoop" jumped immediately to $95.00. But this steep jump seemed to discourage would-be collectors. "Girl with Hoop" remained at $95.00 until December when it edged up another five points to close the year at $100.00 — 45% above issue price.

1979 Pickard *Children of Renoir*
"Girl with Hoop"
(84-P.29-4.3)

Other than these three new issues, the success stories of 1979 were all in the back-issue market. And, as could be expected, 13 of the top 25 gainers were Rockwell issues — 6 of the top 10.

The plate in greatest demand was the Rockwell Society of America's "The Toy Maker" **(84-R.70-3.1)**, the 1977 issue in the *Rockwell Heritage Collection*, issued at $14.50. Trading at $75.00 in January, it doubled over the year to close at $150.00. "Toy Maker" had its most rapid increase of 25 points during January and February but continued to climb through the year. September and October were the only months in which its trading price *didn't* increase.

1977 Royal Devon *Christmas*
(84-R.60-1.3)

1977 Rockwell Society *Heritage*
"The Toy Maker"
(84-R.70-3.1)

1975 Rockwell Society *Christmas*
(84-R.70-1.2)

Five of the next six top gainers were also Rockwells, leading many analysts to call 1979 "the Rockwell year." "The Big Moment" **(84-R.60-1.3)**, 1977 third issue in Royal Devon's *Christmas* series, surged from $32.00 in January to $60.00 in December, an increase of 87.5%. "Angel with a Black Eye" **(84-R.70-1.2)**, 1975 second issue in the Rockwell Society's *Christmas* series, posted a 70% increase over the year to close at $102.00. "Puppy Love" **(84-R.60-2.2)**, the 1976 second issue in Royal Devon's *Mother's Day* series, ended 1979 with a 22-point, 66.6% gain. "The Cobbler," **(84-R.70-3.2)** the 1978 second issue in the *Rockwell Heritage Collection*, went from $45.00 to $74.00, an increase of 64.4%. "Me & My Pal" **(84-G.58-1.5)**, the 1975 fifth issue in Gorham's *Rockwell Four Seasons* series, posted an 85-point gain to close at $220.00, up 62.9%.

Other top Rockwell gainers included "Grand Pals" **(84-G.58-1.6)**, the 1976 Gorham *Rockwell Four Seasons* issue, up 58.6% to $230.00, "A Mother's Love" **(84-R.70-2.1)**, the 1976 Rockwell Society *Mother's Day* issue, up 53.8% to $100.00; and "Good Deeds" **(84-G.58-3.2)**, the 1975 Gorham *Rockwell Christmas* issue, up 50.0% to $45.00.

One series which did not benefit from the Rockwell boom was Franklin Mint's *Christmas* **(84-F.64-1)**. Despite being the only issues on the market with art created by Rockwell specifically for limited-edition plates, the series suffered all year long from the adverse publicity of the CBS-TV "60 Minutes" segment broadcast, in December 1978, which made allegations about the poor resale value of Mint collectibles. The average market price of issues in the series dropped 20% over the year.

1970 Franklin Mint *Christmas*
(84-F.64-1.1)

The only back-issue among the top seven gainers not bearing a Rockwell design was "Freddie the Freeloader" **(84-F.4-2.1)**, the 1976 first issue in Fairmont's *Famous Clowns* series by comedian/artist Red Skelton which finished the year with a 91.3% increase — the second highest gain recorded. Issued at $55.00 and trading at $115.00 as the year began, the plate notched up five points to $120.00 in April, then jumped 42% — to $170.00 — during May and June. Owners were particularly reluctant to part with the issue, and it continued to be bid up throughout the rest of the year, closing at $220.00.

Other plates which posted respectable gains of 50% or more were: "Scarlett" **(84-K.41-3.1)**, the Knowles 1978 *Gone With the Wind* issue, up 62.9% to $35.00; "St. Jakob in Groden" **(38-A.54-1.1)**, the 1971 Anri *Christmas* issue, up 53.3% to $115.00; and "Over the Rainbow" **(84-K.41-1.1)**, Knowles' 1977 *Wizard of Oz* issue, up 50% to $42.00.

The prices of the two most historic plates on the market also rose in 1979. "Behind the Frozen Window" **(14-B.36-1.1)**, the 1895 Bing & Grøndahl *Christmas* issue known as the first true collector's plate, had remained static at $3,170.00 for 18 months. However, when the maker entered the European market to add extra plates to its own collection, "Frozen Window" proved unexpectedly difficult to obtain. News of the maker's troubles reached the U.S. in spring, and the issue jumped 26% in the June Quotations to $4,000.00 where it remained for the rest of the year.

"Deux Oiseaux" **(18-L.3-1.1)**, the 1965 Lalique *Annual* — the famous first crystal plate on the market — also posted a strong gain of $100.00 to $1,850.00 even though it was part of a discontinued series.

The broad market retreat in the last six months of 1979 took its toll on back-issues but revealed no underlying pattern, and losses seemed to reflect only random instances of increased supply/decreased demand. "Raggedy Ann Skates" (42-S.12-5.2), the 1976 second issue in Schmid's *Raggedy Ann Christmas* series sustained the biggest loss. Issued at $13.00 and trading at $30.00 in January, it closed the year at $15.00 — a 50% drop.

1978 Knowles *Gone With the Wind*
(84-K.41-3.1)

1971 Anri *Christmas*
(38-A.54-1.1)

1977 Knowles *Wizard of Oz*
(84-K.41-1.1)

1895 Bing & Grøndahl *Christmas*
(14-B.36-1.1)

1965 Lalique *Annual*
(18-L.3-1.1)

1976 Schmid *Raggedy Ann Christmas*
(42-S.12-5.2)

Other major losers in 1979 were: "Snow Scene" **(22-R.58-1.2)**, the 1973 Royal Bayreuth *Christmas* issue, down 48.5% to $18.00; "Christmas in Wendelstein" **(22-B.20-1.4)**, the 1973 Berlin Design *Christmas* issue, down 47.3% to $20.00; and "Brown's Peace Corps" **(84-R.69-1.3)**, the 1978 RiverShore *Famous Americans* issue, down 42.8% to $80.00.

"CHEVAL" DISAPPOINTS ANALYSTS

One new issue which fell short of expectations in 1979 was *Le Cheval Magique*" (The Magic Horse) **(18-H.6-4.1)**, first issue in the *Mille et un Nuits* series by Haviland of Limoges, France. Although artist Liliane Tellier was a newcomer to the market, many analysts predicted a strong showing based on the maker's substantial reputation, particularly because this was Haviland's first major new series since 1973. But the plate proved to be a striking example of how promising issues were victimized by the surfeit of new plates available. "Le Cheval Magique" ended the year still trading at the issue price of $54.50.

1979 Artists of the World
Children of Aberdeen
(84-A.72-1.1)

Artists of the World began a new series entitled *Children of Aberdeen*, with paintings by Kee Fung Ng inspired by the children of the "floating village" of Aberdeen in Hong Kong harbor. This series was advertised as the first by an artist from the People's Republic of China, a claim also made by Royal Doulton of Great Britain for their *Reflections on China* series **(26-R.62-8)** introduced in 1976. The *Children of Aberdeen* first issue, "Girl with Little Brother" **(84-A.72-1.1)**, traded heavily but ended the year still at the issue price of $50.00.

1979 Haviland *Mille et un Nuits*
(18-H.6-4.1)

One 1979 issue which at mid-year seemed headed for spectacular gains was "The Wedding of David and Bathsheba" **(22-H.31-1.1)**. Analysts were optimistic for two reasons: the plate was both the first issue in a new series by one of the most successful plate artists, Edna Hibel, and also the first proprietary series under the new Hibel Studios hallmark. Previous Hibel plates had been produced by such makers as Royal Doulton **(26-R.62-2)** and Rosenthal **(22-R.55-6 and 22-R.55-8)**. Even at a comparatively high issue price of $250.00, the 5,000-plate edition sold out and was actively sought by Hibel fans on the secondary market. By June, the Exchange quotation was $320.00 and in some areas it traded at $392.00. But by October demand began to slip; "David and Bathsheba" dropped 40 points over the last four months to close at $280.00, only 12% above issue price.

1979 Hibel Studios *King David*
(22-H.31-1.1)

"CHILDREN" STAY AT ISSUE

Although a number of issues carried themes based on the United Nation's 1979 "International Year of the Child" celebration, only two were noteworthy in the market. "The Children's Year" (OTC), called the first cloisonné plate, was created by enamelist Margaret Seeler for the Historic Providence Mint. Despite being billed as "the world's first 24 karat gold and enamel plate" and issued at a relatively modest $95.00, the plate did not sell out over the counter and finished the year still at issue price. Germany's Villeroy & Boch introduced an issue entitled "International Year of the Child" (OTC) through its subsidiary, Heinrich. For each plate sold, the maker agreed to donate $4.50 to UNICEF. The plate was still at its $35.00 issue price when 1979 ended.

Three other over-the-counter issues were noteworthy in 1979. One was "Touch," first issue in *The Five Perceptions of Weo Cho* series from Royal Cornwall, billed as "the first collectibles ever made from deep red Cin-nabar," a material intended to resemble traditional oriental lacquerware. It reputedly was "imported directly from China" — although "China" in this case was Taiwan. Issued at $50.00, "Touch" was trading over the counter at $80.00 by the end of 1979.

Another, "The Man of the Golden West" (OTC), issued after the death of John Wayne by Lynell Studios, prompted Wayne Enterprises, Ltd., to attack Lynell under a claim of exclusive rights to the name and likeness of John Wayne. The conflict was unresolved at year's end, and despite an earlier surge of interest following John Wayne's death, the plate was still at its $45.00 issue price.

A third significant over-the-counter issue was "Spring Flowers," by RiverShore, Ltd., issued at $75.00 and said to be the only still-life ever painted by Norman Rockwell. The 17,000-plate edition failed to generate much secondary market activity; "Spring Flowers" finished the year still at issue price despite the success of other Rockwell issues. It was not part of a series.

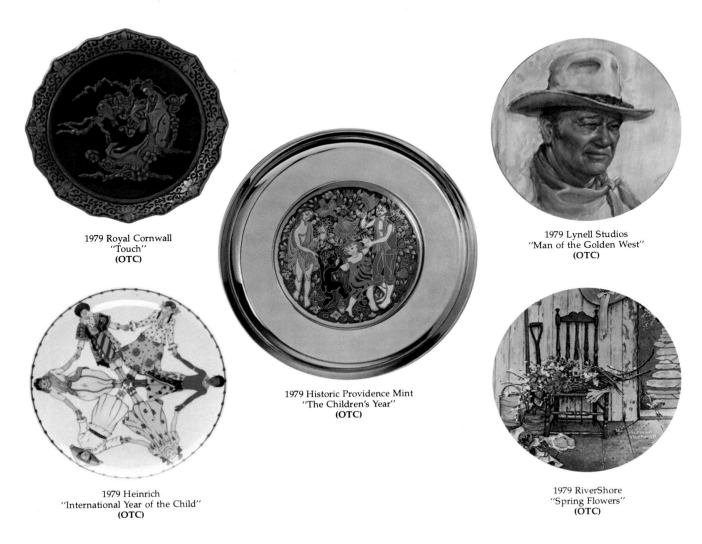

1979 Royal Cornwall
"Touch"
(OTC)

1979 Lynell Studios
"Man of the Golden West"
(OTC)

1979 Historic Providence Mint
"The Children's Year"
(OTC)

1979 Heinrich
"International Year of the Child"
(OTC)

1979 RiverShore
"Spring Flowers"
(OTC)

1907 Rosenthal *Christmas*

1904 Rorstrand *Christmas*

ROSENTHAL WORKED FOR DANES

The year also provided a new chapter in the story of the mysterious 1907 Rosenthal *Christmas* issue which was discovered in 1978. The 1907 plate predated the earliest known Rosenthal collector's issue by three years, and seemed likely to revise collector's plate history. Subsequent investigation established that the design of the plate, as well as those of newly discovered 1908 and 1909 issues, matched those of plates of the same years bearing the hallmark of Buck & Nissen, a defunct Danish department store which commissioned its own proprietary series from the early 1900s until approximately 1924. Discovery of early plates with the same designs bearing both Buck & Nissen and Rosenthal backstamps suggests that Rosenthal in Germany made the plates for Buck & Nissen's Danish market in the Danish blue style made popular by Bing & Grøndahl. Those who have directly compared the Rosenthal and Buck & Nissen issues say that the latter were "cruder" productions with less definition in the artwork.

The Bradford Museum in 1979 acquired a complete set of the rare original Rorstrand *Christmas* series, issued from 1904 to 1925. Never before on public display in North America, the series differs from the current one (**76-R.54-1**, introduced in 1968), being round, rather than distinctively squared.

"BULL" MARKET PERSISTS IN CANADA

The 1979 Canadian market was resistant to the forces which caused the second-half slump in the U.S. The Market Bradex stalled at 320 from June through October after a year-long rise from 300. But with the addition of another three points in November and December, it ended 1979 at an all-time high 323.

The top performing issues on the Canadian market in 1979 paralleled those on the U.S. market. The biggest gainer was the 1977 "Over the Rainbow" (**84-K.41-1.1**),

Plate I in Knowles' *Wizard of Oz Collection*. The plate shot up 36 points over the final four months of 1979 to close at Can. $75.00 — 250% of its Can. $29.00 issue price and a 150% increase on the year. Earlier issues in the series were also in demand. Plate II, "If I Only Had a Brain" (**84-K.41-1.2**), jumped 106% to Can. $60.00 — 206% of its Can. $29.00 issue price. Plates III and IV in the series, "If I Only Had a Heart" (**84-K.41-1.3**) and "If I Were King of the Forest" (**84-K.41-1.4**), gained 10 points each to close at Can. $39.00 — 134% of the Can. $29.00 issue price.

1978 Knowles *Wizard of Oz*
"If I Only Had a Brain"
(**84-K.41-1.2**)

The second best performance for 1979 was registered by "The Toy Maker" (**84-R.70-3.1**), the 1977 *Rockwell Heritage* issue, which benefited from intensive speculation in Rockwell issues. "The Toy Maker" gained 147 points — an increase of 147% — and closed at Can. $247.00, 1008% of its Can. $24.50 issue price. The second plate in the *Rockwell Heritage Collection*, "The Cobbler" (**84-R.70-3.2**), was another top performer of 1979. It rose 67% to close at Can. $75.00 — 254% of its Can. $29.50 issue price.

The third top gainer was "Tiny Tim" **(84-G.58-3.1)**, first issue in the Gorham *Rockwell Christmas* series. It was up 142% and closed at Can. $85.00 — 486% of its Can. $17.50 issue price.

There were a few losers on the 1979 Canadian plate market, most notably the 1970 Wedgwood *Christmas* **(26-W.90-1.2)**, down 40% to $15.00 at year's end; but advances outnumbered declines in every reporting period and the 23-point Bradex increase was a clear indication of market vitality.

1970 Wedgwood *Christmas*
(26-W.90-1.2)

Another indication was the First Annual Canadian Plate Collector's Fair in Montreal October 28 which drew 365 collectors to view makers' exhibits and meet various artists. Despite the small turnout, exhibitors were undismayed, explaining that Quebec province has the lowest concentration of collectors in Canada and that the fair was planned and organized in only eight weeks. A second Canadian fair is planned for Toronto in June, 1980.

The First Annual Canadian Plate
Collector's Fair — Montreal

GERMAN MARKET ALSO UNAFFECTED BY U.S. DOWNTURN

The European plate market also was unaffected by the downturn in the U.S. In Germany, as in Canada, advances outnumbered declines in every reporting period. The two top performers, however, did show how activity on the U.S. market could indirectly affect prices German collectors paid for issues. "The Cobbler" **(84-R.70-3.2)** and "The Toy Maker" **(84-R.70-3.1)** — respectively the second and first plates in the *Rockwell Heritage Collection* — went up 207% and 137%. The increases were generated by collectors of the 1979 third plate in the series, "The Lighthouse Keeper's Daughter" **(84-R.70-3.3)** — the first Rockwell Society plate offered in Germany — going into the back-issue market to fill out their collections. Since "The Cobbler" and "The Toy Maker" were never promoted as new issues in Europe, these collectors were forced to buy specially imported plates at the going U.S. prices, which spiraled ever higher throughout the year. German collectors appeared ready to pay whatever price was necessary. At year's end, "The Cobbler" traded at DM 138.00 (U.S. $80.00), 307% of its DM 45.00 issue price; "The Toy Maker" traded at DM 287.00 (U.S. $166.00), 700% of its DM 41.00 issue price.

The next highest gainer was one which more accurately reflected indigenous trading on the German market. "Franz-Josef Strauss" **(OTC)**, sixth issue in Rosenthal's *Satireteller* series, with a caricature of the political leader who is running for the office of Chancellor in 1980, gained 155 points. It closed up 103% to DM 305.00 (U.S. $177.00), 772% of its DM 39.50 issue price. "*Carl*

Plate VI, Rosenthal *Satireteller*
(OTC)

Larsson Serie I" **(OTC)**, first issue in Bing & Grøndahl's *Marchenteller* series, gained 310 points to close up 62% to DM 810.00 (U.S. $470.00), or 300% of its DM 270.00 issue price.

1977 Bing & Grøndahl *Marchenteller*
(OTC)

The biggest loser for 1979 was "Salvador Dali" **(OTC)**, the 1976 issue in Rosenthal's *Jahresteller (Porzellan)* series. It dropped 25% over the year to close at DM 3120.00 (U.S. $1809.00) — 167% of its DM 1870.00 issue price.

1979 Rosenthal *Jahresteller (Glas)*
(OTC)

Rosenthal more than doubled the price of its Crystal *Jahresteller* issue for 1979 — another plate by Salvador Dali — offering it on the market at DM 1250.00 (U.S. $725.00). Yet collectors who wanted a work by the noted artist were undeterred by the price; the 3,000-plate edition, which was not available in the U.S., sold out and appreciated 60 points by year's end. "Sakura" **(22-R.55-8.3)**, the 1978 Rosenthal *Oriental Gold* plate by Edna Hibel, issued at DM 600.00 (U.S. $348.00), closed at DM 790.00 — a 32% increase. And "Bird of Paradise" **(OTC)**, the 1977 Noritake *Annual*, issued at DM 797.00 (U.S. $462.00), closed at DM 1385.00 — a 74% increase.

NEW EXCHANGE HEADQUARTERS ESTABLISHED IN THE U.K.

For the estimated 100,000 plate collectors in the United Kingdom, the Exchange in 1979 established British headquarters in Banbury, a London suburb. To compute a Market Bradex, ten series widely traded in the U.K. were selected as the key market indicators. The average increase of all issues in these series was estimated, and the U.K. Bradex was tentatively established at 197 as 1980 began.

The Collector Platemaker's Guild Fair in Chicago May 5-6 drew 6,100 people, down from the record 16,627 the previous year in New York, and included appearances by artists Edna Hibel, Frank Russell, Irish McCalla, Roger Brown, Yiannis Koutsis, Mary Vickers, Irene Spencer and Carl Romanelli. Besides meeting the plate artists — many of them at work — collectors could view the "Firsts in Plate Collecting," the Guild's exhibit of the most significant limited-edition plates, including the 1895 Bing & Grøndahl *Christmas* issue — considered to be the first true collector's plate. The Guild scheduled its 1980 fair for September 4-8 at the Los Angeles Century Plaza Hotel and anticipated attendance in the tens of thousands. Fred McGrew, president of the Arizona Plate Collectors' Club and organizer of the previous "Swap & Sell" events at the Plate Collectors Conventions in South Bend, Indiana, planned a greatly expanded version for Los Angeles in the form of a large-scale auction exchange to run for the duration of the 1980 fair.

SOUTH BEND DRAWS 3,980

The Fifth Annual Plate Collectors Convention at South Bend, the oldest yearly convention, was held July 13-15. Industry representatives had expected a banner year; more than 100 exhibitors were on hand and 100 seminars were scheduled. Twenty-seven plate artists attended, including Don Spaulding, Thaddeus Krumeich, Frank Russell and Gertrude Barrer, Donald Zolan and Gayle Bright Appleby. But the number of visitors was a disappointing 3,980 — almost 50% below 1978. At the "Swap & Sell" event, organized by Fred McGrew, more than 400 collectors bought, sold and exchanged plates at a brisk pace. Total sales volume in just the first two hours was $40,000, and by the time the session closed two more hours later the figure stood at $68,500. The 1980 convention in South Bend was scheduled for July 11-13.

An entirely different kind of collector's plate exhibition opened in late August at the Bradford Museum in Niles, Illinois. Entitled "The Originals," it showed the original paintings and graphics used in the creation of such plates as Edna Hibel's "Colette and Child" **(26-R.62-2.1)**; Mary Vickers' "Innocence" **(26-W.90-4.1)**; and Norman Rockwell's "Scotty Gets His Tree" **(84-R.70-1.1)**. Included were 48 works in pencil, gouache, ink, watercolor, fresco, pastel, oil, acrylic and casein. "The Originals" collection was on display through October.

The 1979 American Limited-Edition Association Convention in Anaheim, California, September 7-9, was attended by almost 3,000 collectors, nearly double the number at the 1978 convention. Several celebrities were on hand, including stars from television's "Hollywood Squares" who were promoting a plate inspired by the program. The Association planned to hold the 1980 convention in New York's Madison Square Garden October 4-5.

INTERNATIONAL MARKET GROWS

As typified by the establishment in 1979 of an exchange trading center in the United Kingdom and the First Annual Canadian Plate Collectors Fair, the number of plate collectors in the international market continued to grow. There were signs of resurging collector activity in the Scandinavian countries, an expanding market in Australia, and clear indications of awakening interest in such far-flung and diverse nations as Japan, South Africa and Iceland.

These signs were taken to mean that the American boom years of the 1970s may well be only a prelude to the collector's plate market's greatest period of growth . . . far beyond American shores.

The Exchange gave quotations at the Fifth Annual Plate Collectors Convention in South Bend, Indiana

One hundred seminars were scheduled at the South Bend convention in July

"The Originals" collection was on display at the Bradford Museum from August through October

The Bradford Book of Collector's Plates is the official directory of all major issues regularly traded in the market. It is used to locate and identify all plates quickly and accurately. The plates are arranged by:

    Country of plate's origin in alphabetical order.

    Plate Maker within each country, also in alphabetical order.

    Plate Series of each maker in chronological order beginning with the maker's first series.

    Individual Plates in each series, also in chronological order beginning with the first plate.

To speed identification, each plate is listed by its Bradex number. *These numbers are in sequence but not necessarily consecutive.* The number on the upper outer corner of each page indicates the first plate listed on that page.

THE BRADEX NUMBER

of a plate is made up of five identifiers.

(The number used as an example here is that of the 1979 Anna-Perenna Triptych)

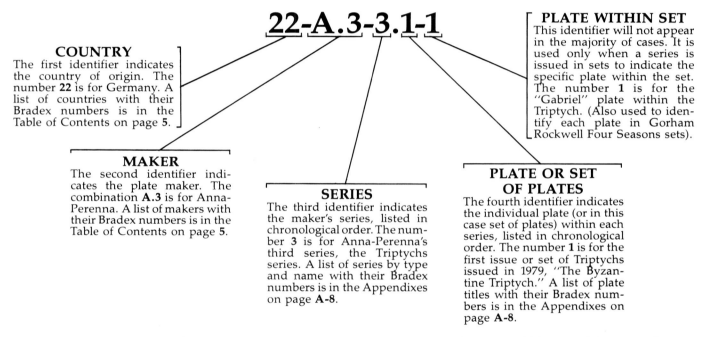

22-A.3-3.1-1

COUNTRY
The first identifier indicates the country of origin. The number **22** is for Germany. A list of countries with their Bradex numbers is in the Table of Contents on page **5**.

MAKER
The second identifier indicates the plate maker. The combination **A.3** is for Anna-Perenna. A list of makers with their Bradex numbers is in the Table of Contents on page **5**.

SERIES
The third identifier indicates the maker's series, listed in chronological order. The number **3** is for Anna-Perenna's third series, the Triptychs series. A list of series by type and name with their Bradex numbers is in the Appendixes on page **A-8**.

PLATE OR SET OF PLATES
The fourth identifier indicates the individual plate (or in this case set of plates) within each series, listed in chronological order. The number **1** is for the first issue or set of Triptychs issued in 1979, "The Byzantine Triptych." A list of plate titles with their Bradex numbers is in the Appendixes on page **A-8**.

PLATE WITHIN SET
This identifier will not appear in the majority of cases. It is used only when a series is issued in sets to indicate the specific plate within the set. The number **1** is for the "Gabriel" plate within the Triptych. (Also used to identify each plate in Gorham Rockwell Four Seasons sets).

Bradex numbers are indexed by *Makers and Sponsors, Plate Titles and Series by Type and Name* and *Artists* in the Appendixes. A Glossary of Commonly Used Terms is also provided in the Appendixes.

LOCATION OF OTHER INFORMATION

Information on history and trademarks is included in each maker's listing; artist, medium, plate diameter, hanging provisions, edition limits and numbering appear with each series listing; Bradex number, plate title, artist and issue price are found below each plate in the series. The listings are complete to 1980 issues, except where the maker did not provide information by press time. Typical edition limits given by makers may be defined as follows:

Edition size limited to 10,000 means the maker established 10,000 plates as the maximum to be produced in the edition, and each plate was numbered.

Edition size limited by announced quantity of 10,000 means only 10,000 plates were issued in the edition, and plates were not numbered.

Edition size undisclosed, limited by period of issue means the edition was limited to the number of plates produced during an announced time period.

Edition size undisclosed, limited by year of issue means the edition was limited to the number of plates produced during the year of issue.

Edition size undisclosed means maker provided no information regarding edition size.

ARGENTINA
PORCELANA GRANADA
(Rosario)

Since 1972, the Porcelana Granada series of Christmas plates has been made by one of Argentina's largest porcelain factories, Porcelanas Verbano. (The 1971 plate was produced in Cali, Colombia.) Porcelanas Verbano is a recognized producer of dinnerware and hand-painted pieces. The Christmas series, *Pax in Terra*, based on the life of Christ, began in 1971 and is to run for fifteen years.

The current artist for the series is Gerry Sparks, noted for her oils and murals which appear in galleries in the United States, Switzerland, Greece and the Bahamas.

PORCELANA GRANADA

(Rosario)

Pax in Terra (Peace on Earth)
Artist: As indicated
Overglaze porcelain decorated in
  cobalt blue
Diameter: 17.8 centimeters
  (7 inches)
Pierced foot rim
Edition size: As indicated
Numbered since 1972, without
  certificate

4-P.61-1.1
1971 *The Annunciation*
Artist: Tom Fennell, Jr
Issue price: $12.00. Edition size limited
to announced quantity of 9,300

4-P.61-1.2
1972 *Mary and Elizabeth*
Artist: Gerry Sparks
Issue price: $13.00
Edition size limited to 6,000

4-P.61-1.3
1973 *Road to Bethlehem*
Artist: Gerry Sparks
Issue price: $14.00
Edition size limited to 5,000

4-P.61-1.4
1974 *No Room at the Inn*
Artist: Gerry Sparks
Issue price: $15.00
Edition size limited to 5,000

4-P.61-1.5
1975 *Shepherds in the Field*
Artist: Gerry Sparks
Issue price: $16.50
Edition size limited to 5,000

4-P.61-1.6
1976 *The Nativity*
Artist: Gerry Sparks
Issue price: $17.50
Edition size limited to 5,000

4-P.61-1.7
1977 *Three Kings*
Artist: Gerry Sparks
Issue price: $18.00
Edition size limited to 5,000

4-P.61-1.8
1978 *Young Carpenter*
Artist: Gerry Sparks
Issue price: $18.00
Edition size limited to 5,000

4-P.61-1.9
1979 *Calling of Disciples*
Artist: Gerry Sparks
Issue price: $19.00
Edition size limited to 5,000

4-P.61-1.10
1980 *Loaves and Fishes*
Artist: Gerry Sparks
Issue price: $20.00
Edition size limited to 5,000

KONGELIG HOFLEVERANDØR

COPENHAGEN PORCELAIN
BING & GRØNDAHL
B&G

Bing & Grøndahl, Denmark's second oldest existing porcelain maker (after Royal Copenhagen), was established in 1853 by Frederick Vilhelm Grøndahl and M. H. and J. H. Bing. Grøndahl, a young sculptor previously employed by Royal Copenhagen, supplied the artistic talent while the Bing brothers provided financial backing. Although Grøndahl died before the manufactory's third year of operation, his name was retained in honor of his contribution. Bing & Grøndahl has continued under the leadership of the Bing family for five generations.

The world's first collector's plate, "Behind the Frozen Window," was issued by Bing & Grøndahl in 1895. This began its *Christmas Series* which has been produced each year without interruption despite wars and economic crises. Plates in this series are now the most widely collected of all plates in the market. In 1969 Bing & Grøndahl issued the first Mother's Day plate, "Dog and Puppies." Besides limited-edition collector's plates, Bing & Grøndahl makes a variety of porcelain articles, including figurines and

tableware. Many of their porcelain works can be found in museums around the world and they have achieved the distinction of appointment to the Royal Courts of Denmark, Sweden and Great Britain. This distinction is symbolized by the crown which is part of their trademark.

Artist Henry Thelander's association with Bing & Grøndahl is unparalleled on the collector's plate market. The 1980 issue marks his eighteenth consecutive design for the *Christmas Series*. He also has designed every Bing & Grøndahl Mother's Day issue — twelve in all. A self-taught artist, Thelander has spent his five-decade-long career living and working in Copenhagen, London and Stockholm, benefitting from the variety of cultures and artistic influences. Known as the "equivalent of a poet laureate" in the field of Danish visual arts, he has designed government-sponsored postage stamps, posters, and a celebrated series of paintings commemorating the Kingdom's 800th anniversary — now displayed in the Copenhagen town hall.

Christmas Series

Artist: As indicated

True underglaze porcelain hand
  painted in Copenhagen blue on
  bas-relief

Diameter: 17.8 centimeters
  (7 inches)

Pierced foot rim

Edition size undisclosed, limited
  by year of issue

Not numbered, without certificate;
  individually initialed on back by
  each painter

14-B.36-1.1
1895 *Behind the Frozen Window*
Artist: F. A. Hallin
Issue price: $.50

14-B.36-1.2
1896 *New Moon over Snow-covered Trees*
Artist: F. A. Hallin
Issue price: $.50

14-B.36-1.3
1897 *Christmas Meal of the Sparrows*
Artist: F. A. Hallin
Issue price: $.75

14-B.36-1.4
1898 *Christmas Roses and Christmas Star*
Artist: Fanny Garde
Issue price: $.75

14-B.36-1.5
1899 *The Crows Enjoying Christmas*
Artist: Dahl Jensen
Issue price: $.75

14-B.36-1.6
1900 *Church Bells Chiming in Christmas*
Artist: Dahl Jensen
Issue price: $.75

14-B.36-1.7
1901 *The Three Wise Men from the East*
Artist: S. Sabra
Issue price: $1.00

14-B.36-1.8
1902 *Interior of a Gothic Church*
Artist: Dahl Jensen
Issue price: $1.00

14-B.36-1.9
1903 *Happy Expectation of Children*
Artist: Margrethe Hyldahl
Issue price: $1.00

14-B.36-1.10
1904 *View of Copenhagen from
Frederiksberg Hill*
Artist: Cathinka Olsen
Issue price: $1.00

14-B.36-1.11
1905 *Anxiety of the Coming Christmas
Night*
Artist: Dahl Jensen
Issue price: $1.00

14-B.36-1.12
1906 *Sleighing to Church on Christmas Eve*
Artist: Dahl Jensen
Issue price: $1.00

14-B.36-1.13
1907 *The Little Match Girl*
Artist: E. Plockross
Issue price: $1.00

14-B.36-1.14
1908 *St. Petri Church of Copenhagen*
Artist: Povl Jorgensen
Issue price: $1.00

14-B.36-1.15
1909 *Happiness over the Yule Tree*
Artist: Aarestrup
Issue price: $1.50

14-B.36-1.16
1910 *The Old Organist*
Artist: C. Ersgaard
Issue price: $1.50

14-B.36-1.17
1911 *First It Was Sung by Angels to
Shepherds in the Fields*
Artist: H. Moltke
Issue price: $1.50

DENMARK
BING & GRØNDAHL
(Copenhagen)

14-B.36-1.18
1912 *Going to Church on Christmas Eve*
Artist: Einar Hansen
Issue price: $1.50

14-B.36-1.19
1913 *Bringing Home the Yule Tree*
Artist: Th. Larsen
Issue price: $1.50

14-B.36-1.20
1914 *Royal Castle of Amalienborg,*
Copenhagen
Artist: Th. Larsen
Issue price: $1.50

14-B.36-1.21
1915 *Chained Dog Getting Double Meal*
on Christmas Eve
Artist: Dahl Jensen
Issue price: $1.50

14-B.36-1.22
1916 *Christmas Prayer of the Sparrows*
Artist: J. Bloch Jorgensen
Issue price: $1.50

14-B.36-1.23
1917 *Arrival of the Christmas Boat*
Artist: Achton Friis
Issue price: $1.50

14-B.36-1.24
1918 *Fishing Boat Returning Home for*
Christmas
Artist: Achton Friis
Issue price: $1.50

14-B.36-1.25
1919 *Outside the Lighted Window*
Artist: Achton Friis
Issue price: $2.00

14-B.36-1.26
1920 *Hare in the Snow*
Artist: Achton Friis
Issue price: $2.00

14-B.36-1.27
1921 *Pigeons in the Castle Court*
Artist: Achton Friis
Issue price: $2.00

14-B.36-1.28
1922 *Star of Bethlehem*
Artist: Achton Friis
Issue price: $2.00

14-B.36-1.29
1923 *Royal Hunting Castle, the Ermitage*
Artist: Achton Friis
Issue price: $2.00

14-B.36-1.30
1924 *Lighthouse in Danish Waters*
Artist: Achton Friis
Issue price: $2.50

14-B.36-1.31
1925 *The Child's Christmas*
Artist: Achton Friis
Issue price: $2.50

14-B.36-1.32
1926 *Churchgoers on Christmas Day*
Artist: Achton Friis
Issue price: $2.50

14-B.36-1.33
1927 *Skating Couple*
Artist: Achton Friis
Issue price: $2.50

14-B.36-1.34
1928 *Eskimos Looking at Village Church in Greenland*
Artist: Achton Friis
Issue price: $2.50

14-B.36-1.35
1929 *Fox Outside Farm on Christmas Eve*
Artist: Achton Friis
Issue price: $2.50

14-B.36-1.36
1930 *Yule Tree in Town Hall Square of Copenhagen*
Artist: H. Flugenring
Issue price: $2.50

14-B.36-1.37
1931 *Arrival of the Christmas Train*
Artist: Achton Friis
Issue price: $2.50

14-B.36-1.38
1932 *Lifeboat at Work*
Artist: H. Flugenring
Issue price: $2.50

14-B.36-1.39
1933 *The Korsor-Nyborg Ferry*
Artist: H. Flugenring
Issue price: $3.00

14-B.36-1.40
1934 *Church Bell in Tower*
Artist: Immanuel Tjerne
Issue price: $3.00

14-B.36-1.41
1935 *Lillebelt Bridge Connecting Funen with Jutland*
Artist: Ove Larsen
Issue price: $3.00

14-B.36-1.42
1936 *Royal Guard Outside Amalienborg Castle in Copenhagen*
Artist: Ove Larsen
Issue price: $3.00

14-B.36-1.43
1937 *Arrival of Christmas Guests*
Artist: Ove Larsen
Issue price: $3.00

14-B.36-1.44
1938 *Lighting the Candles*
Artist: Immanuel Tjerne
Issue price: $3.00

14-B.36-1.45
1939 *Ole Lock-Eye, the Sandman*
Artist: Immanuel Tjerne
Issue price: $3.00

14-B.36-1.46
1940 *Delivering Christmas Letters*
Artist: Ove Larsen
Issue price: $4.00

14-B.36-1.47
1941 *Horses Enjoying Christmas Meal in Stable*
Artist: Ove Larsen
Issue price: $4.00

14-B.36-1.48
1942 *Danish Farm on Christmas Night*
Artist: Ove Larsen
Issue price: $4.00

14-B.36-1.49
1943 *The Ribe Cathedral*
Artist: Ove Larsen
Issue price: $5.00

14-B.36-1.50
1944 *Sorgenfri Castle*
Artist: Ove Larsen
Issue price: $5.00

14-B.36-1.51
1945 *The Old Water Mill*
Artist: Ove Larsen
Issue price: $5.00

14-B.36-1.52
1946 *Commemoration Cross in Honor of Danish Sailors Who Lost Their Lives in World War II*
Artist: Margrethe Hyldahl
Issue price: $5.00

14-B.36-1.53
1947 *Dybbol Mill*
Artist: Margrethe Hyldahl
Issue price: $5.00

DENMARK
BING & GRØNDAHL
(Copenhagen)

14-B.36-1.54
1948 *Watchman, Sculpture of Town Hall, Copenhagen*
Artist: Margrethe Hyldahl
Issue price: $5.50

14-B.36-1.55
1949 *Landsoldaten, 19th Century Danish Soldier*
Artist: Margrethe Hyldahl
Issue price: $5.50

14-B.36-1.56
1950 *Kronborg Castle at Elsinore*
Artist: Margrethe Hyldahl
Issue price: $5.50

14-B.36-1.57
1951 *Jens Bang, New Passenger Boat Running Between Copenhagen and Aalborg*
Artist: Margrethe Hyldahl
Issue price: $6.00

14-B.36-1.58
1952 *Old Copenhagen Canals at Wintertime with Thorvaldsen Museum in Background*
Artist: Borge Pramvig
Issue price: $6.00

14-B.36-1.59
1953 *Royal Boat in Greenland Waters*
Artist: Kjeld Bonfils
Issue price: $7.00

14-B.36-1.60
1954 *Birthplace of Hans Christian Andersen, with Snowman*
Artist: Borge Pramvig
Issue price: $7.50

14-B.36-1.61
1955 *Kalundborg Church*
Artist: Kjeld Bonfils
Issue price: $8.00

14-B.36-1.62
1956 *Christmas in Copenhagen*
Artist: Kjeld Bonfils
Issue price: $8.50

14-B.36-1.63
1957 *Christmas Candles*
Artist: Kjeld Bonfils
Issue price: $9.00

14-B.36-1.64
1958 *Santa Claus*
Artist: Kjeld Bonfils
Issue price: $9.50

14-B.36-1.65
1959 *Christmas Eve*
Artist: Kjeld Bonfils
Issue price: $10.00

14-B.36-1.66
1960 *Danish Village Church*
Artist: Kjeld Bonfils
Issue price: $10.00

14-B.36-1.67
1961 *Winter Harmony*
Artist: Kjeld Bonfils
Issue price: $10.50

14-B.36-1.68
1962 *Winter Night*
Artist: Kjeld Bonfils
Issue price: $11.00

14-B.36-1.69
1963 *The Christmas Elf*
Artist: Henry Thelander
Issue price: $11.00

14-B.36-1.70
1964 *The Fir Tree and Hare*
Artist: Henry Thelander
Issue price: $11.50

14-B.36-1.71
1965 *Bringing Home the Christmas
Tree*
Artist: Henry Thelander
Issue price: $12.00

14-B.36-1.72
1966 *Home for Christmas*
Artist: Henry Thelander
Issue price: $12.00

14-B.36-1.73
1967 *Sharing the Joy of Christmas*
Artist: Henry Thelander
Issue price: $13.00

14-B.36-1.74
1968 *Christmas in Church*
Artist: Henry Thelander
Issue price: $14.00

14-B.36-1.75
1969 *Arrival of Christmas Guests*
Artist: Henry Thelander
Issue price: $14.00

14-B.36-1.76
1970 *Pheasants in the Snow at Christmas*
Artist: Henry Thelander
Issue price: $14.50

14-B.36-1.77
1971 *Christmas at Home*
Artist: Henry Thelander
Issue price: $15.00

14-B.36-1.78
1972 *Christmas in Greenland*
Artist: Henry Thelander
Issue price: $16.50

14-B.36-1.79
1973 *Country Christmas*
Artist: Henry Thelander
Issue price: $19.50

14-B.36-1.80
1974 *Christmas in the Village*
Artist: Henry Thelander
Issue price: $22.00

14-B.36-1.81
1975 *The Old Water Mill*
Artist: Henry Thelander
Issue price: $27.50

14-B.36-1.82
1976 *Christmas Welcome*
Artist: Henry Thelander
Issue price: $27.50

14-B.36-1.83
1977 *Copenhagen Christmas*
Artist: Henry Thelander
Issue price: $29.50

14-B.36-1.84
1978 *A Christmas Tale*
Artist: Henry Thelander
Issue price: $32.00

14-B.36-1.85
1979 *White Christmas*
Artist: Henry Thelander
Issue price: $36.50

14-B.36-1.86
1980 *Christmas in the Woods*
Artist: Henry Thelander
Issue price: $42.50

BING & GRØNDAHL
(Copenhagen)

Mother's Day Series

Artist: Henry Thelander

True underglaze porcelain hand painted in Copenhagen blue on bas-relief

Diameter: 15.2 centimeters (6 inches)

Pierced foot rim

Edition size undisclosed, limited by year of issue

Not numbered, without certificate; individually initialed on back by each painter

14-B.36-3.1
1969 *Dog and Puppies*
Artist: Henry Thelander
Issue price: $9.75

14-B.36-3.2
1970 *Bird and Chicks*
Artist: Henry Thelander
Issue price: $10.00

14-B.36-3.3
1971 *Cat and Kitten*
Artist: Henry Thelander
Issue price: $11.00

14-B.36-3.4
1972 *Mare and Foal*
Artist: Henry Thelander
Issue price: $12.00

14-B.36-3.5
1973 *Duck and Ducklings*
Artist: Henry Thelander
Issue price: $13.00

14-B.36-3.6
1974 *Bear and Cubs*
Artist: Henry Thelander
Issue price: $16.50

14-B.36-3.7
1975 *Doe and Fawns*
Artist: Henry Thelander
Issue price: $19.50

14-B.36-3.8
1976 *Swan Family*
Artist: Henry Thelander
Issue price: $22.50

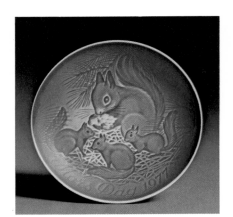

14-B.36-3.9
1977 *Squirrel and Young*
Artist: Henry Thelander
Issue price: $23.50

14-B.36-3.10
1978 *Heron*
Artist: Henry Thelander
Issue price: $24.50

14-B.36-3.11
1979 *Fox and Cubs*
Artist: Henry Thelander
Issue price: $27.50

14-B.36-3.12
1980 *Woodpecker and Young*
Artist: Henry Thelander
Issue price: $29.50

Grande Copenhagen plates are produced at the Eslau porcelain factory near Copenhagen. Grande Copenhagen began its *Christmas Series* of plates depicting Danish winter scenes in 1975.

The artist for Grande Copenhagen's *Christmas Series* is not disclosed.

DENMARK
GRANDE COPENHAGEN
(Copenhagen)

Christmas Series
Artist: Undisclosed

True underglaze porcelain hand
painted in Copenhagen blue on
bas-relief

Diameter: 18.4 centimeters
(7¼ inches)

Pierced foot rim

Edition size undisclosed, limited
by year of issue

Not numbered, without certificate;
individually initialed on back by
each painter

14-G.65-1.1
1975 *Alone Together*
Artist: Undisclosed
Issue price: $24.50

14-G.65-1.2
1976 *Christmas Wreath*
Artist: Undisclosed
Issue price: $24.50

14-G.65-1.3
1977 *Fishwives at Gammelstrand*
Artist: Undisclosed
Issue price: $26.50

14-G.65-1.4
1978 *Hans Christian Andersen*
Artist: Undisclosed
Issue price: $32.50

14-G.65-1.5
1979 Untitled at press time
Artist: Undisclosed
Issue price: $34.50

DENMARK
SVEND JENSEN
(Ringsted)

Svend Jensen plates are made by the Désirée porcelain factory near Copenhagen and are the result of an association between art consultant Svend Jensen and porcelain expert H. C. Torbal. In 1970 they issued the first limited-edition plates in two Svend Jensen annual collections — a *Christmas Series* based on Hans Christian Andersen fairy tales, and a *Mother's Day Series*.

Svend Jensen artist Svend Otto is internationally known for his spare but vigorous illustrations of the beloved Hans Christian Andersen tales. Copenhagen-born Mads Stage received his training at the Royal Danish Academy of Arts and won several prizes for his illustrations of Danish literary works. His perceptive, though child-like style has brought him a wide following, both in Denmark and in the United States.

DENMARK
SVEND JENSEN
(Ringsted)

Christmas Series

Artist: As indicated. Artist's name
  appears on back
True underglaze porcelain hand
  painted in Copenhagen blue on
  bas-relief
Diameter: 17.8 centimeters
  (7 inches)
Pierced foot rim
Edition size undisclosed, limited
  by year of issue
Not numbered, without certificate;
  individually initialed on back by
  each painter

14-J.21-1.1
1970 *Hans Christian Andersen House*
Artist: Gerhard Sausmark
Issue price: $14.50

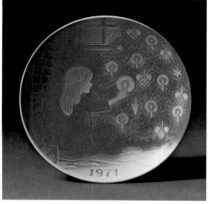

14-J.21-1.2
1971 *The Little Match Girl*
Artist: Mads Stage
Issue price: $15.00

14-J.21-1.3
1972 *Little Mermaid of Copenhagen*
Rights from family of Edvard Eriksen,
sculptor
Issue price: $16.50

14-J.21-1.4
1973 *The Fir Tree*
Artist: Svend Otto
Issue price: $22.00

14-J.21-1.5
1974 *The Chimney Sweep*
Artist: Svend Otto
Issue price: $25.00

14-J.21-1.6
1975 *The Ugly Duckling*
Artist: Svend Otto
Issue price: $27.50

14-J.21-1.7
1976 *The Snow Queen*
Artist: Mads Stage
Issue price: $27.50

14-J.21-1.8
1977 *The Snowman*
Artist: Svend Otto
Issue price: $29.50

14-J.21-1.9
1978 *The Last Dream of the Old Oak Tree*
Artist: Svend Otto
Issue price: $32.00

14-J.21-1.10
1979 *The Old Street Lamp*
Artist: Svend Otto
Issue price: $36.50

14-J.21-1.11
1980 *Willie Winky*
Artist: Svend Otto
Issue price: $42.50

Mother's Day Series

Artist: As indicated. Artist's name
appears on back

True underglaze porcelain hand
painted in Copenhagen blue on
bas-relief

Diameter: 17.8 centimeters
(7 inches)

Pierced foot rim

Edition size undisclosed, limited
by year of issue

Not numbered, with certificate
since 1977; individually initialed
on back by each painter

14-J.21-2.1
1970 *A Bouquet for Mother*
Artist: Maggi Baaring
Issue price: $14.50

14-J.21-2.2
1971 *Mother's Love*
Artist: Nulle Oigaard
Issue price: $15.00

14-J.21-2.3
1972 *Good Night*
Artist: Mads Stage
Issue price: $15.00

14-J.21-2.4
1973 *Flowers for Mother*
Artist: Mads Stage
Issue price: $20.00

14-J.21-2.5
1974 *Daisies for Mother*
Artist: Mads Stage
Issue price: $25.00

14-J.21-2.6
1975 Surprise for Mother
Artist: Mads Stage
Issue price: $27.50

14-J.21-2.7
1976 The Complete Gardener
Artist: Mads Stage
Issue price: $27.50

14-J.21-2.8
1977 Little Friends
Artist: Mads Stage
Issue price: $29.50

14-J.21-2.9
1978 Dreams
Artist: Mads Stage
Issue price: $32.00

14-J.21-2.10
1979 Promenade
Artist: Mads Stage
Issue price: $36.50

14-J.21-2.11
1980 Nursery Scene
Artist: Mads Stage
Issue price: $42.50

DENMARK
ROYAL COPENHAGEN
(Copenhagen)

The Royal Copenhagen Porcelain Manufactory, Denmark's oldest existing porcelain maker, was established by Franz Henrich Muller with the support of Denmark's queen dowager, Juliane Marie, in January 1775. Since the 1760s, members of the Danish royal family had been interested in the white hard-paste porcelain made in China, but it was not until 1772 that Muller, a Danish pharmacist and chemist, was able to duplicate the fine porcelain. In 1779 "The Danish Porcelain Factory," as Royal Copenhagen was then called, came under royal control.

The Danish Court controlled the firm from 1779 to 1867, a period in its history that is still symbolized by the crown in its trademark. The three wavy lines under the crown, part of the factory trademark since 1775, pay tribute to Denmark's tradition as a seafaring nation and represent Denmark's three ancient waterways: the Sound, the Great Belt and the Little Belt. In 1867 the factory was sold and has continued under private ownership. It is still a supplier to the royal court in Denmark.

The first Royal Copenhagen Christmas plate was issued in 1908 and the series had continued every year since then. For the first three years the plates were six inches in diameter. Beginning with the 1911 issue, they were changed to the seven-inch size. From the beginning, the motif for each year's Christmas plate has been selected from suggestions submitted by employees of the Royal Copenhagen factory. Until 1953, small quantities of plates in the *Christmas Series* were created with the word "Christmas" translated into other languages to meet demand from non-Danish collectors.

The Royal Copenhagen *Mother's Day Series* was started in 1971 and the *Historical Series* was introduced in 1975 to celebrate the company's own two-hundredth anniversary. Yearly issues of this series commemorate other bicentennial anniversaries.

Artist Kai Lange has been with Royal Copenhagen from the age of seventeen and after more than half a century with the firm is regarded as one of the most knowledgeable artists working in the porcelain medium today. The first Kai Lange design selected for the annual *Christmas* plate was for the 1940 issue, and since 1963, every plate has been a Kai Lange creation. Ib Spang Olsen, artist for the *Mother's Day Series* is a recipient of the Danish Children's Book Prize.

Christmas Series

Artist: As indicated. Artist's name appears on back since 1955

True underglaze porcelain hand painted in Copenhagen blue on bas-relief

Diameter: 17.8 centimeters (7 inches)

Pierced foot rim

Edition size unannounced, limited by year of issue

Not numbered, without certificate; individually initialed on back by each painter

14-R.59-1.1
1908 *Madonna and Child*
Artist: Chr. Thomsen
Diameter: 6 inches
Issue price: $1.00

14-R.59-1.2
1909 *Danish Landscape*
Artist: St. Ussing
Diameter: 6 inches
Issue price: $1.00

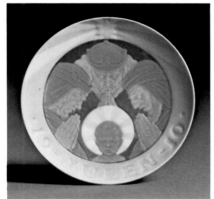

14-R.59-1.3
1910 *The Magi*
Artist: Chr. Thomsen
Diameter: 6 inches
Issue price: $1.00

14-R.59-1.4
1911 *Danish Landscape*
Artist: Oluf Jensen
Issue price: $1.00

14-R.59-1.5
1912 *Elderly Couple by Christmas Tree*
Artist: Chr. Thomsen
Issue price: $1.00

14-R.59-1.6
1913 *Spire of Frederik's Church, Copenhagen*
Artist: A. Boesen
Issue price: $1.50

14-R.59-1.7
1914 *Sparrows in Tree at Church of the Holy Spirit, Copenhagen*
Artist: A. Boesen
Issue price: $1.50

14-R.59-1.8
1915 *Danish Landscape*
Artist: A. Krog
Issue price: $1.50

14-R.59-1.9
1916 *Shepherd in the Field on Christmas Night*
Artist: R. Bocher
Issue price: $1.50

14-R.59-1.10
1917 *Tower of Our Savior's Church, Copenhagen*
Artist: Oluf Jensen
Issue price: $2.00

14-R.59-1.11
1918 *Sheep and Shepherds*
Artist: Oluf Jensen
Issue price: $2.00

14-R.59-1.12
1919 *In the Park*
Artist: Oluf Jensen
Issue price: $2.00

14-R.59-1.13
1920 *Mary with the Child Jesus*
Artist: G. Rode
Issue price: $2.00

14-R.59-1.14
1921 *Aabenraa Marketplace*
Artist: Oluf Jensen
Issue price: $2.00

14-R.59-1.15
1922 *Three Singing Angels*
Artist: Mrs. Selschou Olsen
Issue price: $2.00

14-R.59-1.16
1923 *Danish Landscape*
Artist: Oluf Jensen
Issue price: $2.00

14-R.59-1.17
1924 *Christmas Star over the Sea and Sailing Ship*
Artist: Benjamin Olsen
Issue price: $2.00

14-R.59-1.18
1925 *Street Scene from Christianshavn,*
Copenhagen
Artist: Oluf Jensen
Issue price: $2.00

14-R.59-1.19
1926 *View of Christianshavn Canal,*
Copenhagen
Artist: R. Bocher
Issue price: $2.00

14-R.59-1.20
1927 *Ship's Boy at the Tiller on Christmas*
Night
Artist: Benjamin Olsen
Issue price: $2.00

14-R.59-1.21
1928 *Vicar's Family on Way to Church*
Artist: G. Rode
Issue price: $2.00

14-R.59-1.22
1929 *Grundtvig Church, Copenhagen*
Artist: Oluf Jensen
Issue price: $2.00

14-R.59-1.23
1930 *Fishing Boats on the Way to the*
Harbor
Artist: Benjamin Olsen
Issue price: $2.50

14-R.59-1.24
1931 *Mother and Child*
Artist: G. Rode
Issue price: $2.50

14-R.59-1.25
1932 *Frederiksberg Gardens with Statue of*
Frederik VI
Artist: Oluf Jensen
Issue price: $2.50

14-R.59-1.26
1933 *The Great Belt Ferry*
Artist: Benjamin Olsen
Issue price: $2.50

14-R.59-1.27
1934 *The Hermitage Castle*
Artist: Oluf Jensen
Issue price: $2.50

14-R.59-1.28
1935 *Fishing Boat off Kronborg Castle*
Artist: Benjamin Olsen
Issue price: $2.50

14-R.59-1.29
1936 *Roskilde Cathedral*
Artist: R. Bocher
Issue price: $2.50

14-R.59-1.30
1937 *Christmas Scene in Main Street,
Copenhagen*
Artist: Nils Thorsson
Issue price: $2.50

14-R.59-1.31
1938 *Round Church in Osterlars on
Bornholm*
Artist: Herne Nielsen
Issue price: $3.00

14-R.59-1.32
1939 *Expeditionary Ship in Pack-ice of
Greenland*
Artist: Sv. Nic. Nielsen
Issue price: $3.00

14-R.59-1.33
1940 *The Good Shepherd*
Artist: Kai Lange
Issue price: $3.00

14-R.59-1.34
1941 *Danish Village Church*
Artist: Th. Kjolner
Issue price: $3.00

14-R.59-1.35
1942 *Bell Tower of Old Church in Jutland*
Artist: Nils Thorsson
Issue price: $4.00

14-R.59-1.36
1943 *Flight of Holy Family to Egypt*
Artist: Nils Thorsson
Issue price: $4.00

14-R.59-1.37
1944 *Typical Danish Winter Scene*
Artist: Viggo Olsen
Issue price: $4.00

14-R.59-1.38
1945 *A Peaceful Motif*
Artist: R. Bocher
Issue price: $4.00

14-R.59-1.39
1946 *Zealand Village Church*
Artist: Nils Thorsson
Issue price: $4.00

14-R.59-1.40
1947 *The Good Shepherd*
Artist: Kai Lange
Issue price: $4.50

14-R.59-1.41
1948 *Nodebo Church at Christmastime*
Artist: Th. Kjolner
Issue price: $4.50

14-R.59-1.42
1949 *Our Lady's Cathedral, Copenhagen*
Artist: Hans H. Hansen
Issue price: $5.00

14-R.59-1.43
1950 *Boeslunde Church, Zealand*
Artist: Viggo Olsen
Issue price: $5.00

14-R.59-1.44
1951 *Christmas Angel*
Artist: R. Bocher
Issue price: $5.00

14-R.59-1.45
1952 *Christmas in the Forest*
Artist: Kai Lange
Issue price: $5.00

14-R.59-1.46
1953 *Frederiksberg Castle*
Artist: Th. Kjolner
Issue price: $6.00

14-R.59-1.47
1954 *Amalienborg Palace, Copenhagen*
Artist: Kai Lange
Issue price: $6.00

14-R.59-1.48
1955 *Fano Girl*
Artist: Kai Lange
Issue price: $7.00

14-R.59-1.49
1956 *Rosenborg Castle, Copenhagen*
Artist: Kai Lange
Issue price: $7.00

14-R.59-1.50
1957 *The Good Shepherd*
Artist: Hans H. Hansen
Issue price: $8.00

14-R.59-1.51
1958 *Sunshine over Greenland*
Artist: Hans H. Hansen
Issue price: $9.00

14-R.59-1.52
1959 *Christmas Night*
Artist: Hans H. Hansen
Issue price: $9.00

14-R.59-1.53
1960 *The Stag*
Artist: Hans H. Hansen
Issue price: $10.00

ROYAL COPENHAGEN
(Copenhagen)

14-R.59-1.54
1961 *Training Ship Danmark*
Artist: Kai Lange
Issue price: $10.00

14-R.59-1.55
1962 *The Little Mermaid at Wintertime*
Specific artist not named because of
special nature of this motif
Issue price: $11.00

14-R.59-1.56
1963 *Hojsager Mill*
Artist: Kai Lange
Issue price: $11.00

14-R.59-1.57
1964 *Fetching the Christmas Tree*
Artist: Kai Lange
Issue price: $11.00

14-R.59-1.58
1965 *Little Skaters*
Artist: Kai Lange
Issue price: $12.00

14-R.59-1.59
1966 *Blackbird at Christmastime*
Artist: Kai Lange
Issue price: $12.00

14-R.59-1.60
1967 *The Royal Oak*
Artist: Kai Lange
Issue price: $13.00

14-R.59-1.61
1968 *The Last Umiak*
Artist: Kai Lange
Issue price: $13.00

14-R.59-1.62
1969 *The Old Farmyard*
Artist: Kai Lange
Issue price: $14.00

14-R.59-1.63
1970 *Christmas Rose and Cat*
Artist: Kai Lange
Issue price: $14.00

14-R.59-1.64
1971 *Hare in Winter*
Artist: Kai Lange
Issue price: $15.00

14-R.59-1.65
1972 *In the Desert*
Artist: Kai Lange
Issue price: $16.00

14-R.59-1.66
1973 *Train Homeward Bound for Christmas*
Artist: Kai Lange
Issue price: $22.00

14-R.59-1.67
1974 *Winter Twilight*
Artist: Kai Lange
Issue price: $22.00

14-R.59-1.68
1975 *Queen's Palace*
Artist: Kai Lange
Issue price: $27.50

14-R.59-1.69
1976 *Danish Watermill*
Artist: Sven Vestergaard
Issue price: $27.50

14-R.59-1.70
1977 *Immervad Bridge*
Artist: Kai Lange
Issue price: $32.00

14-R.59-1.71
1978 *Greenland Scenery*
Artist: Kai Lange
Issue price: $35.00

14-R.59-1.72
1979 *Choosing the Christmas Tree*
Artist: Kai Lange
Issue price: $42.50

14-R.59-1.73
1980 *Bringing Home the Christmas Tree*
Artist: Kai Lange
Issue price: $49.50

Mother's Day Series

Artist: As indicated

True underglaze porcelain hand painted in Copenhagen blue on bas-relief

Diameter: 15.9 centimeters (6¼ inches)

Pierced foot rim

Edition size unannounced, limited by year of issue

Not numbered, without certificate; individually initialed on back by each painter

14-R.59-2.1
1971 *American Mother*
Artist: Kamma Svensson
Issue price: $12.50

14-R.59-2.2
1972 *Oriental Mother*
Artist: Kamma Svensson
Issue price: $14.00

14-R.59-2.3
1973 *Danish Mother*
Artist: Arne Ungermann
Issue price: $16.00

14-R.59-2.4
1974 *Greenland Mother*
Artist: Arne Ungermann
Issue price: $16.50

14-R.59-2.5
1975 *Bird in Nest*
Artist: Arne Ungermann
Issue price: $20.00

14-R.59-2.6
1976 *Mermaids*
Artist: Arne Ungermann
Issue price: $20.00

14-R.59-2.7
1977 *The Twins*
Artist: Arne Ungermann
Issue price: $24.00

14-R.59-2.8
1978 *Mother and Child*
Artist: Ib Spang Olsen
Issue price: $26.00

14-R.59-2.9
1979 *A Loving Mother*
Artist: Ib Spang Olsen
Issue price: $29.50

14-R.59-2.10
1980 *An Outing with Mother*
Artist: Ib Spang Olsen
Issue price: $37.50

Historical Series

Artist: Sven Vestergaard

True underglaze porcelain hand painted in Copenhagen blue on bas-relief

Diameter: 19 centimeters (7½ inches)

Pierced foot rim

Edition size unannounced, limited by year of issue

Not numbered, without certificate; individually initialed on back by each painter

14-R.59-3.1
1975 *Royal Copenhagen Bicentennial*
Artist: Sven Vestergaard
Issue price: $30.00

14-R.59-3.2
1976 *United States Bicentennial*
Artist: Sven Vestergaard
Issue price: $35.00

DENMARK
ROYAL COPENHAGEN
(Copenhagen)

14-R.59-3.3
1977 *The Discovery of Electro-Magnetism*
Artist: Sven Vestergaard
Issue price: $35.00

14-R.59-3.4
1978 *Captain Cook Landing on Hawaii*
Artist: Sven Vestergaard
Issue price: $37.50

14-R.59-3.5
1979 *Adam Oehlenschlager*
Artist: Sven Vestergaard
Issue price: $42.50

14-R.59-3.6
1980 *Amagertorv*
Artist: Sven Vestergaard
Issue price: $52.50

In 1873 Arabia was founded as a subsidiary of the Swedish firm Rorstrand (see Sweden, RORSTRAND). The factory was located on the outskirts of Helsinki, a site chosen in hopes of supplying the growing markets for ceramics in Finland and the Russian Empire. Early products included dinner services, pitchers, and mugs, almost all based on Rorstrand designs.

In 1884 Arabia was reorganized as a Finnish company, Arabia Aktiefabrik, and developed its own designs from that time on. The company won a gold medal at the Paris World Exhibition in 1900, and is the only pottery producing both household and art ceramics in Finland today.

To celebrate the one-hundredth anniversary of the firm in 1973, Arabia produced a limited-edition anniversary plate. Its success, in turn, led to the introduction in 1976 of an annual limited-edition series based on the Finnish national epic, the *Kalevala*.

Artist for the series is Raija Uosikkinen, a designer of Arabia creations since 1947. Works in her distinctive contemporary folk art style have been exhibited in Helsinki, Milan and Brussels, and won a Gold Medal at a 1961 exhibition in California.

FINLAND
ARABIA
(Helsinki)

Kalevala Series
Artist: Raija Uosikkinen
Stoneware
Diameter: 19 centimeters square
   (7½ inches square)
Pierced foot rim
Edition size undisclosed
Not numbered, without certificate

16-A.69-1.1
1976 *Vainamoinen's Sowing*
Artist: Raija Uosikkinen
Issue price: $30.00

16-A.69-1.2
1977 *Aino's Fate*
Artist: Raija Uosikkinen
Issue price: $30.00

16-A.69-1.3
1978 *Lemminkainen's Chase*
Artist: Raija Uosikkinen
Issue price: $39.00

16-A.69-1.4
1979 *Kullervo's Revenge*
Artist: Raija Uosikkinen
Issue price $39.50

16-A.69-1.5
1980 *Vainamoinen's Rescue*
Artist: Raija Uosikkinen
Issue price: $45.00

The hallmark of Henri d'Arceau L. et Fils is one of the most prestigious in the famous porcelain center of Limoges. The firm, which claims to adhere to the original "Grellet Standard" of 1768 for handcraftsmanship, is today directed by Gerard Boyer, a descendant of the founder.

The firm was commissioned by L'Association l'Esprit de Lafayette to produce the six-plate bicentennial series *Collection Le Patrimoine de Lafayette (Lafayette Legacy Series)*. 1973-1975, which chronicles the role of the Marquis de Lafayette in America's War of Independence. The D'Arceau-Limoges *Christmas Series, Noel Vitrail*, begun in 1975, was inspired by the stained-glass windows of the cathedral at Chartres. *Les Femmes du Siecle (Women of the Century)*, a twelve-plate series commissioned by the Chambre Syndicale de la Couture Parisienne, began in 1976. This series with United Nations recognition, depicts Western Women's fashions from 1865 to 1965. Introduced in 1978 was *Les Jeunes Filles des Saisons (Girls of the Seasons)*, and in 1979 *Les Tres Riches Heures (The Book of Hours)*, which adapts its artwork from an early fifteenth-century illuminated manuscript. In 1980, the firm, in collaboration with *La Société de Paris et Son Histoire*, issued Louis Dali's *La Ville de Paris (City of Paris) Series*, a collection of the artist's unique impressions of the famous city.

Among the artists who have designed works for D'Arceau-Limoges are the late André Restieau, world authority on the techniques of re-creating medieval stained glass coloration in porcelain; neo-Classicist Guy Cambier, winner of numerous awards from the *Prix de la Jeune Peinture Méditerranée* in 1955 to the *Médaille d'or au Prix Leonardo da Vinciin* 1972; and François Ganeau, resident consultant to the theatre *Comedie Française*. In 1980 the noted Impressionist Louis Dali, a Fellow of the *Salon de l'Ecole Française* and the *Salon des Independants*, joined D'Arceau-Limoges artists with his *La Ville de Paris Series*.

FRANCE
D'ARCEAU-LIMOGES
(Limoges)

Collection Le Patrimoine de Lafayette *(The Lafayette Legacy Collection)*

Artist: André Restieau. Artist's signature appears on front, initials on back

Overglaze porcelain

Diameter: 21.6 centimeters (8½ inches)

Attached back hanger

Edition size undisclosed, limited by announced period of issue

Numbered with certificate

18-D.15-1.1
1973 *The Secret Contract*
Artist: André Restieau
Issue price: $14.82

18-D.15-1.2
1973 *The Landing at North Island*
Artist: André Restieau
Issue price: $19.82

18-D.15-1.3
1974 *The Meeting at City Tavern*
Artist: André Restieau
Issue price: $19.82

18-D.15-1.4
1974 *The Battle of Brandywine*
Artist: André Restieau
Issue price: $19.82

18-D.15-1.5
1975 *The Messages to Franklin*
Artist: André Restieau
Issue price: $19.82

18-D.15-1.6
1975 *The Siege at Yorktown*
Artist: André Restieau
Issue price: $19.82

Noël Vitrail
(Stained-glass Christmas)

Artist: André Restieau. Artist's signature appears on front, initials on back

Overglaze porcelain

Diameter: 21 centimeters (8¼ inches)

Attached back hanger

Edition size undisclosed, limited by announced period of issue

Numbered with certificate

18-D.15-2.1
1975 *La Fuite en Egypte*
(Flight into Egypt)
Artist: André Restieau
Issue price: $24.32

18-D.15-2.2
1976 *Dans la Crèche*
(In the Manger)
Artist: André Restieau
Issue price: $24.32

18-D.15-2.3
1977 *Le Refus d'Hebèrgement*
(No Room at the Inn)
Artist: André Restieau
Issue price: $24.32

18-D.15-2.4
1978 *La Purification*
(The Purification)
Artist: André Restieau
Issue price: $26.81

18-D.15-2.5
1979 *L'Adoration des Rois*
(The Adoration of Kings)
Artist: André Restieau
Issue price: $26.81

18-D.15-2.6
1980 *Nouvelles de Grande
Rejouissance*
(Tidings of Great Joy)
Artist: André Restieau
Issue price: $28.61

FRANCE
D'ARCEAU-LIMOGES
(Limoges)

Les Femmes du Siècle

(The Women of the Century)

Artist: François Ganeau. Artist's
  signature appears on front,
  initials on back
Overglaze porcelain
Diameter: 21.6 centimeters
  (8½ inches)
Attached back hanger
Edition size undisclosed, limited
  by announced period of issue
Numbered with certificate

18-D.15-3.1
1976 *Scarlet en Crinoline*
Artist: François Ganeau
Issue price: $14.80

18-D.15-3.2
1976 *Sarah en Tournure*
Artist: François Ganeau
Issue price: $22.74

18-D.15-3.3
1976 *Colette, la Femme Sportive*
Artist: François Ganeau
Issue price: $22.74

18-D.15-3.4
1976 *Léa, la Femme Fleur*
Artist: François Ganeau
Issue price: $22.74

18-D.15-3.5
1977 *Albertine, la Femme Liane*
Artist: François Ganeau
Issue price: $22.74

18-D.15-3.6
1977 *Edith, la Femme Pratique*
Artist: François Ganeau
Issue price: $22.74

18-D.15-3.7
1977 *Daisy, la Garconne*
Artist: François Ganeau
Issue price: $22.74

18-D.15-3.8
1977 *Marlène, la Vamp*
Artist: François Ganeau
Issue price: $22.74

18-D.15-3.9
1978 *Hélène, l'Intrépide*
Artist: François Ganeau
Issue price: $22.74

18-D.15-3.10
1978 *Sophie, la Féminité Retrouvée*
Artist: François Ganeau
Issue price: $22.74

18-D.15-3.11
1979 *Francoise en Pantalon*
Artist: François Ganeau
Issue price: $22.74

18-D.15-3.12
1979 *Brigitte en Mini-jupe*
Artist: François Ganeau
Issue price: $22.74

Les Jeunes Filles des Saisons

(The Girls of the Seasons)
Artist: Guy Cambier
Overglaze porcelain banded
  in gold
Diameter: 24.8 centimeters
  (9¾ inches)
No hanger
Edition size limited to 15,000
Numbered with certificate

18-D.15-4.1
1978 *La Jeune Fille d'Eté*
(Summer Girl)
Artist: Guy Cambier
Issue price: $105.00

18-D.15-4.2
1979 *La Jeune Fille d'Hiver*
(Winter Girl)
Artist: Guy Cambier
Issue price: $105.00

FRANCE
D'ARCEAU-LIMOGES
(Limoges)

18-D.15-4.3
1980 *La Jeune Fille Printaniere*
(Spring Girl)
Artist: Guy Cambier
Issue price: $105.00

18-D.15-4.4
1980 *La Jeune Fille d'Automne*
(Autumn Girl)
Artist: Guy Cambier
Issue price: $105.00

Les Très Riches Heures
(The Book of Hours Series)

Artist: Jean Dutheil
Overglaze porcelain
Diameter: 24.8 centimeters
  (9¾ inches)
Attached back hanger
Edition size unannounced
Numbered with certificate

18-D.15-5.1
1979 *Janvier*
(January)
Artist: Jean Dutheil
Issue price: $75.48

18-D.15-5.2
1980 *Avril*
(April)
Artist: Jean Dutheil
Issue price: $75.48

La Ville de Paris
(City of Paris)

Artist: Louis Dali
Overglaze porcelain
Diameter: 21 centimeters
  (8¼ inches)
Attached back hanger
Edition size undisclosed, limited
  by announced period of issue
Numbered with certificate

18-D.15-6.1
1980 *L'Arc de Triomphe*
(The Arch of Triumph)
Artist: Louis Dali
Issue price: Undetermined at
press time

18-D.15-6.2
1980 *La Cathedrale Notre-Dame*
(Notre Dame Cathedral)
Artist: Louis Dali
Issue price: Undetermined at
press time

In 1839 David Haviland of New York City became the first American importer of Limoges porcelain made from white kaolin clay. When, in 1842, he realized that French factories would not adjust methods to meet the tastes of his American market, Haviland established his own pottery in Limoges.

In 1892 his son, Theodore, left the firm but remained in Limoges to set up Theodore Haviland & Company for production of porcelain dinnerware and decorative pieces. In the 1930s, Theodore Haviland & Company opened an American Haviland factory to produce tableware; the firm also bought the original Haviland & Company established by David Haviland.

All Haviland collector's plates are produced in Limoges, France. The *Christmas Series*, begun in 1970, is based on the carol "The Twelve Days of Christmas." The five-plate *Bicentennial Series*, introduced in 1972, commemorates events leading to the American Declaration of Independence. In 1973, the *Mother's Day Series* of seven plates, entitled *The French Collection*, was started.

And 1979 marked the beginning of *Mille et Un Nuits Series* based on the literary classic *One Thousand One Arabian Nights*.

Adept in a variety of styles, French painter Remy Hétreau is the principal artist for Haviland collector's plates, with three distinctively different series to his credit — from historical chronicle to whimsical sketches of modern family life. Noted watercolorist Liliane Tellier, creator of the *Mille et Un Nuits Series*, has an extensive following among connoisseurs of the medium.

The Twelve Days of Christmas Series

Artist: Remy Hétreau. Artist's
  signature appears on back
Overglaze porcelain
Diameter: 21.3 centimeters
  (8⅜ inches)
No hanger
Edition size limited to announced
  quantity of 30,000
Not numbered, without certificate

18-H.6-1.1
1970 *A Partridge in a Pear Tree*
Artist: Remy Hétreau
Issue price: $25.00

18-H.6-1.2
1971 *Two Turtle Doves*
Artist: Remy Hétreau
Issue price: $25.00

18-H.6-1.3
1972 *Three French Hens*
Artist: Remy Hétreau
Issue price: $27.50

18-H.6-1.4
1973 *Four Colly Birds*
Artist: Remy Hétreau
Issue price: $28.50

18-H.6-1.5
1974 *Five Golden Rings*
Artist: Remy Hétreau
Issue price: $30.00

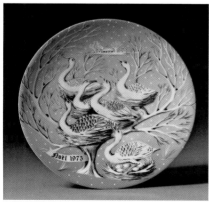

18-H.6-1.6
1975 *Six Geese A'Laying*
Artist: Remy Hétreau
Issue price: $32.50

18-H.6-1.7
1976 *Seven Swans A'Swimming*
Artist: Remy Hétreau
Issue price: $38.00

18-H.6-1.8
1977 *Eight Maids A'Milking*
Artist: Remy Hétreau
Issue price: $40.00

18-H.6-1.9
1978 *Nine Ladies Dancing*
Artist: Remy Hétreau
Issue price: $45.00

18-H.6-1.10
1979 *Ten Lords A'Leaping*
Artist: Remy Hétreau
Issue price: $50.00

18-H.6-1.11
1980 *Eleven Pipers Piping*
Artist: Remy Hétreau
Issue price: $55.00

Bicentennial Series

Artist: Remy Hétreau. Artist's
  signature appears on back
Overglaze porcelain
Diameter: 24.8 centimeters
  (9¾ inches)
No hanger
Edition size limited to announced
  quantity of 10,000
Not numbered, without certificate

18-H.6-2.1
1972 *Burning of the Gaspee*
Artist: Remy Hétreau
Issue price: $39.95

18-H.6-2.2
1973 *Boston Tea Party*
Artist: Remy Hétreau
Issue price: $39.95

18-H.6-2.3
1974 *First Continental Congress*
Artist: Remy Hétreau
Issue price: $39.95

18-H.6-2.4
1975 *Ride of Paul Revere*
Artist: Remy Hétreau
Issue price: $40.00

18-H.6-2.5
1976 *The Declaration of Independence*
Artist: Remy Hétreau
Issue price: $48.00

FRANCE
HAVILAND
(Limoges)

The French Collection
Artist: Remy Hétreau. Artist's
  signature appears on front
Overglaze porcelain
Diameter: 21 centimeters
  (8¼ inches)
No hanger
Edition size limited to 10,000
Numbered without certificate

18-H.6-3.1
1973 Breakfast
Artist: Remy Hétreau
Issue price: $29.95

18-H.6-3.2
1974 The Wash
Artist: Remy Hétreau
Issue price: $29.95

18-H.6-3.3
1975 In the Park
Artist: Remy Hétreau
Issue price: $30.00

18-H.6-3.4
1976 To Market
Artist: Remy Hétreau
Issue price: $38.00

18-H.6-3.5
1977 A Wash Before Dinner
Artist: Remy Hétreau
Issue price: $38.00

18-H.6-3.6
1978 An Evening at Home
Artist: Remy Hétreau
Issue price: $40.00

18-H.6-3.7
1979 Happy Mother's Day
Artist: Remy Hétreau
Issue price: $45.00

Mille et Un Nuits
(1001 Arabian Nights)

Artist: Liliane Tellier
Porcelain banded in gold
Diameter: 24.1 centimeters
(9½ inches)
No hanger
Edition size unannounced
Numbered with certificate

18-H.6-4.1
1979 *Le Cheval Magique*
(The Magic Horse)
Artist: Liliane Tellier
Issue price: $54.50

18-H.6-4.2
No information available
at press time

Haviland Parlon is a chapter in the intricate Haviland porcelain story. In 1853 Robert Haviland left New York City to work for his brother David Haviland in Limoges (see France, HAVILAND). In 1870 Robert's son Charles Field Haviland, established a porcelain factory in Limoges also, using "Ch. Field Haviland" as his trade name. After he retired in 1881, the firm was known by several different names until 1942, when Robert Haviland (Robert's great-grandson) purchased it. The firm is now known as Robert Haviland & C. Parlon but retains the "Ch. Field Haviland" trademark.

The *Tapestry Series*, begun in 1971 reproduced six scenes from the French medieval tapestries, "The Hunt of the Unicorn" now hanging in the Cloisters of New York's Metropolitan Museum of Art. The *Christmas Series* of famous Renaissance Madonnas began in 1972, and the *Mother's Day Series*, in 1975. A second *Tapestry Series* of six plates began in 1977 and reproduces scenes from "The Lady and the Unicorn" tapestries hanging in the Cluny Museum in Paris.

Designs for the *Christmas Series* are taken from works by the great masters as indicated. Marian Carlsen is an American artist who is well-known for her portraits of children.

FRANCE
HAVILAND PARLON
(Limoges)

Tapestry Series
Reproduced from French medieval
  tapestries
Overglaze porcelain banded in
  gold
Diameter: 25.4 centimeters
  (10 inches)
No hanger
Edition size limited to announced
  quantity of 10,000
Not numbered, without certificate

18-H.8-1.1
1971 *The Unicorn in Captivity*
Artist: Unknown
Issue price: $35.00

18-H.8-1.2
1972 *Start of the Hunt*
Artist: Unknown
Issue price: $35.00

18-H.8-1.3
1973 *Chase of the Unicorn*
Artist: Unknown
Issue price: $35.00

18-H.8-1.4
1974 *End of the Hunt*
Artist: Unknown
Issue price: $37.50

18-H.8-1.5
1975 *The Unicorn Surrounded*
Artist: Unknown
Issue price: $40.00

18-H.8-1.6
1976 *The Unicorn Is Brought to the
Castle*
Artist: Unknown
Issue price: $42.50

18-H.8-2.1

Christmas Series
Artist: As indicated
Overglaze porcelain banded in
  gold
Diameter: 25.4 centimeters
  (10 inches)
No hanger
Edition size: As indicated
Numbered without certificate

18-H.8-2.1
1972 Madonna and Child
Artist: Rafael
Issue price: $35.00
Edition size limited to 5,000

18-H.8-2.2
1973 Madonnina
Artist: Feruzzi
Issue price: $40.00
Edition size limited to 5,000

18-H.8-2.3
1974 Cowper Madonna and Child
Artist: Rafael
Issue price: $42.50
Edition size limited to 5,000

18-H.8-2.4
1975 Madonna and Child
Artist: Murillo
Issue price: $42.50
Edition size limited to 7,500

18-H.8-2.5
1976 Madonna and Child
Artist: Botticelli
Issue price: $45.00
Edition size limited to 7,000

18-H.8-2.6
1977 Madonna and Child
Artist: Bellini
Issue price: $48.00
Edition size limited to 7,500

18-H.8-2.7
1978 Madonna and Child
Artist: Fra Filippo Lippi
Issue price: $48.00
Edition size limited to 7,500

Maker had
no photo at
press time

18-H.8-2.8
1979 Madonna of the Eucharist
Artist: Botticelli
Issue price: $49.50
Edition size limited to 7,500

FRANCE
HAVILAND PARLON

(Limoges)

Mother's Day Series
Artist: Marian Carlsen
Overglaze porcelain banded
  in gold
Diameter: 19.7 centimeters
  (7¾ inches)
No hanger
Edition size: As indicated
Not numbered, without certificate

18-H.8-3.1
1975 *Laura and Child*
Artist: Marian Carlsen
Issue price: $37.50. Edition size limited
to announced quantity of 15,000

18-H.8-3.2
1976 *Pinky and Baby*
Artist: Marian Carlsen
Issue price: $42.50. Edition size limited
to announced quantity of 15,000

18-H.8-3.3
1977 *Amy and Snoopy*
Artist: Marian Carlsen
Issue price: $45.00. Edition size limited
to announced quantity of 10,000

Lady and the Unicorn Series

Reproduced from French medieval
   tapestries

Overglaze porcelain banded in
   gold

Diameter: 25.4 centimeters
   (10 inches)

No hanger

Edition size: As indicated

Not numbered, without certificate

18-H.8-4.1
1977 *To My Only Desire*
Artist: Unknown
Issue price: $45.00
Edition size limited to 20,000

18-H.8-4.2
1978 *Sight*
Artist: Unknown
Issue price: $45.00
Edition size limited to 20,000

18-H.8-4.3
1979 *Sound*
Artist: Unknown
Issue price: $47.50
Edition size limited to 20,000

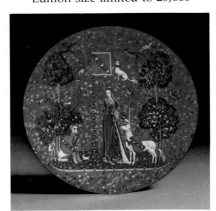

18-H.8-4.4
1980 *Touch*
Artist: Unknown
Issue price: $52.50
Edition size limited to 15,000

Rene Lalique, founder of the firm that bears his name, began his career as a goldsmith and jeweler in the late nineteenth century. His clients included such notables as Sarah Bernhardt and the dealers Cartier and Boucheron.

In 1902 his interests turned to glassmaking and he acquired a small glassworks at Clairfontaine, France. In 1909 he opened a glass factory near Paris where he produced bottles for the leading Parisian *parfumiers*, and in 1918 he opened the present Lalique factory in Alsace. Here he began to produce glass items in the Art Deco style. His designs, usually created in pressed lead crystal, are noted for the frosted and satin effects of the glass. Until his death in 1945, Lalique produced numerous commercial glass objects such as perfume bottles, vases and figurines.

Upon Rene's death in 1945, his son Marc — himself a noted artist — inherited the firm and served as its president until his death in 1977.

The firm is headed by Marc's daughter, Marie-Claude. As Lalique's chief designer she created the *Annual Series* of Lalique crystal collector's plates which began in 1965 and ended in 1976.

The third generation in a distinguished family of artists, Madame Lalique is known for her versatility, being an accomplished painter, sculptor, glass-blower and jewelry designer. She is a graduate of *L'Ecole Normale Superiore des Arts Decoratifs de Paris* and exhibits a preference for animal motifs in art nouveau and art deco styles.

FRANCE
LALIQUE

(Alsace)

Annual Series

Artist: Marie-Claude Lalique

Full lead crystal with incised designs

Diameter: 21.6 centimeters (8½ inches)

No hanger

Edition size: As indicated. Announced between 5,000 and 8,000 from 1967 to 1975

Not numbered, without certificate; engraved "Lalique-France" on back

18-L.3-1.1
1965 *Deux Oiseaux*
(Two Birds)
Artist: Marie-Claude Lalique
Issue price: $25.00. Limited by
announced edition size of 2,000

18-L.3-1.2
1966 *Rose de Songerie*
(Dream Rose)
Artist: Marie-Claude Lalique
Issue price: $25.00. Limited by
announced edition size of 5,000

18-L.3-1.3
1967 *Ballet de Poisson*
(Fish Ballet)
Artist: Marie-Claude Lalique
Issue price: $25.00

18-L.3-1.4
1968 *Gazelle Fantaisie*
(Gazelle Fantasy)
Artist: Marie-Claude Lalique
Issue price: $25.00

18-L.3-1.5
1969 *Papillon*
(Butterfly)
Artist: Marie-Claude Lalique
Issue price: $30.00

18-L.3-1.6
1970 *Paon*
(Peacock)
Artist: Marie-Claude Lalique
Issue price: $30.00

18-L.3-1.7
1971 *Hibou*
(Owl)
Artist: Marie-Claude Lalique
Issue price: $35.00

18-L.3-1.8
1972 *Coquillage*
(Shell)
Artist: Marie-Claude Lalique
Issue price: $40.00

18-L.3-1.9
1973 *Petit Geai*
(Jayling)
Artist: Marie-Claude Lalique
Issue price: $42.50

18-L.3-1.10
1974 *Sous d'Argent*
(Silver Pennies)
Artist: Marie-Claude Lalique
Issue price: $47.50

18-L.3-1.11
1975 *Duo de Poisson*
(Fish Duet)
Artist: Marie-Claude Lalique
Issue price: $50.00. Limited by
announced edition size of 8,000

18-L.3-1.12
1976 *Aigle*
(Eagle)
Artist: Marie-Claude Lalique
Issue price: $60.00

The porcelain house of Limoges-Turgot draws upon a tradition of porcelain making which began with A.-R.-J. Turgot, Baron de l'Aulne, Louis XVI's administrator for the Limousin province of which Limoges was the capital. When kaolin clay, the key ingredient in true hard-fire porcelain, was discovered in 1768 at the nearby town of Saint-Yrieix, it was largely due to Turgot's efforts that the Limoges porcelain industry was established and achieved world renown.

Les Enfants de Durand, (Durand's Children Collection), began in 1978 and is the first proprietary series by Limoges-Turgot.

The late artist, Paul Durand, achieved an international reputation for his illustrations of such children's classics as *The Three Musketeers*, and *Treasure Island*. His art was personally chosen by General Charles de Gaulle to illustrate his 1969 Christmas message to French children.

Les Enfants de Durand

(Durand's Children Series)
Artist: Paul Durand
Overglaze porcelain
Diameter: 20.3 centimeters
  (8 inches)
Attached back hanger
Edition size undisclosed, limited
  by year of issue
Numbered with certificate

18-L.52-1.1
1978 *Marie-Ange*
Artist: Paul Durand
Issue price: $36.40

18-L.52-1.2
1979 *Emilie et Philippe*
Artist: Paul Durand
Issue price: $36.40

18-L.52-1.3
1980 *Christiane et Fifi*
Artist: Paul Durand
Issue price: $36.40

18-L.52-1.4
1980 *Cecile et Raoul*
Artist: Paul Durand
Issue price: $36.40

Named for Anna Perenna, the Roman goddess associated with health, abundance, and the rebirth of spring, ANNA-PERENNA, Inc. was founded in 1977 by its president, Klaus D. Vogt. With offices in Stuttgart and New York, the company imports and distributes exclusive limited-edition items made by Rosenthal and is the American importer of KPM plates.

"The Byzantine Triptych," first issue in a *Triptych Series* inspired by the portable alter-pieces of the Middle Ages, was issued in 1979 and is a three-plate set which reinterprets ancient Byzantine religious motifs. In 1980, ANNA-PERENNA introduced *Romantic Loves*, a four-plate series celebrating great romantic loves of history. Their four-plate series, *Uncle Tad's Cats*, also began in 1980.

The *Byzantine Triptych* and the *Romantic Loves* series are the work of the husband-and-wife team Frank Russell and Gertrude Barrer. Their work, characterized by bold coloring, has been exhibited at the Art Institute of Chicago and the Whitney Museum of American Art.

Thaddeus Krumeich is master of the style known as *trompe l'oeil*, which he calls "magic realism." He has had shows throughout the United States, is represented in such private collections as those of Mrs. Paul Mellon, "Doc" Severinson, and His Excellency Seydou Traori, Mali Ambassador to the United States, and his work was selected for a 1980 series of UNICEF Christmas cards.

The Triptych Series

Artist: Frank Russell and Gertrude Barrer

Hard-paste porcelain with wood frame

Diameter: plates one and three, 22 centimeters (8½ inches); plate two, 24.8 centimeters (9¾ inches); overall triptych, 89 centimeters x 46 centimeters (35 inches x 18 inches)

Attached back hanger

Edition size: As indicated

Individually hand-numbered with certificate

A triptych is a set of three panels hinged side-by-side, bearing paintings or carvings usually on a religious theme and often used as a portable altarpiece.

22-A.3-3.1-1
1979 *Gabriel*
Artist: Frank Russell and
Gertrude Barrer
Issue price: $325.00 the set
Edition size limited to 5,000 sets

22-A.3-3.1-2
1979 *Madonna and Child*

22-A.3-3.1-3
1979 *Michael*

The Byzantine Triptych

22-A.3-3.2-1
1980 *Saul*
Artist: Frank Russell and
Gertrude Barrer
Issue price: $350.00 the set
Edition size limited to 7,500 sets

22-A.3-3.2-2
1980 *David*

22-A.3-3.2-3
1980 *Solomon*

The Jerusalem Triptych

Romantic Loves Series

Artist: Frank Russell and
Gertrude Barrer

Hard-paste porcelain banded
in gold

Diameter: 25 centimeters
(9⅞ inches)

Attached back hanger

Edition size limited to 7,500

Individually hand-numbered
with certificate

22-A.3-4.1
1979 *Romeo and Juliet*
Artist: Frank Russell and
Gertrude Barrer
Issue price: $95.00

22-A.3-4.2
1980 *Lancelot and Guinevere*
Artist: Frank Russell and
Gertrude Barrer
Issue price: $95.00

The Bareuther & Company porcelain factory began to produce dinnerware, vases and giftware in 1867. The small shop was established with a porcelain kiln and an annular brick kiln by sculptor Johann Matthaeus Ries. In 1884 Ries's son sold the shop to Oskar Bareuther who continued to produce fine tableware.

To observe the one-hundredth anniversary of the factory in 1967, Bareuther began a series of limited-edition *Christmas* plates. A *Father's Day Series*, depicting the great castles of Germany, was started in 1969.

Hans Mueller, a German plate artist known especially for his dramatic landscapes, designs both series for Bareuther.

Christmas Series

Artist: Hans Mueller except 1971
Underglaze porcelain decorated in
  cobalt blue
Diameter: 20.3 centimeters
  (8 inches)
Edition size limited to announced
  quantity of 10,000
Pierced foot rim
Not numbered, without certificate

22-B.7-1.1
1967 *Stiftskirche*
Artist: Hans Mueller
Issue price: $12.00

22-B.7-1.2
1968 *Kappl*
Artist: Hans Mueller
Issue price: $12.00

22-B.7-1.3
1969 *Christkindlesmarkt*
Artist: Hans Mueller
Issue price: $12.00

22-B.7-1.4
1970 *Chapel in Oberndorf*
Artist: Hans Mueller
Issue price: $12.50

22-B.7-1.5
1971 *Toys for Sale*
From drawing by Ludwig Richter
Issue price: $12.75

22-B.7-1.6
1972 *Christmas in Munich*
Artist: Hans Mueller
Issue price: $14.50

22-B.7-1.7
1973 *Christmas Sleigh Ride*
Artist: Hans Mueller
Issue price: $15.00

22-B.7-1.8
1974 *Church in the Black Forest*
Artist: Hans Mueller
Issue price: $19.00

22-B.7-1.9
1975 Snowman
Artist: Hans Mueller
Issue price: $21.50

22-B.7-1.10
1976 Chapel in the Hills
Artist: Hans Mueller
Issue price: $23.50

22-B.7-1.11
1977 Story Time
Artist: Hans Mueller
Issue price: $24.50

22-B.7-1.12
1978 Mittenwald
Artist: Hans Mueller
Issue price: $27.50

22-B.7-1.13
1979 Winter Day
Artist: Hans Mueller
Issue price: $35.00

22-B.7-1.14
1980 Miltenberg
Artist: Hans Mueller
Issue price: $37.50

GERMANY
BAREUTHER
(Waldsassen)

Father's Day Series
Artist: Hans Mueller
Underglaze porcelain decorated in
cobalt blue
Diameter: 20.3 centimeters
(8 inches)
Edition size limited to announced
quantity of 2,500
Pierced foot rim
Not numbered, without certificate

22-B.7-2.1
1969 *Castle Neuschwanstein*
Artist: Hans Mueller
Issue price: $10.50

22-B.7-2.2
1970 *Castle Pfalz*
Artist: Hans Mueller
Issue price: $12.50

22-B.7-2.3
1971 *Castle Heidelberg*
Artist: Hans Mueller
Issue price: $12.75

22-B.7-2.4
1972 *Castle Hohenschwangau*
Artist: Hans Mueller
Issue price: $14.50

22-B.7-2.5
1973 *Castle Katz*
Artist: Hans Mueller
Issue price: $15.00

22-B.7-2.6
1974 *Wurzburg Castle*
Artist: Hans Mueller
Issue price: $19.00

22-B.7-2.7
1975 *Castle Lichtenstein*
Artist: Hans Mueller
Issue price: $21.50

22-B.7-2.8
1976 *Castle Hohenzollern*
Artist: Hans Mueller
Issue price: $23.50

22-B.7-2.9
1977 *Castle Eltz*
Artist: Hans Mueller
Issue price: $24.50

22-B.7-2.10
1978 *Castle Falkenstein*
Artist: Hans Mueller
Issue price: $27.50

22-B.7-2.11
1979 *Castle Rheinstein*
Artist: Hans Mueller
Issue price: $35.00

22-B.7-2.12
1980 *Castle Cochum*
Artist: Hans Mueller
Issue price: $37.50

Berlin Design's limited-edition plates, mugs, and other collectibles are manufactured by the Kaiser Porcelain Company (see Germany, KAISER), and are identified by the distinctive bear and crown symbol of the city of Berlin.

The *Christmas Series*, introduced in 1970, depicts Yule festivities in German towns. The *Mother's Day Series* of animal mothers and their young began in 1971.

Artists for Berlin Design plates are not disclosed.

GERMANY
BERLIN DESIGN
(Staffelstein)

Christmas Series
Artist: Undisclosed
Underglaze porcelain decorated in
  cobalt blue
Diameter: 19.7 centimeters
  (7¾ inches)
Edition size: As indicated
Pierced foot rim
Not numbered, without certificate

22-B.20-1.1
1970 *Christmas in Bernkastel*
Artist: Undisclosed
Issue price: $14.50. Edition size limited
to announced quantity of 4,000

22-B.20-1.2
1971 *Christmas in Rothenburg on Tauber*
Artist: Undisclosed
Issue price: $14.50. Edition size limited
to announced quantity of 20,000

22-B.20-1.3
1972 *Christmas in Michelstadt*
Artist: Undisclosed
Issue price: $15.00. Edition size limited
to announced quantity of 20,000

22-B.20-1.4
1973 *Christmas in Wendelstein*
Artist: Undisclosed
Issue price: $20.00. Edition size limited
to announced quantity of 20,000

22-B.20-1.5
1974 *Christmas in Bremen*
Artist: Undisclosed
Issue price: $25.00. Edition size limited
to announced quantity of 20,000

22-B.20-1.6
1975 *Christmas in Dortland*
Artist: Undisclosed
Issue price: $30.00. Edition size limited
to announced quantity of 20,000

22-B.20-1.7
1976 *Christmas Eve in Augsburg*
Artist: Undisclosed
Issue price: $32.00. Edition size limited
to announced quantity of 20,000

22-B.20-1.8
1977 *Christmas Eve in Hamburg*
Artist: Undisclosed
Issue price: $32.00. Edition size limited
to announced quantity of 20,000

22-B.20-1.9
1978 *Christmas Market at the Berlin Cathedral*
Artist: Undisclosed
Issue price: $36.00. Edition size limited to announced quantity of 20,000

22-B.20-1.10
1979 *Christmas Eve in Greetsiel*
Artist: Undisclosed
Issue price: $47.50. Edition size limited to announced quantity of 20,000

22-B.20-1.11
1980 *Children Play with Snow and Skate*
Artist: Undisclosed
Issue price: $50.00. Edition size limited to announced quantity of 20,000

Mother's Day Series
Artist: Undisclosed
Underglaze porcelain decorated in cobalt blue
Diameter: 19.7 centimeters (7¾ inches)
Edition size: As indicated
Pierced foot rim
Not numbered, without certificate

22-B.20-3.1
1971 *Grey Poodles*
Artist: Undisclosed
Issue price: $14.50. Edition size limited to announced quantity of 20,000

22-B.20-3.2
1972 *Fledglings*
Artist: Undisclosed
Issue price: $15.00. Edition size limited to announced quantity of 10,000

22-B.20-3.3
1973 *Duck Family*
Artist: Undisclosed
Issue price: $16.50. Edition size limited to announced quantity of 6,000

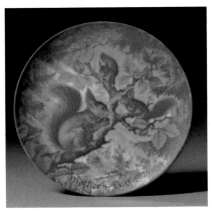

22-B.20-3.4
1974 *Squirrels*
Artist: Undisclosed
Issue price: $22.50. Edition size limited to announced quantity of 6,000

22-B.20-3.5
1975 *Cats*
Artist: Undisclosed
Issue price: $30.00. Edition size limited to announced quantity of 6,000

GERMANY
BERLIN DESIGN
(Staffelstein)

22-B.20-3.6
1976 *A Doe and Her Fawn*
Artist: Undisclosed
Issue price: $32.00. Edition size limited
to announced quantity of 6,000

22-B.20-3.7
1977 *Storks*
Artist: Undisclosed
Issue price: $32.00. Edition size limited
to announced quantity of 6,000

22-B.20-3.8
1978 *Mare with Foal*
Artist: Undisclosed
Issue price: $36.00. Edition size limited
to announced quantity of 6,000

22-B.20-3.9
1979 *Swans and Cygnets*
Artist: Undisclosed
Issue price: $47.50. Edition size limited
to announced quantity of 6,000

22-B.20-3.10
1980 *Goat Family*
Artist: Undisclosed
Issue price: $55.00. Edition size limited
to announced quantity of 6,000

Danish Church plates, formerly called Roskilde Church plates, are produced by a division of Bareuther & Company (see Germany, BAREUTHER). The *Church Series*, started in 1968, is of famous Danish churches.

Artists for Danish Church plates are not disclosed.

GERMANY
DANISH CHURCH
(Waldsassen)

Church Series
Artist: Undisclosed
Underglaze porcelain decorated in
cobalt blue
Diameter: 19.7 centimeters
(7¾ inches)
Edition size undisclosed, limited
by year of issue
Pierced foot rim
Not numbered, without certificate

22-D.5-1.1
1968 *Roskilde Cathedral*
Artist: Undisclosed
Issue price: $12.00

22-D.5-1.2
1969 *Ribe Cathedral*
Artist: Undisclosed
Issue price: $13.00

22-D.5-1.3
1970 *Marmor Church*
Artist: Undisclosed
Issue price: $13.00

22-D.5-1.4
1971 *Ejby Church*
Artist: Undisclosed
Issue price: $13.00

22-D.5-1.5
1972 *Kalundborg Church*
Artist: Undisclosed
Issue price: $13.00

22-D.5-1.6
1973 *Grundtvig Church*
Artist: Undisclosed
Issue price: $15.00

22-D.5-1.7
1974 *Broager Church*
Artist: Undisclosed
Issue price: $15.00

22-D.5-1.8
1975 *Sct. Knuds Church*
Artist: Undisclosed
Issue price: $18.00

22-D.5-1.9
1976 *Osterlars Church*
Artist: Undisclosed
Issue price: $22.00

22-D.5-1.10
1977 *Budolfi Church*
Artist: Undisclosed
Issue price: $15.95

22-D.5-1.11
1978 *Haderslev Cathedral*
Artist: Undisclosed
Issue price: $19.95

Maker had
no photo at
press time

Maker had
no photo at
press time

22-D.5-1.12
1979 *Holmens Church*
Artist: Undisclosed
Issue price: $19.95

22-D.5-1.13
1980 *Sct. Bendts Church*
Artist: Undisclosed
Issue price: Undetermined
at press time

The Dresden trademark was originated in 1971 by Porzellanzfabrik Tirschenreuth in honor of the famous early porcelain making region of that name. Porzellanzfabrik Tirschenreuth was established in the Dresden-Meissen area in 1838. In 1927, the firm merged with Lorenz Hutschenreuther A. G. and moved to Selb, Bavaria.

Dresden introduced its *Christmas Series* in 1971 and its *Mother's Day Series* in 1972. Both series ended in 1977.

Hans Waldheimer, the German wildlife and landscape artist noted for his strong compositional unity, created both series.

DRESDEN

(Selb)

Christmas Series

Artist: Hans Waldheimer

Underglaze porcelain centers
decorated in cobalt blue, white
baroque rims in relief trimmed
with matte gold edges

Diameter: 19 centimeters
(7½ inches)

Edition size: As indicated

Attached back hanger

Not numbered, without certificate

22-D.68-1.1
1971 *Shepherd Scene*
Artist: Hans Waldheimer
Issue price: $14.50. Edition size limited
to announced quantity of 3,500

22-D.68-1.2
1972 *Niklas Church*
Artist: Hans Waldheimer
Issue price: $18.00. Edition size limited
to announced quantity of 6,000

22-D.68-1.3
1973 *Schwanstein Church*
Artist: Hans Waldheimer
Issue price: $18.00. Edition size limited
to announced quantity of 6,000

22-D.68-1.4
1974 *Village Scene*
Artist: Hans Waldheimer
Issue price: $20.00. Edition size limited
to announced quantity of 5,000

22-D.68-1.5
1975 *Rothenberg Scene*
Artist: Hans Waldheimer
Issue price: $24.00. Edition size limited
to announced quantity of 5,000

22-D.68-1.6
1976 *Bavarian Village Church*
Artist: Hans Waldheimer
Issue price: $26.00. Edition size limited
to announced quantity of 5,000

22-D.68-1.7
1977 *Old Mill in the Hexenloch Valley*
Artist: Hans Waldheimer
Issue price: $28.00. Edition size limited
to announced quantity of 5,000

Mother's Day Series

Artist: Hans Waldheimer

Underglaze porcelain centers decorated in cobalt blue, white baroque rims in relief, trimmed with matte gold edges

Diameter: 19 centimeters (7½ inches)

Edition size: As indicated

Attached back hanger

Not numbered, without certificate

22-D.68-2.1
1972 Doe and Fawns
Artist: Hans Waldheimer
Issue price: $15.00. Edition size limited to announced quantity of 8,000

22-D.68-2.2
1973 Mare and Colt
Artist: Hans Waldheimer
Issue price: $16.00. Edition size limited to announced quantity of 6,000

22-D.68-2.3
1974 Tiger and Cub
Artist: Hans Waldheimer
Issue price: $20.00. Edition size limited to announced quantity of 5,000

22-D.68-2.4
1975 Dachshund Family
Artist: Hans Waldheimer
Issue price: $24.00. Edition size limited to announced quantity of 5,000

22-D.68-2.5
1976 Mother Owl and Young
Artist: Hans Waldheimer
Issue price: $26.00. Edition size limited to announced quantity of 5,000

22-D.68-2.6
1977 Chamois
Artist: Hans Waldheimer
Issue price: $28.00. Edition size limited to announced quantity of 5,000

Furstenberg, West Germany's oldest existing porcelain factory, was established in 1747 in the fourteenth-century castle of Furstenberg by order of Duke Karl I of Brunswick. He decreed that each piece of porcelain be initialed with a blue *F* which was later surmounted by a crown.

The factory, privately owned since 1859, presently occupies a modern plant on the grounds of Furstenberg Castle and produces tableware, vases and other decorative accessories as well as figurines and plaques.

The Furstenberg collector's plates began with a *Christmas Series* introduced in 1971. A second *Deluxe Christmas Series* began the same year. They were followed in 1972 by a *Mother's Day Series*. All series have ended.

Eva Grossberg — one of Furstenberg's best-known artists — is a Primitivist noted for her bold coloring and dynamic compositions.

Christmas Series
Artist: As indicated
Underglaze porcelain decorated in
 cobalt blue
Diameter: 19 centimeters
 (7½ inches)
Attached back hanger
Edition size: As indicated
Not numbered, without certificate

22-F.82-1.1
1971 *Rabbits*
Artist: Walter Schoen
Issue price: $15.00. Edition size limited
to announced quantity of 8,500

22-F.82-1.2
1972 *Snowy Village*
Artist: Walter Schoen
Issue price: $15.00. Edition size limited
to announced quantity of 6,000

22-F.82-1.3
1973 *Christmas Eve*
Artist: Walter Schoen
Issue price: $18.00. Edition size limited
to announced quantity of 5,000

22-F.82-1.4
1974 *Sparrows*
Artist: Walter Schoen
Issue price: $20.00. Edition size limited
to announced quantity of 4,000

22-F.82-1.5
1975 *Deer Family*
Artist: Walter Schoen
Issue price: $24.00. Edition size limited
to announced quantity of 4,000

22-F.82-1.6
1976 *Winter Birds Feeding from Pine
Cones*
Artist: I. Gahries
Issue price: $25.00. Edition size limited
to announced quantity of 4,000

Deluxe Christmas Series

Artist: Eva Grossberg. Artist's
   signature appears on back
Overglaze porcelain decorated in
   18k gold
Diameter: 24.1 centimeters
   (9½ inches)
No hanger
Edition size: As indicated
Numbered without certificate

22-F.82-2.1
1971 *Three Wise Men*
Artist: Eva Grossberg
Issue price: $45.00
Edition size limited to 1,500

22-F.82-2.2
1972 *Holy Family and Angel*
Artist: Eva Grossberg
Issue price: $45.00
Edition size limited to 2,000

22-F.82-2.3
1973 *Christmas Eve*
Artist: Eva Grossberg
Issue price: $60.00
Edition size limited to 2,000

Mother's Day Series

Artist: As indicated
Underglaze porcelain decorated in
   cobalt blue
Diameter: 19 centimeters
   (7½ inches)
Attached back hanger
Edition size: As indicated
Not numbered, without certificate

22-F.82-4.1
1972 *Hummingbird*
Artist: Undisclosed
Issue price: $15.00. Edition size limited
to announced quantity of 7,500

22-F.82-4.2
1973 *Hedgehogs*
Artist: Undisclosed
Issue price: $16.00. Edition size limited
to announced quantity of 5,000

GERMANY
FURSTENBERG
(Hoxter)

22-F.82-4.3
1974 *Doe with Fawn*
Artist: Undisclosed
Issue price: $20.00. Edition size limited
to announced quantity of 4,000

22-F.82-4.4
1975 *Swan Family*
Artist: Undisclosed
Issue price: $24.00. Edition size limited
to announced quantity of 4,000

22-F.82-4.5
1976 *Koala Bear and Young*
Artist: I. Gahries
Issue price: $25.00. Edition size limited
to announced quantity of 4,000

W. Goebel Porzellanfabrik was established in 1871 in Oeslau by Franz Deleff Goebel and his son William. Headed by Wilhelm Goebel, who represents the fifth generation of the founding family, Goebel produces handcrafted figurines, plates, dinnerware and gift items.

In 1935 Goebel introduced the famous M. I. Hummel figurines based on sketches by the late Franciscan nun. In 1971, to celebrate the one-hundredth anniversary of the firm, Goebel inaugurated an *Annual Series* of limited-edition plates with the M. I. Hummel designs.

The Hummel *Anniversary Series* began in 1975, with a new plate to be issued every five years. Other Goebel plate series include the *Wildlife Series*, which began in 1974, and a *Mothers Series* started in 1975.

The late Sister Maria Innocentia Hummel in her years at the Franciscan convent at Siessen produced stylized drawings of children — quite often with a religious theme — which Goebel has translated into both porcelain figurines and bas-relief stoneware plates.

Hummel Annual Series

Artist: Sister M. I. Hummel
  Artist's signature appears on
  front
Stoneware with hand-painted
  bas-relief
Diameter: 19 centimeters
  (7½ inches)
Pierced foot rim
Edition size undisclosed, limited
  by year of issue
Not numbered, without certificate

22-G.54-1.1
1971 *Heavenly Angel*
Artist: Sister M. I. Hummel
Issue price: $25.00

22-G.54-1.2
1972 *Hear Ye, Hear Ye*
Artist: Sister M. I. Hummel
Issue price: $30.00

22-G.54-1.3
1973 *Globe Trotter*
Artist: Sister M. I. Hummel
Issue price: $32.50

22-G.54-1.4
1974 *Goose Girl*
Artist: Sister M. I. Hummel
Issue price: $40.00

22-G.54-1.5
1975 *Ride into Christmas*
Artist: Sister M. I. Hummel
Issue price: $50.00

22-G.54-1.6
1976 *Apple Tree Girl*
Artist: Sister M. I. Hummel
Issue price: $50.00

22-G.54-1.7
1977 *Apple Tree Boy*
Artist: Sister M. I. Hummel
Issue price: $50.00

22-G.54-1.8
1978 *Happy Pastime*
Artist: Sister M. I. Hummel
Issue price: $65.00

22-G.54-1.9
1979 *Singing Lesson*
Artist: Sister M. I. Hummel
Issue price: $90.00

22-G.54-1.10
1980 *School Girl*
Artist: Sister M. I. Hummel
Issue price: $100.00

Wildlife Series

Artist: Undisclosed
Stoneware with hand-painted
  bas-relief
Diameter: 19 centimeters
  (7½ inches)
Pierced foot rim
Edition size undisclosed, limited
  by year of issue
Not numbered, without certificate

22-G.54-2.1
1974 *Robin*
Artist: Undisclosed
Issue price: $45.00

22-G.54-2.2
1975 *Blue Titmouse*
Artist Undisclosed
Issue price: $50.00

22-G.54-2.3
1976 *Barn Owl*
Artist: Undisclosed
Issue price: $50.00

22-G.54-2.4
1977 *Bullfinch*
Artist: Undisclosed
Issue price: $50.00

22-G.54-2.5
1978 *Sea Gull*
Artist: Undisclosed
Issue price: $55.00

GERMANY
GOEBEL
(Oeslau)

22-G.54-2.6
No information available
at press time

Hummel Anniversary Series

Artist: Sister M. I. Hummel.
  Artist's signature appears on
  front
Stoneware with hand-painted
  bas-relief
Diameter: 25.4 centimeters
  (10 inches)
Pierced foot rim
Edition size undisclosed, limited
  by year of issue
Not numbered, without certificate

22-G.54-3.1
1975 *Stormy Weather*
Artist: Sister M. I. Hummel
Issue price: $100.00

22-G.54-3.2
1980 *Spring Dance*
Artist: Sister M. I. Hummel
Issue price: $225.00

Mothers Series

Artist: Gerhard Bochmann
Stoneware with hand-painted
  bas-relief
Diameter: 19 centimeters
  (7½ inches)
Pierced foot rim
Edition size undisclosed, limited
  by year of issue for plates
  through 1978, other years as
  indicated

22-G.54-4.1
1975 *Rabbits*
Artist: Gerhard Bochmann
Issue price: $45.00

22-G.54-4.2
1976 *Cats*
Artist: Gerhard Bochmann
Issue price: $45.00

22-G.54-4.3
1977 Panda Bear with Baby
Artist: Gerhard Bochmann
Issue price: $45.00

22-G.54-4.4
1978 Doe and Fawn
Artist: Gerhard Bochmann
Issue price: $50.00

22-G.54-4.5
1979 Long Eared Owl
Artist: Gerhard Bochmann
Issue price: $65.00. Edition size limited
to announced quantity of 10,000

Maker had
no photo at
press time

22-G.54-4.6
1980 Raccoon and Baby
Artist: Gerhard Bochmann
Issue price: $75.00. Edition size limited
to announced quantity of 10,000

GERMANY
HIBEL STUDIO
(Staffelstein)

Hibel Studio was founded in 1976. Headquartered in Riviera Beach, Florida, the studio specializes in porcelain figurines, lithographs on porcelain and limited-edition collector's plates. All artwork is approved by Edna Hibel, and plates are made by Kaiser Porcelain (see Germany, KAISER).

Hibel Studio began its first series of collector's plates, the *David Series*, in 1979. The four-plate series is based on the biblical story of King David with artwork by Edna Hibel.

Edna Hibel, at 22, became the youngest living artist to have a painting in a major American museum when the Boston Museum purchased one of her canvases in 1939. She is an elected member of the Royal Society of Arts in London, and is the only living female artist with a U.S. museum devoted to her works. In 1979, she gave a one-woman show at the Monaco Fine Arts Gallery under the patronage of Prince Ranier and Princess Grace, and won the "International Year of the Child" award in the United States.

GERMANY
HIBEL STUDIO
(Staffelstein)

David Series
Artist: Edna Hibel
Porcelain highlighted and banded
  in gold
Diameter: 25.7 centimeters
  (10⅛ inches)
Pierced foot rim
Edition size limited to 5,000
Numbered with certificate

22-H.31-1.1
1979 *The Wedding of David and
Bathsheba*
Artist: Edna Hibel
Issue price: $250.00

22-H.31-1.2
1980 *David, Bathsheba and Solomon*
Artist: Edna Hibel
Issue price: $275.00

The history of Kaiser porcelain began in 1872 when porcelain painter August Alboth set up his own workshop in Coburg. When he retired in 1899, his son Ernst moved the pottery to Bavaria. Marriage united the Alboth and Kaiser families in 1922, resulting in the ALKA trademark — a combination of the first two letters of both names.

In 1938 the firm purchased the old Bavarian pottery of Silbermann Brothers, which had been awarded a royal diploma in 1882 for its "magnificent" cobalt blue underglaze. The company opened its modern factory in Staffelstein in 1953 and in 1970 the trademark was changed to Kaiser Porcelain.

Long a producer of porcelain coffee sets, dinnerware and figurines, Kaiser introduced its first series of limited-edition plates, the *Christmas Series*, in 1970. The series ended in 1978. The *Mother's Day Series* began in 1971, and to observe the company's own centennial, the *Anniversary Series* began a year later.

Until his death in 1978, artist Toni Schoener was Chief Designer for Kaiser — noted for his stylistic blend of Western classicism in composition with Oriental mysticism in shading.

KAISER
(Staffelstein)

Christmas Series
Artist: As indicated
Underglaze porcelain decorated in
  cobalt blue
Diameter: 19 centimeters
  (7½ inches)
Pierced foot rim
Edition size undisclosed, limited
  by year of issue except 1974
Not numbered, without certificate

22-K.4-1.1
1970 *Waiting for Santa Claus*
Artist: Toni Schoener
Issue price: $12.50

22-K.4-1.2
1971 *Silent Night*
Artist: Kurt Bauer
Issue price: $13.50

22-K.4-1.3
1972 *Welcome Home*
Artist: Kurt Bauer
Issue price: $16.50

22-K.4-1.4
1973 *Holy Night*
Artist: Toni Schoener
Issue price: $18.00

22-K.4-1.5
1974 *Christmas Carolers*
Artist: Kurt Bauer
Issue price: $25.00. Edition size limited
to announced quantity of 8,000

22-K.4-1.6
1975 *Bringing Home the Christmas Tree*
Artist: Joann Northcott
Issue price: $25.00

22-K.4-1.7
1976 *Christ the Saviour Is Born*
Artist: Carlo Maratta
Issue price: $25.00

22-K.4-1.8
1977 *The Three Kings*
Artist: Toni Schoener
Issue price: $25.00

22-K.4-1.9
1978 *Shepherds in the Fields*
Artist: Toni Schoener
Issue price: $30.00

22-K.4-1.10
1979 *Christmas Eve*
Artist: H. Blum
Issue price: $32.00

22-K.4-1.11
1980 *Joys of Winter*
Artist: H. Blum
Issue price: $40.00

Mother's Day Series

Artist: As indicated
Underglaze porcelain decorated in cobalt blue
Diameter: 19 centimeters (7½ inches)
Pierced foot rim
Edition size undisclosed, limited by year of issue except 1974
Not numbered, without certificate

22-K.4-2.1
1971 *Mare and Foal*
Artist: Toni Schoener
Issue price: $13.00

22-K.4-2.2
1972 *Flowers for Mother*
Artist: Toni Schoener
Issue price: $16.50

22-K.4-2.3
1973 *Cats*
Artist: Toni Schoener
Issue price: $17.00

22-K.4-2.4
1974 *Fox*
Artist: Toni Schoener
Issue price: $22.00. Edition size limited to announced quantity of 7,000

22-K.4-2.5
1975 *German Shepherd*
Artist: Toni Schoener
Issue price: $25.00

22-K.4-2.6
1976 *Swan and Cygnets*
Artist: Toni Schoener
Issue price: $25.00

22-K.4-2.7
1977 *Mother Rabbit and Young*
Artist: Toni Schoener
Issue price: $25.00

22-K.4-2.8
1978 *Hen and Chicks*
Artist: Toni Schoener
Issue price: $30.00

22-K.4-2.9
1979 *A Mother's Devotion*
Artist: Nori Peter
Issue price: $32.00

22-K.4-2.10
1980 *Raccoon Family*
Artist: Joann Northcott
Issue price: $40.00

Anniversary Series

Artist: As indicated

Underglaze porcelain decorated in cobalt blue

Diameter: 19 centimeters (7½ inches)

Pierced foot rim

Edition size undisclosed, limited by year of issue except 1974 and 1975

Not numbered, without certificate

22-K.4-3.1
1972 *Love Birds*
Artist: Toni Schoener
Issue price: $16.50

22-K.4-3.2
1973 *In the Park*
Artist: Toni Schoener
Issue price: $18.00

22-K.4-3.3
1974 *Canoeing down River*
Artist: Toni Schoener
Issue price: $22.00. Edition size limited
to announced quantity of 7,000

22-K.4-3.4
1975 *Tender Moment*
Artist: Toni Schoener
Issue price: $25.00. Edition size limited
to announced quantity of 7,000

22-K.4-3.5
1976 *Serenade for Lovers*
Artist: Toni Schoener
Issue price: $25.00

22-K.4-3.6
1977 *A Simple Gift*
Artist: Toni Schoener
Issue price: $25.00

22-K.4-3.7
1978 *Viking Toast*
Artist: Toni Schoener
Issue price: $30.00

22-K.4-3.8
1979 *Romantic Interlude*
Artist: H. Blum
Issue price: $32.00

22-K.4-3.9
1980 *Love at Play*
Artist: H. Blum
Issue price: $40.00

Königszeit Bavaria entered the collector's plate market in 1979 with the first issue in its *Christmas Series*, more than a century after the creation of the first porcelain bearing the hallmark of Königszelt of Silesia. The likeness of Wilhelm I (1797 - 1888), king of Prussia and first sovereign of a united Germany, is incorporated in the hallmark of Königszelt Bavaria — a tribute to his early patronage under which Bavarian porcelain began its rise to prominence among the porcelain creations of the world.

The artist for the *Christmas Series* is Hedi Keller, the Bavarian-born Primitivist whose work has received major showings in Berlin, Munich and Dusseldorf.

GERMANY
KÖNIGSZELT BAVARIA
(Waldsassen)

Hedi Keller Christmas Series

Artist: Hedi Keller
Porcelain
Diameter: 24.1 centimeters
   (9½ inches)
Attached back hanger
Edition size unannounced
Numbered with certificate

22-K.46-1.1
1979 *The Adoration*
Artist: Hedi Keller
Issue price: $29.50

Maker had
no photo at
press time

22-K.46-1.2
1980 *Flight Into Egypt*
Artist: Hedi Keller
Issue price: $29.50

The Lindner porcelain factory was established by Ernst Lindner in the 1930s in Kueps, Bavaria. Collector's plates by Lihs-Lindner were the product of collaboration between Lindner and Helmut H. Lihs of Long Beach, California. Lihs provided motifs and sketches which were finished by Lindner's artist, Josef Neubauer. Lindner also produces bells, vases and various porcelain items.

The *Christmas Series* started in 1972 and ended in 1977. In 1978 Lihs-Lindner introduced a second Christmas series, *A Child's Christmas*.

Joseph Neubauer, a native of Bavaria, is prominent among German porcelain artists as a master of *Volkskurst* (Folk art). H. Ferner, the artist for *A Child's Christmas* is a recognized master of the old art of Meissner-style porcelain painting.

Christmas Series

Artist: Josef Neubauer
Overglaze porcelain decorated in cobalt blue and 24k gold
Diameter: 19 centimeters (7½ inches)
Pierced foot rim
Edition size: As indicated
Numbered, with certificate since 1976

22-L.31-1.1
1972 *Little Drummer Boy*
Artist: Josef Neubauer
Issue price: $25.00
Edition size limited to 6,000

22-L.31-1.2
1973 *The Little Carolers*
Artist: Josef Neubauer
Issue price: $25.00
Edition size limited to 6,000

22-L.31-1.3
1974 *Peace on Earth*
Artist: Josef Neubauer
Issue price: $25.00
Edition size limited to 6,000

22-L.31-1.4
1975 *Christmas Cheer*
Artist: Josef Neubauer
Issue price: $30.00
Edition size limited to 6,000

22-L.31-1.5
1976 *The Joy of Christmas*
Artist: Josef Neubauer
Issue price: $30.00
Edition size undisclosed

22-L.31-1.6
1977 *Have a Holly-Jolly Christmas*
Artist: Josef Neubauer
Issue price: $30.00
Edition size undisclosed

A Child's Christmas Series
Artist: H. Ferner
Overglaze porcelain decorated in
  cobalt blue and 24k gold
Diameter: 19.7 centimeters
  (7¾ inches)
Attached back hanger
Edition size limited to 5,000
Numbered with certificate

22-L.31-5.1
1978 *Holy Night*
Artist: H. Ferner
Issue price: $40.00

Philip Rosenthal began his business in 1879 in the town of Selb in Bavaria. He initially purchased "white ware" from various porcelain manufacturers in Selb (including Hutschenreuther) and painted it with his own designs.

In 1895 he established his own factory in Kronach where he produced fine porcelain signed *Rosenthal* on the back, making him one of the first porcelain makers to use his name rather than a symbol. Philip died in 1937 and the business was taken over by his son, Philip Jr., who still heads the firm.

Rosenthal's *Traditional Christmas Series* began in 1910 and ended with the 1974 issue. From 1969 to 1971 some of the earlier plates were reissued in small quantities (no more than 500 per reissue). Reissued plates, regardless of the year depicted, have a post-1957 backstamp and their foot rims are not pierced. After 1971, the firm discontinued the practice of reissuing plates from previous years, and each Rosenthal collector's plate is now produced only during its current year. The *Traditional Christmas* plates now qualify as limited editions. A second *Christmas Series* was introduced in 1974 bearing Rosenthal's Classic Rose Collection backstamp.

In 1971 Rosenthal began the first of its Studio-Linie collections with the *Wiinblad*

Christmas Series. These plates carry intricate modern designs partially hand painted in as many as eighteen colors and are embellished with platinum and 18k gold. A second Wiinblad series, consisting of two plates, began in 1976 and is entitled the *Fantasies and Fables Series*. It also carries the Rosenthal Studio-Linie backstamp. The *Nobility of Children Series* and the *Oriental Gold Series* were also begun in 1976 and carry Rosenthal's Classic Rose Collection backstamp.

Danish artist Bjorn Wiinblad received his education at the Royal Academy of Fine Art from 1940 to 1943. His works now hang in The Museum of Decorative Art in Copenhagen, The Museum of Decorative Art in Bergen, Norway, the Faenza Museum in Italy and the National Museum of Sweden in Stockholm. Edna Hibel, at 22, became the youngest living artist to have a painting in a major American museum when the Boston Museum purchased one of her canvases in 1939. She is an elected member of the Royal Society of Arts in London, and is the only living female artist with a U.S. museum devoted to her works. In 1979, she gave a one-woman show at the Monaco Fine Arts Gallery under the patronage of Prince Ranier and Princess Grace, and won the "International Year of the Child" award in the United States.

ROSENTHAL

(Selb, Rothbühl, Selb-Plössberg, München, Kronach, Amberg, Bad Soden, Neusorg)

Traditional Christmas Series

Artist: As indicated. Artist's name appears on back

Overglaze porcelain, many in series have gold inner rim and lettering

Diameter: 21.6 centimeters (8½ inches)

Pierced foot rim until 1971, attached back hanger thereafter

Edition size: Undisclosed

Not numbered, without certificate

22-R.55-1.1
1910 *Winter Peace*
Artist: Jul V. Guldbrandson
Issue price: Unknown

22-R.55-1.2
1911 *The Three Wise Men*
Artist: Heinrich Vogeler
Issue price: Unknown

22-R.55-1.3
1912 *Stardust*
Artist: Paul Rieth
Issue price: Unknown

22-R.55-1.4
1913 *Christmas Lights*
Artist: Julius Dietz
Issue price: Unknown

22-R.55-1.5
1914 *Christmas Song*
Artist: Prof. L. V. Zumbusch
Issue price: Unknown

22-R.55-1.6
1915 *Walking to Church*
Artist: Jul V. Guldbrandson
Issue price: Unknown

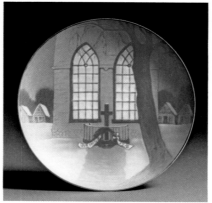

22-R.55-1.7
1916 *Christmas During War*
Artist: Jul V. Guldbrandson
Issue price: Unknown

22-R.55-1.8
1917 *Angel of Peace*
Artist: Moere
Issue price: Unknown

22-R.55-1.9
1918 *Peace on Earth*
Artist: Pfeifer
Issue price: Unknown

22-R.55-1.10
1919 *St. Christopher with the Christ Child*
Artist: Dr. W. Schertel
Issue price: Unknown

22-R.55-1.11
1920 *The Manger in Bethlehem*
Artist: Dr. W. Schertel
Issue price: Unknown

22-R.55-1.12
1921 *Christmas in the Mountains*
Artist: Jupp Wiertz
Issue price: Unknown

22-R.55-1.13
1922 *Advent Branch*
Artist: F. Nicolai
Issue price: Unknown

22-R.55-1.14
1923 *Children in the Winter Wood*
Artist: Ernst Hofer
Issue price: Unknown

22-R.55-1.15
1924 *Deer in the Woods*
Artist: Theo Karner
Issue price: Unknown

22-R.55-1.16
1925 *The Three Wise Men*
Artist: Tauschek
Issue price: Unknown

22-R.55-1.17
1926 *Christmas in the Mountains*
Artist: Theo Schmutz-Baudess
Issue price: Unknown

GERMANY
ROSENTHAL

(Selb, Rothbühl, Selb-Plössberg, München, Kronach, Amberg, Bad Soden, Neusorg)

22-R.55-1.18
1927 *Station on the Way*
Artist: Theo Schmutz-Baudess
Issue price: Unknown

22-R.55-1.19
1928 *Chalet Christmas*
Artist: Heinrich Fink
Issue price: Unknown

22-R.55-1.20
1929 *Christmas in the Alps*
Artist: Heinrich Fink
Issue price: Unknown

22-R.55-1.21
1930 *Group of Deer Under the Pines*
Artist: Theo Karner
Issue price: Unknown

22-R.55-1.22
1931 *Path of the Magi*
Artist: Heinrich Fink
Issue price: Unknown

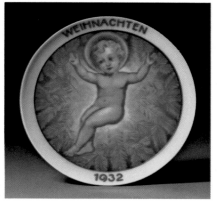

22-R.55-1.23
1932 *Christ Child*
Artist: Otto Koch
Issue price: Unknown

22-R.55-1.24
1933 *Through the Night to Light*
Artist: Hans Schiffner
Issue price: Unknown

22-R.55-1.25
1934 *Christmas Peace*
Artist: Heinrich Fink
Issue price: Unknown

22-R.55-1.26
1935 *Christmas by the Sea*
Artist: Heinrich Fink
Issue price: Unknown

22-R.55-1.27
1936 *Nurnberg Angel*
Artist: Heinrich Fink
Issue price: Unknown

22-R.55-1.28
1937 *Berchtesgaden*
Artist: Heinrich Fink
Issue price: Unknown

22-R.55-1.29
1938 *Christmas in the Alps*
Artist: Heinrich Fink
Issue price: Unknown

22-R.55-1.30
1939 *Schneekoppe Mountain*
Artist: Heinrich Fink
Issue price: Unknown

22-R.55-1.31
1940 *Marien Church in Danzig*
Artist: Walter Mutze
Issue price: Unknown

22-R.55-1.32
1941 *Strassburg Cathedral*
Artist: Walter Mutze
Issue price: Unknown

22-R.55-1.33
1942 *Marianburg Castle*
Artist: Walter Mutze
Issue price: Unknown

22-R.55-1.34
1943 *Winter Idyll*
Artist: Amadeus Dier
Issue price: Unknown

22-R.55-1.35
1944 *Wood Scape*
Artist: Willi Hein
Issue price: Unknown

GERMANY
ROSENTHAL

(Selb, Rothbühl, Selb-Plössberg, München, Kronach, Amberg,
Bad Soden, Neusorg)

22-R.55-1.36
1945 *Christmas Peace*
Artist: Alfred Mundel
Issue price: Unknown

22-R.55-1.37
1946 *Christmas in an Alpine Valley*
Artist: Willi Hein
Issue price: Unknown

22-R.55-1.38
1947 *The Dillingen Madonna*
Artist: Louis Hagen
Issue price: Unknown

22-R.55-1.39
1948 *Message to the Shepherds*
Artist: Richard Hoffman
Issue price: Unknown

22-R.55-1.40
1949 *The Holy Family*
Artist: Prof. Karl
Issue price: Unknown

22-R.55-1.41
1950 *Christmas in the Forest*
Artist: Willi Hein
Issue price: Unknown

22-R.55-1.42
1951 *Star of Bethlehem*
Artist: Anne V. Groote
Issue price: Unknown

22-R.55-1.43
1952 *Christmas in the Alps*
Artist: Willi Hein
Issue price: Unknown

22-R.55-1.44
1953 *The Holy Light*
Artist: Willi Hein
Issue price: Unknown

22-R.55-1.45
1954 *Christmas Eve*
Artist: Willi Hein
Issue price: Unknown

22-R.55-1.46
1955 *Christmas in a Village*
Artist: Willi Hein
Issue price: Unknown

22-R.55-1.47
1956 *Christmas in the Alps*
Artist: Willi Hein
Issue price: Unknown

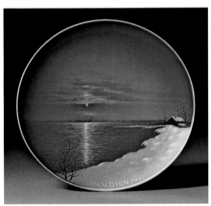

22-R.55-1.48
1957 *Christmas by the Sea*
Artist: Willi Hein
Issue price: Unknown

22-R.55-1.49
1958 *Christmas Eve*
Artist: Willi Hein
Issue price: Unknown

22-R.55-1.50
1959 *Midnight Mass*
Artist: Willi Hein
Issue price: Unknown

22-R.55-1.51
1960 *Christmas in a Small Village*
Artist: Willi Hein
Issue price: Unknown

22-R.55-1.52
1961 *Solitary Christmas*
Artist: Willi Hein
Issue price: Unknown

22-R.55-1.53
1962 *Christmas Eve*
Artist: Willi Hein
Issue price: Unknown

GERMANY
ROSENTHAL

(Selb, Rothbühl, Selb-Plössberg, München, Kronach, Amberg,
Bad Soden, Neusorg)

22-R.55-1.54
1963 *Silent Night*
Artist: Willi Hein
Issue price: Unknown

22-R.55-1.55
1964 *Christmas Market in Nurnberg*
Artist: Georg Kuspert
Issue price: Unknown

22-R.55-1.56
1965 *Christmas in Munich*
Artist: Georg Kuspert
Issue price: Unknown

22-R.55-1.57
1966 *Christmas in Ulm*
Artist: Georg Kuspert
Issue price: Unknown

22-R.55-1.58
1967 *Christmas in Regensburg*
Artist: Georg Kuspert
Issue price: Unknown

22-R.55-1.59
1968 *Christmas in Bremen*
Artist: Georg Kuspert
Issue price: Unknown

22-R.55-1.60
1969 *Christmas in Rothenburg*
Artist: Georg Kuspert
Issue price: Unknown

22-R.55-1.61
1970 *Christmas in Cologne*
Artist: Georg Kuspert
Issue price: Unknown

22-R.55-1.62
1971 *Christmas in Garmisch*
Artist: Georg Kuspert
Issue price: $66.00

22-R.55-1.63
1972 *Christmas Celebration in Franconia*
Artist: Georg Kuspert
Issue price: $66.00

22-R.55-1.64
1973 *Christmas in Lübeck-Holstein*
Artist: Georg Kuspert
Issue price: $84.00

22-R.55-1.65
1974 *Christmas in Wurzburg*
Artist: Georg Kuspert
Issue price: $85.00

Wiinblad Christmas Series

Artist: Bjørn Wiinblad. Artist's signature appears on front

Overglaze porcelain partially hand painted in 18 colors with 18k gold design on border

Diameter: 29.2 centimeters (11½ inches)

Attached back hanger

Edition size: Undisclosed

Not numbered, without certificate

22-R.55-2.1
1971 *Maria and Child*
Artist: Bjørn Wiinblad
Issue price: $100.00

22-R.55-2.2
1972 *Caspar*
Artist: Bjørn Wiinblad
Issue price: $100.00

22-R.55-2.3
1973 *Melchior*
Artist: Bjørn Wiinblad
Issue price: $125.00

22-R.55-2.4
1974 *Balthazar*
Artist: Bjørn Wiinblad
Issue price: $125.00

22-R.55-2.5
1975 *The Annunciation*
Artist: Bjørn Wiinblad
Issue price: $195.00

(Selb, Rothbühl, Selb-Plössberg, München, Kronach, Amberg, Bad Soden, Neusorg)

22-R.55-2.6
1976 Angel with Trumpet
Artist: Bjørn Wiinblad
Issue price: $195.00

22-R.55-2.7
1977 Adoration of the Shepherds
Artist: Bjørn Wiinblad
Issue price: $225.00

22-R.55-2.8
1978 Angel with Harp
Artist: Bjørn Wiinblad
Issue price: $275.00

22-R.55-2.9
1979 Exodus from Egypt
Artist: Bjørn Wiinblad
Issue price: $310.00

22-R.55-2.10
1980 Angel with a Glockenspiel
Artist: Bjørn Wiinblad
Issue price: $360.00

Fantasies and Fables Series

Artist: Bjørn Wiinblad. Artist's
signature appears on front
Overglaze porcelain highlighted
in gold
Diameter: 16.5 centimeters
(6½ inches)
Attached back hanger
Edition size: Undisclosed
Not numbered, without certificate

22-R.55-4.1
1976 Oriental Night Music
Artist: Bjørn Wiinblad
Issue price: $50.00

22-R.55-4.2
1977 The Mandolin Players
Artist: Bjørn Wiinblad
Issue price: $55.00

The Nobility of Children Series

Artist: Edna Hibel. Artist's signature appears on front

Overglaze porcelain banded in gold

Diameter: 25.4 centimeters (10 inches)

Attached back hanger

Edition size limited to 12,750

Numbered with certificate

22-R.55-6.1
1976 *La Contessa Isabella*
Artist: Edna Hibel
Issue price: $120.00

22-R.55-6.2
1977 *Le Marquis Maurice-Pierre*
Artist: Edna Hibel
Issue price: $120.00

22-R.55-6.3
1978 *Baronesse Johanna-Maryke Van Vollendam Tot Marken*
Artist: Edna Hibel
Issue price: $130.00

22-R.55-6.4
1979 *Chief Red Feather*
Artist: Edna Hibel
Issue price: $140.00

Oriental Gold Series

Artist: Edna Hibel. Artist's signature appears on front

Overglaze porcelain highlighted in gold

Diameter: 25.4 centimeters (10 inches)

Attached back hanger

Edition size limited to 2,000

Numbered with certificate

22-R.55-8.1
1976 *Yasuko*
Artist: Edna Hibel
Issue price: $275.00

22-R.55-8.2
1977 *Mr. Obata*
Artist: Edna Hibel
Issue price: $275.00

GERMANY
ROSENTHAL

(Selb, Rothbühl, Selb-Plössberg, München, Kronach, Amberg,
Bad Soden, Neusorg)

22-R.55-8.3
1978 *Sakura*
Artist: Edna Hibel
Issue price: $295.00

22-R.55-8.4
1979 *Michio*
Artist: Edna Hibel
Issue price: $325.00

Christmas Series
(The Classic Rose Collection)
Artist: Helmut Drexler. Artist's
  name appears on back
Overglaze porcelain with gold
  inner rim and lettering
Diameter: 21.6 centimeters
  (8½ inches)
Attached back hanger
Edition size: Undisclosed
Not numbered, without certificate

Photo unavailable
at press time

22-R.55-11.1
1974 *Memorial Church in Berlin*
Artist: Helmut Drexler
Issue price: $84.00

22-R.55-11.2
1975 *Freiburg Cathedral*
Artist: Helmut Drexler
Issue price: $75.00

22-R.55-11.3
1976 *The Castle of Cochem*
Artist: Helmut Drexler
Issue price: $95.00

22-R.55-11.4
1977 *Hannover Town Hall*
Artist: Helmut Drexler
Issue price: $125.00

22-R.55-11.5
1978 *Cathedral at Aachen*
Artist: Helmut Drexler
Issue price: $150.00

22-R.55-11.6
1979 *Cathedral in Luxemburg*
Artist: Helmut Drexler
Issue price: $165.00

22-R.55-11.7
1980 *Christmas in Brussels*
Artist: Helmut Drexler
Issue price: $190.00

The pottery now known as Royal Bayreuth began in 1794 in the mountain village of Tettau as the Koniglich Privilegierter Porzellanfabrik Tettau, the first porcelain manufacturer in Bavaria. Now a subsidiary of Royal Tettau, Royal Bayreuth began its first limited-edition *Christmas Series* in 1972. The series, which depicts Bavarian winter scenes, was followed in 1973 by a *Mother's Day Series* with art by contemporary artists.

Artists from several nationalities contribute to the Royal Bayreuth series. Self-taught landscape artist Ken Zylla and American Frank Kecskes are among the designers whose works appear in the *Christmas Series*. Brazilian Ozz Franka, a specialist in the art of children's portraiture, began the *Mother's Day Series* in 1973. Since then, Dutch artist Leo Jansen, renowned for his Interpretive style of portraiture, has created the artwork for the series.

GERMANY
ROYAL BAYREUTH
(Tettau)

Christmas Series
Artist: As indicated
Overglaze porcelain banded in
  gold since 1976
Diameter: 20.3 centimeters
  (8 inches)
Attached back hanger
Edition size: As indicated
Numbered without certificate

22-R.58-1.1
1972 *Carriage in the Village*
Artist: Unknown
Issue price: $15.00
Edition size limited to 4,000

22-R.58-1.2
1973 *Snow Scene*
Artist: Unknown
Issue price: $16.50
Edition size limited to 5,000

22-R.58-1.3
1974 *The Old Mill*
Artist: Unknown
Issue price: $24.00
Edition size limited to 4,000

22-R.58-1.4
1975 *Forest Chalet 'Serenity'*
Artist: Georg Rotger
Issue price: $27.50
Edition size limited to 4,000

22-R.58-1.5
1976 *Christmas in the Country*
Artist: Ken Zylla
Issue price: $40.00
Edition size limited to 5,000

22-R.58-1.6
1977 *Peace on Earth*
Artist: Frank Kecskes, Jr.
Issue price: $40.00
Edition size limited to 5,000

22-R.58-1.7
1978 *Peaceful Interlude*
Artist: Ron Stewart
Issue price: $45.00
Edition size limited to 5,000

22-R.58-1.8
1979 *Homeward Bound*
Artist: Ron Stewart
Issue price: $50.00
Edition size limited to 5,000

Mother's Day Series

Artist: As indicated. Artist's
signature appears on back until
1975, on front thereafter
Overglaze porcelain
Diameter: 19.7 centimeters
(7¾ inches)
Attached back hanger
Edition size: as indicated
Numbered without certificate

22-R.58-2.1
1973 *Consolation*
Artist: Ozz Franka
Issue price: $16.50
Edition size limited to 4,000

22-R.58-2.2
1974 *Young Americans*
Artist: Leo Jansen
Issue price: $25.00
Edition size limited to 4,000

22-R.58-2.3
1975 *Young Americans II*
Artist: Leo Jansen
Issue price: $25.00
Edition size limited to 5,000

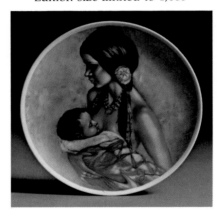

22-R.58-2.4
1976 *Young Americans III*
Artist: Leo Jansen
Issue price: $30.00
Edition size limited to 5,000

22-R.58-2.5
1977 *Young Americans IV*
Artist: Leo Jansen
Issue price: $40.00
Edition size limited to 5,000

22-R.58-2.6
1978 *Young Americans V*
Artist: Leo Jansen
Issue price: $45.00
Edition size limited to 5,000

22-R.58-2.7
1979 *Young Americans VI*
Artist: Leo Jansen
Issue price: $60.00
Edition size limited to 5,000

22-R.58-2.8
1980 *Young Americans VII*
Artist: Leo Jansen
Issue price: $65.00
Edition size limited to 5,000

Schmid was established in Boston in the 1930s. Since then the firm has been a specialized importer of porcelain bells and mugs as well as plates. Schmid limited-edition plates are produced by the Hutschenreuther factory in Germany, a noted manufacturer of porcelain figurines and tableware.

Both the *Christmas Series*, which began in 1971, and the *Mother's Day Series*, which started the following year, feature art created by the late Berta Hummel. The Hummel plates bear her signature depending on whether Berta Hummel had signed the original artwork. The *Ferrandiz Mother and Child Series* began in 1977.

Both Hummel series feature art created by Berta Hummel before she entered the Franciscan order at Siessen in 1934 and took the name Sister Maria Innocentia. (See Germany, GOEBEL). Prior to taking her vows, she had received extensive training at art academies in Simbach and Munich, where she evolved the distinctive style that instantly identifies her work to collectors worldwide.

GERMANY
SCHMID
(Selb)

Christmas Series

Artist: Berta Hummel. Artist's
   signature or initials appear on
   front except 1975 and 1977
Overglaze porcelain
Diameter: 19.7 centimeters
   (7¾ inches)
Attached back hanger
Edition size undisclosed, limited
   by year of issue
Not numbered, without certificate

22-S.12-1.1
1971 *Angel in a Christmas Setting*
Artist: Berta Hummel
Issue price: $15.00

22-S.12-1.2
1972 *Angel with Flute*
Artist: Berta Hummel
Issue price: $15.00

22-S.12-1.3
1973 *The Nativity*
Artist: Berta Hummel
Issue price: $15.00

22-S.12-1.4
1974 *The Guardian Angel*
Artist: Berta Hummel
Issue price: $18.50

22-S.12-1.5
1975 *Christmas Child*
Artist: Berta Hummel
Issue price: $25.00

22-S.12-1.6
1976 *Sacred Journey*
Artist: Berta Hummel
Issue price: $27.50

22-S.12-1.7
1977 *Herald Angel*
Artist: Berta Hummel
Issue price: $27.50

22-S.12-1.8
1978 *Heavenly Trio*
Artist: Berta Hummel
Issue price: $32.50

22-S.12-1.9
1979 *Starlight Angel*
Artist: Berta Hummel
Issue price: $38.00

22-S.12-1.10
1980 *Parade into Toyland*
Artist: Berta Hummel
Issue price: $45.00

Mother's Day Series

Artist: Berta Hummel. Artist's signature or initials appears on front except 1976, 1978, 1979 and 1980

Overglaze porcelain

Diameter: 19.7 centimeters (7¾ inches)

Attached back hanger

Edition size undisclosed, limited by year of issue

Not numbered, without certificate

22-S.12-2.1
1972 *Playing Hooky*
Artist: Berta Hummel
Issue price: $15.00

22-S.12-2.2
1973 *The Little Fisherman*
Artist: Berta Hummel
Issue price: $15.00

22-S.12-2.3
1974 *The Bumblebee*
Artist: Berta Hummel
Issue price: $18.50

22-S.12-2.4
1975 *Message of Love*
Artist: Berta Hummel
Issue price: $25.00

22-S.12-2.5
1976 *Devotion for Mother*
Artist: Berta Hummel
Issue price: $27.50

22-S.12-2.6
1977 *Moonlight Return*
Artist: Berta Hummel
Issue price: $27.50

22-S.12-2.7
1978 *Afternoon Stroll*
Artist: Berta Hummel
Issue price: $32.50

22-S.12-2.8
1979 *Cherub's Gift*
Artist: Berta Hummel
Issue price: $38.00

22-S.12-2.9
1980 *Mother's Little Helpers*
Artist: Berta Hummel
Issue price: $45.00

Ferrandiz Mother and Child Series

Artist: Juan Ferrandiz
Overglaze porcelain banded in gold
Diameter: 25.4 centimeters (10 inches)
Pierced foot rim
Edition size limited to 10,000
Numbered without certificate

22-S.12-3.1
1977 *Orchard Mother and Child*
Artist: Juan Ferrandiz
Issue price: $65.00

22-S.12-3.2
1978 *Pastoral Mother and Child*
Artist: Juan Ferrandiz
Issue price: $75.00

22-S.12-3.3
1979 *Floral Mother*
Artist: Juan Ferrandiz
Issue price: $95.00

22-S.12-3.4
1980 *Avian Mother*
Artist: Juan Ferrandiz
Issue price: $100.00

GREAT BRITAIN
BELLEEK
(Belleek, County Fermanagh)

Belleek Pottery Ltd., maker of thin, translucent parian china, was established in 1857 by David McBirney and Robert W. Armstrong on the banks of the River Erne near the small village of Belleek in County Fermanagh, Ireland. The site is near deposits of clay discovered when the owner of Castle Caldwell in Fermanagh became interested in the brilliant whitewash used on local cottages and found that his entire estate lay on a bed of feldspar clay.

When combined with metallic washes, this clay produces the unique iridescent effect for which Belleek is known — a mother-of-pearl luster that has been used on tea sets, figurines and tableware. Queen Victoria and her son, the Prince of Wales, were among those who commissioned elaborate table services from the firm.

During the 1880s and 1890s some workers from Belleek were brought to the United States to produce an American Belleek, but the resulting porcelain was heavier and less translucent than the Irish product. Belleek ware is still made today much as it was a century ago.

Belleek's *Christmas Series*, based on Irish subjects, began in 1970 and ended in 1977. The *Irish Wildlife Christmas Series* began in 1978.

Artists for Belleek plates are not disclosed.

BELLEEK

(Belleek, County Fermanagh)

Christmas Series
Artist: Undisclosed
Parian china
Diameter: 19 centimeters
   (7½ inches)
No hanger
Edition size limited to announced
   quantity of 7,500
Not numbered, without certificate

26-B.18-1.1
1970 *Castle Caldwell*
Artist: Undisclosed
Issue price: $25.00

26-B.18-1.2
1971 *Celtic Cross*
Artist: Undisclosed
Issue price: $25.00

26-B.18-1.3
1972 *Flight of the Earls*
Artist: Undisclosed
Issue price: $30.00

26-B.18-1.4
1973 *Tribute to W. B. Yeats*
Artist: Undisclosed
Issue price: $38.50

26-B.18-1.5
1974 *Devenish Island*
Artist: Undisclosed
Issue price: $45.00

26-B.18-1.6
1975 *The Celtic Cross*
Artist: Undisclosed
Issue price: $48.00

26-B.18-1.7
1976 *Dove of Peace*
Artist: Undisclosed
Issue price: $55.00

26-B.18-1.8
1977 *Wren*
Artist: Undisclosed
Issue price: $55.00

26-B.18-2.1

*Irish Wildlife
Christmas Series*
Artist: Undisclosed
Parian china
Diameter: 22.9 centimeters
   (9 inches)
No hanger
Edition size undisclosed
Not numbered, without certificate

26-B.18-2.1
1978 *A Leaping Salmon*
Artist: Undisclosed
Issue price: $55.00

Maker had
no photo at
press time

26-B.18-2.2
1979 *Hare at Rest*
Artist: Undisclosed
Issue price: $58.50

26-B.18-2.3
No information available
at press time

One of the oldest surviving English china manufacturers, Doulton & Company traces its origin in 1815 to the small stoneware pottery of John Doulton and John Watts near Vauxhall Gardens, London. Within a few years the pottery was moved to Lambeth, where it remained until it was relocated to its present site at Burslem in 1877. There Doulton took over an established pottery and began producing fine earthenware and china.

In 1887 the honor of knighthood was bestowed upon Henry Doulton by Queen Victoria and in 1901 the company received the Royal warrant giving it authority to use *Royal* with its name.

The Royal Doulton Christmas *Around the World Series* produced by Royal Doulton's Beswick Potteries, was issued from 1972 to 1978, depicting foreign Christmas traditions.

The Collector's International collection began with the *Mother and Child Series* in 1973. These plates show mothers and children of various countries. Other series in the Collector's International group are by contemporary artists and include the *Commedia Dell' Arte Series* begun in 1974 and ended in 1978; the *Flower Garden Series* started in 1975; and *The Log of the "Dashing Wave"* and *Reflections on China Series* which

began in 1976. The *Valentine's Day Series* also began in 1976 with artwork from Victorian period prints. The *Christmas Series* was introduced in 1977.

Royal Doulton has recruited several important artists to design its collector's plates. The maker was the first to commission Edna Hibel to work in the limited-edition plate medium. She has since become one of the most successful plate artists (see Germany, HIBEL STUDIOS). Another famous Royal Doulton artist is LeRoy Neiman, recipient of the gold medal of the *Salon d'Art Moderne* in Paris. His work has appeared on the covers of *Time* and *Newsweek* magazines and is in the permanent collection of Oxford University. Artist for the *Reflections on China* series is Chen Chi, whose lyrical style blends Western Impressionism with Oriental settings. Artist John Stobart's marine works are highly praised for their historical accuracy and are in the permanent collections of maritime museums around the world, including the National Maritime Museum in Greenwich, England. Argentine Hahn Vidal, designer of the *Flower Garden Series*, was the first western floral artist to be invited to exhibit officially in Japan and Taiwan.

GREAT BRITAIN
ROYAL DOULTON
(Burslem, Stoke-on-Trent, Staffordshire)

Beswick Christmas Series
Artist: As indicated
Earthenware in hand-cast
 bas-relief hand painted in
 15 colors
Diameter: 20.5 centimeters
 (8 inches square)
Pierced foot rim
Edition size limited to 15,000
Numbered without certificate

26-R.62-1.1
1972 *Christmas in England*
Artist: Harry Sales
Issue price: $35.00

26-R.62-1.2
1973 *Christmas in Mexico*
Artist: Chavela Castrejon
Issue price: $37.50

26-R.62-1.3
1974 *Christmas in Bulgaria*
Artist: Dimitri Yordanov
Issue price: $37.50

26-R.62-1.4
1975 *Christmas in Norway*
Artist: Alton Toby
Issue price: $45.00

26-R.62-1.5
1976 *Christmas in Holland*
Artist: Alton Toby
Issue price: $50.00

26-R.62-1.6
1977 *Christmas in Poland*
Artist: Alton Toby
Issue price: $50.00

26-R.62-1.7
1978 *Christmas in America*
Artist: Alton Toby
Issue price: $55.00

Mother and Child Series

Artist: Edna Hibel. Artist's
  signature appears on front
Bone china banded in gold
Diameter: 21 centimeters
  (8¼ inches)
No hanger
Edition size limited to 15,000
Numbered since 1974, without
  certificate

26-R.62-2.1
1973 *Colette and Child*
Artist: Edna Hibel
Issue price: $40.00

26-R.62-2.2
1974 *Sayuri and Child*
Artist: Edna Hibel
Issue price: $40.00

26-R.62-2.3
1975 *Kristina and Child*
Artist: Edna Hibel
Issue price: $50.00

26-R.62-2.4
1976 *Marilyn and Child*
Artist: Edna Hibel
Issue price: $55.00

26-R.62-2.5
1977 *Lucia and Child*
Artist: Edna Hibel
Issue price: $60.00

Maker had
no photo at
press time

26-R.62-2.6
1978 *Kathleen and Child*
Artist: Edna Hibel
Issue price: $65.00

Commedia Dell' Arte Series

Artist: LeRoy Neiman. Artist's
  signature appears on front
Bone china banded in gold
Diameter: 25.4 centimeters
  (10 inches)
No hanger
Edition size limited to 15,000
Numbered without certificate

26-R.62-3.1
1974 *Harlequin*
Artist: LeRoy Neiman
Issue price: $50.00

26-R.62-3.2
1975 *Pierrot*
Artist: LeRoy Neiman
Issue price: $60.00

26-R.62-3.3
1977 *Columbine*
Artist: LeRoy Neiman
Issue price: $70.00

26-R.62-3.4
1978 *Punchinello*
Artist: LeRoy Neiman
Issue price: $70.00

Flower Garden Series

Artist: Hahn Vidal. Artist's
  signature appears on front
Bone china banded in gold
Diameter: 26.7 centimeters
  (10½ inches)
No hanger
Edition size limited to 15,000
Numbered without certificate

26-R.62-4.1
1975 *Spring Harmony*
Artist: Hahn Vidal
Issue price: $60.00

26-R.62-4.2
1976 *Dreaming Lotus*
Artist: Hahn Vidal
Issue price: $65.00

26-R.62-4.3
1977 *From a Poet's Garden*
Artist: Hahn Vidal
Issue price: $70.00

26-R.62-4.4
1978 *Country Bouquet*
Artist: Hahn Vidal
Issue price: $70.00

26-R.62-4.5
No information available
at press time

The Log of the "Dashing Wave" Series

Artist: John Stobart. Artist's
signature appears on front
Bone china banded in gold
Diameter: 26.7 centimeters
(10½ inches)
No hanger
Edition size limited to 15,000
Numbered without certificate

26-R.62-6.1
1976 *Sailing with the Tide*
Artist: John Stobart
Issue price: $65.00

26-R.62-6.2
1977 *Running Free*
Artist: John Stobart
Issue price: $70.00

26-R.62-6.3
1978 *Rounding the Horn*
Artist: John Stobart
Issue price: $70.00

26-R.62-6.4
1979 *Hong Kong*
Artist: John Stobart
Issue price: $75.00

26-R.62-6.5
No information available
at press time

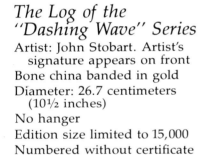
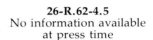

ROYAL DOULTON

(Burslem, Stoke-on-Trent, Staffordshire)

Valentine's Day Series

Artist: Unknown. Reproduced
   from nineteenth-century
   Victorian prints
Bone china banded in gold
Diameter: 21 centimeters
   (8¼ inches)
No hanger
Edition size undisclosed, limited
   by period of issue
Not numbered, without certificate

26-R.62-7.1
1976 *Victorian Boy and Girl*
Artist: Unknown
Issue price: $25.00

26-R.62-7.2
1977 *My Sweetest Friend*
Artist: Unknown
Issue price: $25.00

26-R.62-7.3
1978 *If I Loved You*
Artist: Unknown
Issue price: $25.00

26-R.62-7.4
1979 *My Valentine*
Artist: Unknown
Issue price: $29.95

26-R.62-7.5
1980 Untitled at press time
Artist: Unknown
Issue price: $32.95

Reflections on China Series
Artist: Chen Chi. Artist's signature
    appears on front
Bone china
Diameter: 26.7 centimeters
    (10½ inches)
No hanger
Edition size limited to15,000
Numbered without certificate

26-R.62-8.1
1976 *Garden of Tranquility*
Artist: Chen Chi
Issue price: $70.00

26-R.62-8.2
1977 *Imperial Palace*
Artist: Chen Chi
Issue price: $70.00

26-R.62-8.3
1978 *Temple of Heaven*
Artist: Chen Chi
Issue price: $75.00

26-R.62-8.4
No information available
at press time

The Worcester Porcelain Company, the oldest porcelain manufactory in England today, was established at Worcester, England, in 1751. Two of its original stockholders — Dr. John Wall, a physician and amateur artist, and William Davis, an apothecary — are credited with perfecting a formula for making soft-paste porcelain from soapstone (steatite). Their formula was used until the introduction of bone china in the nineteenth century.

In 1788, King George III gave the company permission to call itself "Manufacturers to their Majesties." After undergoing a number of changes in ownership, the firm was reorganized in 1862 and the Royal Worcester Porcelain Company in recognition of its long history of royal patronage. More recently in 1976, Royal Worcester merged with Spode; however, each company has retained its own trademark.

Royal Worcester makes two types of collector's plates: bone china, made at Worcester, England; and pewter, made in the United States (see United States, ROYAL WORCESTER).

In 1972, Royal Worcester introduced a series of twelve annual plates, the *Doughty Bird Series*, based on the porcelain sculptures of American birds by Dorothy Doughty.

Dorothy Doughty is a prominent English sculptor of wildlife.

Doughty Bird Series

Artist: Dorothy Doughty. Artist's
  signature appears on back
Bone china with hand-painted
  bas-relief and gold scalloped rim
Diameter: 20.3 centimeters
  (8 inches)
No hanger
Edition size: As indicated
Not numbered, without certificate

26-R.76-1.1
1972 *Redstarts and Beech*
Artist: Dorothy Doughty
Issue price: $125.00. Edition size
limited to announced quantity of 2,750

26-R.76-1.2
1973 *Myrtle Warbler and Cherry*
Artist: Dorothy Doughty
Issue price: $175.00. Edition size
limited to announced quantity of 3,000

26-R.76-1.3
1974 *Blue-Grey Gnatcatchers*
Artist: Dorothy Doughty
Issue price: $195.00. Edition size
limited to announced quantity of 3,000

26-R.76-1.4
1975 *Blackburnian Warbler*
Artist: Dorothy Doughty
Issue price: $195.00. Edition size
limited to announced quantity of 3,000

26-R.76-1.5
1976 *Blue-Winged Sivas and Bamboo*
Artist: Dorothy Doughty
Issue price: $195.00. Edition size
limited to announced quantity of 3,000

26-R.76-1.6
1977 *Paradise Wydah*
Artist: Dorothy Doughty
Issue price: $195.00. Edition size
limited to announced quantity of 3,000

26-R.76-1.7
1978 *Bluetits and Witch Hazel*
Artist: Dorothy Doughty
Issue price: $195.00. Edition size
limited to announced quantity of 3,000

26-R.76-1.8
1979 *Mountain Bluebird and Pine*
Artist: Dorothy Doughty
Issue price: $195.00. Edition size
limited to announced quantity of 3,000

26-R.76-1.9
1980 *Cerulean Warblers and Beech*
Artist: Dorothy Doughty
Issue price: $195.00. Edition size
limited to announced quantity of 3,000

Spode

Josiah Spode I established the Spode Works at Stoke-on-Trent, England, in 1776 after spending nearly thirty years learning every facet of the pottery business. From the beginning, the Spode name was highly respected, and the firm has been awarded the Royal warrant by each English monarch since George III.

Josiah Spode perfected the process by which animal bone ash is added to china clay to produce bone china, which is creamy white and translucent. His formula came to be known as English bone china and remains the standard to this day.

Upon Spode's death in 1797, his son, Josiah Spode II, continued the trade, with William Copeland in charge of sales. Josiah Spode III in turn headed the business, but upon his death, Copeland became sole owner and from 1827 his descendants operated the firm. Under their direction it was called W. T. Copeland & Sons, Ltd., but retained the Spode trademark. Between 1967 and 1976, the firm was owned by Carborundum Company, but in 1976 Spode merged with Royal Worcester of England. The Spode trademark has been retained and the present factory is located on the site of the original pottery.

Spode's bone china *Christmas Series* began in 1970 and draws its theme from old English carols. The plate itself reproduces an original eighteenth-century Spode model. Decorations of the 1970 and 1971 plates are in gold; thereafter, decorations are gold with a second color which is changed every two years.

Designs for Spode *Christmas* plates are inspired by the originals of Gillian West, a prominent nineteenth-century British ceramics artist.

GREAT BRITAIN
SPODE
(Stoke-on-Trent, Staffordshire)

Christmas Series
Artist: As indicated
Bone china decorated in gold
Diameter: 20.3 centimeters
(8 inches)
No hanger
Edition size undisclosed, limited
by year of issue
Not numbered, without certificate

26-S.63-1.1
1970 *Partridge in a Pear Tree*
Artist: Gillian West
Issue price: $35.00

26-S.63-1.2
1971 *In Heaven the Angels Singing*
Artist: Gillian West
Issue price: $35.00

26-S.63-1.3
1972 *We Saw Three Ships A-Sailing*
Artist: Gillian West
Issue price: $35.00

26-S.63-1.4
1973 *We Three Kings of Orient Are*
Artist: Gillian West
Issue price: $35.00

26-S.63-1.5
1974 *Deck the Halls*
Artist: Gillian West
Issue price: $35.00

26-S.63-1.6
1975 *Christbaum*
Artist: Gillian West
Issue price: $45.00

26-S.63-1.7
1976 *Good King Wenceslas*
Artist: Gillian West
Issue price: $45.00

26-S.63-1.8
1977 *The Holly and the Ivy*
Artist: Gillian West
Issue price: $45.00

26-S.63-1.9
1978 *While Shepherds Watched*
Artist: Gillian West
Issue price: $45.00

26-S.63-1.10
1979 *Away in a Manger*
Artist: Gillian West
Issue price: $50.00

26-S.63-1.11
1980 Untitled at press time
Artist: Paul Wood
Issue price: $60.00

Josiah Wedgwood I, Fellow of the Royal Society, was known as the "father of English potters." He founded the firm that bears his name in 1759 and built a new factory which he called "Etruria" ten years later.

Wedgwood himself developed many of the processes and materials used by the firm to this day. He is perhaps best known for his "Jasperware" which he perfected in 1774. A vitreous, unglazed stoneware, Jasper is pure white in its original form but can be stained to produce a wide variety of colored backgrounds — green, lilac, yellow, maroon, black, and most popular of all, classic "Wedgwood blue" — onto which white bas-relief decorations are applied by hand.

Although potters in England and abroad tried to duplicate Jasperware, none were successful and the Wedgwood name is so firmly linked with Jasper to this day that many people mistakenly think it is the only ware Wedgwood produces, and that it is made only in blue. In 1940, having outgrown the pottery at Etruria, the firm moved to what has been described as the most up-to-date pottery in the world near the village of Barlaston, Stoke-on-Trent, Staffordshire, England.

There, in 1969, the firm celebrated the two-hundredth anniversary of the Etruria pottery by introducing a *Christmas Series* of classic Wedgwood blue and white Jasper collector's plates commemorating famous English monuments. In 1972 Wedgwood began a series of *Mothers* plates, issued annually, made in Jasperware, and bearing designs created for Wedgwood in the late eighteenth century. The *Bicentennial of American Independence Series*, also in blue and white Jasper, is a six-plate series which began in 1972 and closed in 1976. It commemorates events which led to American Independence. *The Blossoming of Suzanne Series* started in 1977.

Artists for Wedgwood over the past two centuries have included some of the most distinguished names in plate design. William Hackwood was a modeler for Wedgwood from 1769 to 1832, and his eighteenth-century designs have been used on Wedgwood Jasperware for generations. Lady Elizabeth Templetown was a designer for Wedgwood from 1783 to 1787. Most of her designs were modeled by William Hackwood. Among the staff artists of the Wedgwood Design Studio over the past thirty years are Rex Whistler, Eric Ravilious, Edward Bawden, Arnold Machin, Richard Guyatt and Eduardo Paolozzi. Mary Vickers is considered one of the leading Romantic painters. Her works are exhibited in major galleries on both sides of the Atlantic, and in private collections such as that of the Duke and Duchess of Marlborough.

GREAT BRITAIN
WEDGWOOD
(Barlaston, Stoke-on-Trent, Staffordshire)

Christmas Series

Modeler: As indicated
Jasper stoneware
Diameter: 20.3 centimeters
  (8 inches)
No hanger
Edition size undisclosed, limited
  by year of issue
Not numbered, without certificate

26-W.90-1.1
1969 *Windsor Castle*
Modeler: Tom Harper
Issue price: $25.00

26-W.90-1.2
1970 *Christmas in Trafalgar Square*
Modeler: Tom Harper
Issue price: $30.00

26-W.90-1.3
1971 *Picadilly Circus, London*
Modeler: Tom Harper
Issue price: $30.00

26-W.90-1.4
1972 *St. Paul's Cathedral*
Modeler: Tom Harper
Issue price: $35.00

26-W.90-1.5
1973 *The Tower of London*
Modeler: Tom Harper
Issue price: $40.00

26-W.90-1.6
1974 *The Houses of Parliament*
Modeler: Tom Harper
Issue price: $40.00

26-W.90-1.7
1975 *Tower Bridge*
Modeler: Tom Harper
Issue price: $45.00

26-W.90-1.8
1976 *Hampton Court*
Modeler: Tom Harper
Issue price: $55.00

26-W.90-1.9
1977 *Westminster Abbey*
Modeler: Tom Harper
Issue price: $55.00

26-W.90-1.10
1978 *The Horse Guards*
Modeler: Tom Harper
Issue price: $60.00

26-W.90-1.11
1979 *Buckingham Palace*
Modeler: Wedgwood Design Studio
Issue price: $65.00

26-W.90-1.12
No information available
at press time

Mothers Series

Artist: As indicated
Jasper stoneware in varying colors
Diameter: 16.5 centimeters
(6½ inches)
No hanger
Edition size undisclosed, limited
by year of issue
Not numbered, without certificate

26-W.90-2.1
1971 *Sportive Love*
Artist: Lady Elizabeth Templetown
Issue price: $20.00

26-W.90-2.2
1972 *The Sewing Lesson*
Artist: Emma Crewe
Issue price: $20.00

26-W.90-2.3
1973 The Baptism of Achilles
Artist: Lady Elizabeth Templetown
Issue price: $25.00

26-W.90-2.4
1974 Domestic Employment
Artist: Lady Elizabeth Templetown
Issue price: $30.00

26-W.90-2.5
1975 Mother and Child
Artist: Lady Elizabeth Templetown
Issue price: $35.00

26-W.90-2.6
1976 The Spinner
Artist: William Hackwood
Issue price: $35.00

26-W.90-2.7
1977 Leisure Time
Artist: William Hackwood
Issue price: $35.00

26-W.90-2.8
1978 Swan and Cygnets
Artist: Wedgwood Design Studio
Barlaston
Issue price: $40.00

26-W.90-2.9
1979 Deer and Fawn
Artist: Wedgwood Design Studio
Issue price: $45.00

26-W.90-2.10
1980 Birds
Artist: Wedgwood Design Studio
Issue price: $47.50

Bicentennial of American Independence Series
Modeler: Undisclosed
Jasper stoneware
Diameter: 20.3 centimeters
(8 inches)
No hanger
Edition size undisclosed, limited
by year of issue
Not numbered, without certificate

26-W.90-3.1
1972 Boston Tea Party
Modeler: Undisclosed
Issue price: $30.00

26-W.90-3.2
1973 Paul Revere's Ride
Modeler: Undisclosed
Issue price: $35.00

26-W.90-3.3
1974 Battle of Concord
Modeler: Undisclosed
Issue price: $40.00

26-W.90-3.4
1975 Across the Delaware
Modeler: Undisclosed
Issue price: $45.00

26-W.90-3.5
1975 Victory at Yorktown
Modeler: Undisclosed
Issue price: $45.00

26-W.90-3.6
1976 Declaration Signed
Modeler: Undisclosed
Issue price: $45.00

(Barlaston, Stoke-on-Trent, Staffordshire)

*Blossoming of
Suzanne Series*
Artist: Mary Vickers
Bone china banded in gold
Diameter: 23.5 centimeters
  (9¼ inches)
No hanger
Edition size: As indicated
Numbered with certificate

26-W.90-4.1
1977 Innocence
Artist: Mary Vickers
Issue price: $60.00
Edition size limited to 17,000

26-W.90-4.2
1978 Cherish
Artist: Mary Vickers
Issue price: $60.00
Edition size limited to 24,000

26-W.90-4.3
1979 Daydream
Artist: Mary Vickers
Issue price: Undetermined at press
time. Edition size limited to 24,000

26-W.90-4.4
1980 Wistful
Artist: Mary Vickers
Issue price: Undetermined at press
time. Edition size limited to 24,000

ITALY
ANRI
(Santa Christina)

The House of Anri, which claims to be the world's largest wood-carving manufactory, is a family firm established in 1916 by Anton Riffeser Sr. and is headed by his son, Anton Jr. The factory is located in the Tyrolean Alps, an area with a long tradition of wood carving.

Anri's *Christmas Series* began in 1971. Using a process known as "toriart," the plates are molded and carved in wood material and hand painted to produce a three-dimensional effect. Each plate is mounted in a circular European maple frame.

The artist for the Anri *Christmas Series* is currently undisclosed. Former series artist Joseph Malfertheiner was Master Carver for Anri, working with the company from 1966. His creations are exhibited throughout Italy, Austria and Germany.

ITALY
ANRI
(Santa Christina)

Christmas Series

Artist: Joseph Malfertheiner

Hand-painted molded wood
  material

Diameter: 30.5 centimeters
  (12 inches)

Attached back hanger

Edition size: As indicated

Numbered since 1972, without
  certificate

38-A.54-1.1
1971 *St. Jakob in Groden*
Artist: Joseph Malfertheiner
Issue price: $37.50. Edition size limited
to announced quantity of 10,000

38-A.54-1.2
1972 *Pipers at Alberobello*
Artist: Joseph Malfertheiner
Issue price: $45.00
Edition size limited to 10,000

38-A.54-1.3
1973 *Alpine Horn*
Artist: Joseph Malfertheiner
Issue price: $45.00
Edition size limited to 10,000

38-A.54-1.4
1974 *Young Man and Girl*
Artist: Joseph Malfertheiner
Issue price: $50.00
Edition size limited to 10,000

38-A.54-1.5
1975 *Christmas in Ireland*
Artist: Joseph Malfertheiner
Issue price: $60.00
Edition size limited to 10,000

38-A.54-1.6
1976 *Alpine Christmas*
Artist: Joseph Malfertheiner
Issue price: $65.00
Edition size limited to 10,000

38-A.54-1.7
1977 *Legend of Heiligenblut*
Artist: Joseph Malfertheiner
Issue price: $65.00
Edition size limited to 6,000

38-A.54-1.8
1978 *The Klöckler Singers*
Artist: Joseph Malfertheiner
Issue price: $80.00
Edition size limited to 6,000

38-A.54-1.9
1979 *The Moss Gatherers of Villnoess*
Artist: Undisclosed
Issue price: $135.00
Edition size limited to 6,000

38-A.54-1.10
1980 *Wintry Churchgoing in Santa Christina*
Artist: Undisclosed
Issue price: $165.00
Edition size limited to 6,000

King's Porcelain was established in the original Giuseppe Cappe factory in the 1960s. The factory had been known for its Cappe figurines of which King's has retained the original molds.

King's *Flowers of America Series* began in 1973 and ended in 1977.

Chief sculptor for King's Porcelain is the Italian artist Aldo Falchi, who studied sculpture in Milan and later collaborated with Bjorn Wiinblad on works for Rosenthal of Germany. Some of his pieces in terra cotta can be found in Verona, Mantova and Bozzolo, Italy.

ITALY
KING'S
(Usmate, Milan)

Flowers of America Series

Artist: Aldo Falchi

Artist's signature appears on back since 1975

High relief, hand-painted porcelain banded in gold

Diameter: 22.3 centimeters (8¾ inches)

Attached back hanger

Edition size limited to 1,000

Numbered without certificate

38-K.32-2.1
1973 Pink Carnation
Artist: Aldo Falchi
Issue price: $85.00

38-K.32-2.2
1974 Red Roses
Artist: Aldo Falchi
Issue price: $100.00

38-K.32-2.3
1975 Yellow Dahlia
Artist: Aldo Falchi
Issue price: $110.00

38-K.32-2.4
1976 Bluebells
Artist: Aldo Falchi
Issue price: $130.00

38-K.32-2.5
1977 Anemones
Artist: Aldo Falchi
Issue price: $130.00

The Veneto Flair was established in 1946 by a consortium of potters and painters. Creative World of White Plains, New York, acts as importer and distributor of the Veneto Flair collector's plates.

A centuries-old technique is used to create the Veneto Flair plates. The resulting decorated and glazed earthenware is known as majolica or faience pottery. In this ancient process, terra cotta is hand thrown on a potter's wheel and the design is incised with a scalpel on the baked clay. Colors are then hand applied and the plates undergo a series of paintings and firings before a final firing with a secret-formula glaze which produces Veneto Flair's unique mosaic-effect finish.

In 1971, Veneto Flair entered the limited-edition plate market with a single issue, the Bellini "Madonna" plate. The *Last Supper Series*, based on da Vinci's painting, and a *Dog Series* both began in 1972 and ended in 1976. Veneto Flair's *Mosaic Series* began in 1973, closed after the '74 issue, but reopened in 1977 for a single issue. The annual *Christmas Card Series* started in 1975 and ended in 1978.

Vincente Tiziano is credited with reviving ancient Etruscan techniques of ceramic production, and his classical style was greatly influenced by the ceramic traditions of the sixteenth century. He is a recipient of the Amerigo Longhi Award from the International Ceramic Show of Deruta. Many of his works are on display at the Deruta Ceramic Museum.

ITALY
VENETO FLAIR
(Treviso)

Bellini Plate
Artist: Vincente Tiziano
(after Bellini's *Madonna*)
Terra cotta banded in gold
Diameter: 21.6 centimeters
(8½ inches)
Pierced foot rim
Edition size limited to 500
Numbered with certificate

38-V.22-1.1
1971 *Madonna*
Artist: Vincente Tiziano
Issue price: $45.00

Dog Series
Artist: Vincente Tiziano
Terra cotta banded in gold
Diameter: 21.6 centimeters
(8½ inches)
Pierced foot rim
Edition size limited to 2,000
Numbered with certificate

38-V.22-5.1
1972 *German Shepherd*
Artist: Vincente Tiziano
Issue price: $37.50

38-V.22-5.2
1973 *Poodle*
Artist: Vincente Tiziano
Issue price: $37.50

38-V.22-5.3
1974 *Doberman*
Artist: Vincente Tiziano
Issue price: $37.50

38-V.22-5.4
1975 *Collie*
Artist: Vincente Tiziano
Issue price: $40.00

38-V.22-5.5
1976 *Dachshund*
Artist: Vincente Tiziano
Issue price: $45.00

Last Supper Series

Artist: Vincente Tiziano (after
    Leonardo da Vinci's *Last Supper*)
Terra cotta banded in gold
Diameter: 21.6 centimeters
    (8½ inches)
Pierced foot rim
Edition size limited to 2,000
Numbered with certificate

38-V.22-6.1
1973 *Last Supper - Scene I*
Artist: Vincente Tiziano
Issue price: $100.00

38-V.22-6.2
1973 *Last Supper - Scene II*
Artist: Vincente Tiziano
Issue price: $70.00

38-V.22-6.3
1974 *Last Supper - Scene III*
Artist: Vincente Tiziano
Issue price: $70.00

38-V.22-6.4
1975 *Last Supper - Scene IV*
Artist: Vincente Tiziano
Issue price: $70.00

38-V.22-6.5
1976 *Last Supper - Scene V*
Artist: Vincente Tiziano
Issue price: $70.00

Mosaic Series

Artist: Vincente Tiziano
Terra cotta banded in gold
Diameter: 16.5 centimeters
    (6½ inches)
Pierced foot rim
Edition size: As indicated
Numbered with certificate

38-V.22-9.1
1973 *Justinian*
Artist: Vincente Tiziano
Issue price: $50.00
Edition size limited to 500

38-V.22-9.2
1974 *Pelican*
Artist: Vincente Tiziano
Issue price: $50.00
Edition size limited to 1,000

38-V.22-9.3
1977 Theodora
Artist: Vincente Tiziano
Issue price: $50.00
Edition size limited to 500

Christmas Card Series
Artist: Vincente Tiziano
Terra cotta banded in gold
Diameter: 18.4 centimeters
  (7¼ inches)
Pierced foot rim
Edition size limited to 5,000
Numbered with certificate

38-V.22-11.1
1975 Christmas Eve
Artist: Vincente Tiziano
Issue price: $45.00

38-V.22-11.2
1976 The Old North Church
Artist: Vincente Tiziano
Issue price: $50.00

38-V.22-11.3
1977 Log Cabin Christmas
Artist: Vincente Tiziano
Issue price: $50.00

38-V.22-11.4
1978 Dutch Christmas
Artist: Vincente Tiziano
Issue price: $50.00

Located near Volterra in Tuscany, world center for the mining and carving of alabaster, the Studio Dante di Volteradici continues the Italian tradition of alabaster sculpturing.

Di Volteradici's *Grand Opera Series*, commissioned by the Museo Teatrale alla Scala to commemorate the two-hundredth anniversary of La Scala Opera House, began in 1976. *Madonna Viventi (Living Madonnas)*, its first proprietary series, began in 1978.

Gino Ruggeri, a sculptor in the neo-classic tradition, is best known for his work "The Crucifix," sculpted for the Casa Serena Institute of Cecina Mare, and his two "Memorials to the Fallen," sculptures which pay tribute to World War I victims. Now in his late 70s, Ruggeri's last completed work was the "Aida" plate. His successor as designer of the Grand Opera series is Franco Ingargiola, whom Ruggeri personally tutored and who works in onyx and ceramics as well as alabaster. Alberto Santangela, current sculptor of the *Madonne Viventi Series*, sculpts in the style of the Italian High Renaissance.

ITALY
STUDIO DANTE DI VOLTERADICI
(Volterra)

Grand Opera Series

Artist: Gino Ruggeri. Artist's
   signature appears on front
Ivory alabaster
Diameter: 21.6 centimeters
   (8½ inches)
Attached back hanger
Edition size undisclosed, limited
   by period of issue
Numbered with certificate

38-V.90-1.1
1976 Rigoletto
Artist: Gino Ruggeri
Issue price: $35.00

38-V.90-1.2
1977 Madama Butterfly
Artist: Gino Ruggeri
Issue price: $35.00

38-V.90-1.3
1978 Carmen
Artist: Gino Ruggeri
Issue price: $40.00

38-V.90-1.4
1979 Aida
Artist: Gino Ruggeri
Issue price: $40.00

38-V.90-1.5
1980 The Barber of Seville
Artist: Gino Ruggeri
Issue price: $40.00

Madonne Viventi Series

(Living Madonnas Series)

Artist: As indicated. Artist's
   signature appears on front
Ivory alabaster
Diameter: 21.6 centimeters
   (8½ inches)
Attached back hanger
Edition size undisclosed, limited
   by period of issue
Numbered with certificate

38-V.90-2.1
1978 Madonna Pensosa
(The Pensive Madonna)
Artist: Ado Santini
Issue price: $45.00

38-V.90-2.2
1979 Madonna Serena
(The Serene Madonna)
Artist: Alberto Santangela
Issue price: $45.00

38-V.90-2.3
1980 *Madonna Beata*
(The Beatific Madonna)
Artist: Alberto Santangela
Issue price: $45.00

Although the present Fukagawa Porcelain factory was organized in the 1880s in Arita by the Fukagawa family, the heritage of its Izumistone porcelain goes back some three centuries to the discovery of kaolin deposits on the island of Kyushu, Japan. It was there, on the slopes of Mount Izumi, that the Korean master potter Ri Sampei ended his twenty-year search for a pure white clay base to be used in the manufacture of fine porcelain. As the direct result of his discovery, a number of small porcelain workshops — the first in all Japan — sprang up in the nearby town of Arita, and delicate plates and saucers were being shipped to the West from the harbor city of Imari decades before porcelain manufacture began in Europe.

The establishment of Fukagawa Porcelain was actually a merger of a number of small workshops whose standards and techniques dated to the time of Ri Sampei. In 1913, Fukagawa was granted the title "Purveyor to the Imperial Household," which indicates patronage from the royal family of Japan. In recognition of this honor, all Fukagawa ceramics bear the imprint "Imperial." The factory, which is still in the hands of the Fukagawa family, continues to employ the original Izumiyama clay from Mount Izumi to give its porcelain a uniquely white body.

In 1977, Fukagawa began its first series of collector's plates — the *Warabe No Haiku (Haiku about Children) Series*.

Master of the traditional "Sea of Whiteness" motif, Suetomi is the principal artist for Fukagawa and is the recipient of the Gold Prize from Japan's Ministry of International Trade.

JAPAN
FUKAGAWA
(Arita)

Warabe No Haiku Series
(Haiku about children)

Artist: Suetomi. Artist's signature
and seal appear on front

Overglaze porcelain

Diameter: 25.7 centimeters
(10¼ inches)

No hanger

Edition size undisclosed, limited
by period of issue

Numbered with certificate

Original Haiku poem appears
on front

42-F.78-1.1
1977 Beneath the Plum Branch
Artist: Suetomi
Issue price: $38.00

42-F.78-1.2
1978 Child of Straw
Artist: Suetomi
Issue price: $42.00

42-F.78-1.3
1979 Dragon Dance
Artist: Suetomi
Issue price: $42.00

Maker had
no photo at
press time

42-F.78-1.4
1980 Mask Dancing
Artist: Suetomi
Issue price: $42.00

Dave Grossman Designs, Inc., headquartered in St. Louis, was formed in 1969 to market metal sculptures created by Dave Grossman. The firm entered the collectibles market in 1973 with a series of handcrafted porcelain figurines based on the *Saturday Evening Post* covers painted by Norman Rockwell. Subsequent creations have included porcelain mugs, Christmas ornaments and limited-edition lithographs — all based on Rockwell works.

In 1979, the first issue in the *Dave Grossman Designs Annual Series* was introduced, with the bas-relief design inspired by a famous Rockwell *Post* cover. Plates in the series are produced for the firm by Goto, of Seito City, Japan.

Dave Grossman, a noted sculptor who has been commissioned to create works for Presidents Johnson and Nixon, sculpts the master for each plate in the series.

JAPAN
DAVE GROSSMAN DESIGNS
(Seito City)

*Dave Grossman Designs
Annual Series*

Modeler: Dave Grossman

Porcelain with hand-painted bas-relief

Diameter: 19 centimeters
(7½ inches)

Pierced foot rim

Edition size undisclosed, limited by year of issue

Not numbered, without certificate

42-G.74-1.1
1979 *Leapfrog*
Modeler: Dave Grossman
Issue price: $50.00

42-G.74-1.2
1980 *The Lovers*
Modeler: Dave Grossman
Issue price: $60.00

A Japanese subsidiary of Schmid (see Germany, SCHMID) produces several series of plates based on contemporary cartoon characters.

The *Peanuts Christmas Series* and the *Peanuts Mother's Day Series* began in 1972. The *Peanuts Valentine's Day Series* began in 1977. The *Disney Christmas Series* was introduced in 1973 and the *Disney Mother's Day Series* in 1974. The *Raggedy Ann Christmas Series* was issued from 1975 to 1979. The *Raggedy Ann Mother's Day Series* was issued from 1976 to 1979 and the *Raggedy Ann Valentine's Day Series* from 1978 to 1979. The *Raggedy Ann Annual Series* started in 1980.

Cartoonist Charles Schulz, creator of the widely-syndicated cartoon strip "Peanuts," designs or approves all plates in the three *Peanuts* series. Walt Disney Productions staff artists design both *Disney* series. Designs for all *Raggedy Ann* series are from artists of the Bobbs-Merrill Company.

Peanuts Christmas Series

Artist: Charles Schulz. Artist's
  signature appears on front
Overglaze porcelain
Diameter: 19 centimeters
  (7½ inches)
Attached back hanger
Edition size undisclosed, limited
  by year of issue, except as
  indicated
Not numbered except as indicated,
  without certificate

42-S.12-1.1
1972 *Snoopy Guides the Sleigh*
Artist: Charles Schulz
Issue price: $10.00

42-S.12-1.2
1973 *Christmas Eve at the Doghouse*
Artist: Charles Schulz
Issue price: $10.00

42-S.12-1.3
1974 *Christmas Eve at the Fireplace*
Artist: Charles Schulz
Issue price: $10.00

42-S.12-1.4
1975 *Woodstock, Santa Claus*
Artist: Charles Schulz
Issue price: $12.50

42-S.12-1.5
1976 *Woodstock's Christmas*
Artist: Charles Schulz
Issue price: $13.00

42-S.12-1.6
1977 *Deck the Doghouse*
Artist: Charles Schulz
Issue price: $13.00

42-S.12-1.7
1978 *Filling the Stocking*
Artist: Charles Schulz
Issue price: $15.00

42-S.12-1.8
1979 *Christmas at Hand*
Artist: Charles Schulz
Issue price: $17.50
Edition size limited to 15,000

42-S.12-1.9

42-S.12-1.9
1980 *Waiting for Santa*
Artist: Charles Schulz
Issue price: $17.50
Edition size limited to 15,000

Peanuts Mother's Day Series

Artist: Charles Schulz. Artist's signature appears on front except 1975

Overglaze porcelain

Diameter: 19 centimeters (7½ inches)

Attached back hanger

Edition size undisclosed, limited by year of issue, except as indicated

Not numbered except as indicated, without certificate

42-S.12-2.1
1972 *Linus*
Artist: Charles Schulz
Issue price: $10.00

42-S.12-2.2
1973 *Mom?*
Artist: Charles Schulz
Issue price: $10.00

42-S.12-2.3
1974 *Snoopy and Woodstock on Parade*
Artist: Charles Schulz
Issue price: $10.00

42-S.12-2.4
1975 *A Kiss for Lucy*
Artist: Charles Schulz
Issue price: $12.50

42-S.12-2.5
1976 *Linus and Snoopy*
Artist: Charles Schulz
Issue price: $13.00

42-S.12-2.6
1977 *Dear Mom*
Artist: Charles Schulz
Issue price: $13.00

42-S.12-2.7
1978 *Thoughts that Count*
Artist: Charles Schulz
Issue price: $15.00

42-S.12-2.8
1979 *A Special Letter*
Artist: Charles Schulz
Issue price: $17.50
Edition size limited to 10,000

42-S.12-2.9
1980 *A Tribute to Mom*
Artist: Charles Schulz
Issue price: $17.50
Edition size limited to 10,000

Disney Christmas Series
Artist: Walt Disney Productions
Overglaze porcelain
Diameter: 19 centimeters
 (7½ inches)
Attached back hanger
Edition size undisclosed, limited
 by year of issue, except as
 indicated
Not numbered except as
 indicated, without certificate

42-S.12-3.1
1973 *Sleigh Ride*
Artist: Walt Disney Productions
Issue price: $10.00

42-S.12-3.2
1974 *Decorating the Tree*
Artist: Walt Disney Productions
Issue price: $10.00

42-S.12-3.3
1975 *Caroling*
Artist: Walt Disney Productions
Issue price: $12.50

42-S.12-3.4
1976 *Building a Snowman*
Artist: Walt Disney Productions
Issue price: $13.00

42-S.12-3.5
1977 *Down the Chimney*
Artist: Walt Disney Productions
Issue price: $13.00

42-S.12-3.6
1978 *Night Before Christmas*
Artist: Walt Disney Productions
Issue price: $15.00

42-S.12-3.7
1979 *Santa's Surprise*
Artist: Walt Disney Productions
Issue price: $17.50
Edition size limited to 15,000

42-S.12-3.8
1980 *Sleigh Ride*
Artist: Walt Disney Productions
Issue price: $17.50
Edition size limited to 15,000

Disney Mother's Day Series
Artist: Walt Disney Productions
Overglaze porcelain
Diameter: 19 centimeters
(7½ inches)
Attached back hanger
Edition size undisclosed, limited
by year of issue, except as
indicated
Not numbered except as indicated,
without certificate

42-S.12-4.1
1974 *Flowers for Mother*
Artist: Walt Disney Productions
Issue price: $10.00

42-S.12-4.2
1975 *Snow White and the Seven Dwarfs*
Artist: Walt Disney Productions
Issue price: $12.50

42-S.12-4.3
1976 Minnie Mouse and Friends
Artist: Walt Disney Productions
Issue price: $13.00

42-S.12-4.4
1977 Pluto's Pals
Artist: Walt Disney Productions
Issue price: $13.00

42-S.12-4.5
1978 Flowers for Bambi
Artist: Walt Disney Productions
Issue price: $15.00

42-S.12-4.6
1979 Happy Feet
Artist: Walt Disney Productions
Issue price: $17.50
Edition size limited to 10,000

42-S.12-4.7
1980 Minnie's Surprise
Artist: Walt Disney Productions
Issue price: $17.50
Edition size limited to 10,000

Raggedy Ann Christmas Series

Artist: The Bobbs-Merrill
Company, Inc.
Overglaze porcelain
Diameter: 19 centimeters
(7½ inches)
Attached back hanger
Edition size undisclosed, limited
by year of issue, except as
indicated
Not numbered except as indicated,
without certificate

42-S.12-5.1
1975 Gifts of Love
Artist: The Bobbs-Merrill
Company, Inc.
Issue price: $12.50

42-S.12-5.2
1976 Raggedy Ann Skates
Artist: The Bobbs-Merrill
Company, Inc.
Issue price: $13.00

42-S.12-5.3
1977 Decorating Tree
Artist: The Bobbs-Merrill
Company, Inc.
Issue price: $13.00

42-S.12-5.4
1978 Checking the List
Artist: The Bobbs-Merrill
Company, Inc.
Issue price: $15.00

42-S.12-5.5
1979 Little Helper
Artist: The Bobbs-Merrill
Company, Inc.
Issue price: $17.50
Edition size limited to 15,000

Raggedy Ann Mother's Day Series

Artist: The Bobbs-Merrill
Company, Inc.

Overglaze porcelain

Diameter: 19 centimeters
(7½ inches)

Attached back hanger

Edition size undisclosed, limited
by year of issue, except as
indicated

Not numbered except as indicated,
without certificate

42-S.12-6.1
1976 Motherhood
Artist: The Bobbs-Merrill
Company, Inc.
Issue price: $13.00

42-S.12-6.2
1977 Bouquet of Love
Artist: The Bobbs-Merrill
Company, Inc.
Issue price: $13.00

42-S.12-6.3
1978 Hello Mom
Artist: The Bobbs-Merrill
Company, Inc.
Issue price: $15.00

42-S.12-6.4
1979 High Spirits
Artist: The Bobbs-Merrill
Company, Inc.
Issue price: $17.50
Edition size limited to 10,000

Peanuts Valentine's Day Series

Artist: Charles Schulz. Artist's signature appears on front

Overglaze porcelain

Diameter: 19 centimeters (7½ inches)

Attached back hanger

Edition size undisclosed, limited by year of issue

Not numbered, without certificate

42-S.12-7.1
1977 *Home Is Where the Heart Is*
Artist: Charles Schulz
Issue price: $13.00

42-S.12-7.2
1978 *Heavenly Bliss*
Artist: Charles Schulz
Issue price: $13.00

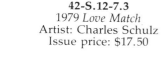

42-S.12-7.3
1979 *Love Match*
Artist: Charles Schulz
Issue price: $17.50

42-S.12-7.4
1980 *From Snoopy, With Love*
Artist: Charles Schulz
Issue price: $17.50

Raggedy Ann Valentine's Day Series

Artist: The Bobbs-Merrill Company, Inc.

Overglaze porcelain

Diameter: 19 centimeters (7½ inches)

Attached back hanger

Edition size undisclosed, limited by year of issue

Not numbered, without certificate

42-S.12-8.1
1978 *As Time Goes By*
Artist: The Bobbs-Merrill Company, Inc.
Issue price: $13.00

42-S.12-8.2
1979 *Daisies Do Tell*
Artist: The Bobbs-Merrill Company, Inc.
Issue price: $17.50

*Raggedy Ann
Annual Series*
Artist: The Bobbs-Merrill
 Company, Inc.
Overglaze porcelain
Diameter: 19 centimeters
 (7½ inches)
Attached back hanger
Edition size: As indicated
Numbered without certificate

42-S.12-9.1
1980 *The Sunshine Wagon*
Artist: The Bobbs-Merrill
Company, Inc.
Issue price: $17.50
Edition size limited to 10,000

Johan Jeremiason established Porsgrund, Norway's only porcelain factory, in 1885. Jeremiason began his business by importing English clay which was modeled by ceramist Carl Bauer. Porcelain tableware and decorative wares have been produced since then. Porsgrund's first collector's plate was a 1909 Christmas issue entitled "Christmas Flowers." The series was abandoned after a single issue.

A *Christmas Series* based on religious themes was introduced in 1968 and ended with the 1977 issue. In 1978 Porsgrund began a nostalgic Christmas series entitled the *Traditional Norwegian Christmas Series*. The *Mother's Day Series* began in 1970 and the *Father's Day Series* in 1971.

Gunnar Bratlie is the principal designer for Porsgrund. Master of the Norwegian folk art known as "Rosemaling," he has received the Norwegian Design Award and is represented in galleries in France, Italy and the United States, as well as his native Norway.

Christmas Series

Artist: Gunnar Bratlie
Underglaze porcelain decorated in cobalt blue
Diameter: 17.8 centimeters (7 inches)
Pierced foot rim
Edition size undisclosed, limited by year of issue
Not numbered, without certificate

54-P.62-1.1
1968 *Church Scene*
Artist: Gunnar Bratlie
Issue price: $12.00

54-P.62-1.2
1969 *Three Kings*
Artist: Gunnar Bratlie
Issue price: $12.00

54-P.62-1.3
1970 *Road to Bethlehem*
Artist: Gunnar Bratlie
Issue price: $12.00

54-P.62-1.4
1971 *A Child Is Born in Bethlehem*
Artist: Gunnar Bratlie
Issue price: $12.00

54-P.62-1.5
1972 *Hark, the Herald Angels Sing*
Artist: Gunnar Bratlie
Issue price: $12.00

54-P.62-1.6
1973 *Promise of the Savior*
Artist: Gunnar Bratlie
Issue price: $15.00

54-P.62-1.7
1974 *The Shepherds*
Artist: Gunnar Bratlie
Issue price: $15.00

54-P.62-1.8
1975 *Jesus on the Road to the Temple*
Artist: Gunnar Bratlie
Issue price: $19.50

54-P.62-1.9
1976 *Jesus and the Elders*
Artist: Gunnar Bratlie
Issue price: $22.00

54-P.62-1.10
1977 *The Draught of Fish*
Artist: Gunnar Bratlie
Issue price: $24.00

Mother's Day Series

Artist: Gunnar Bratlie
Underglaze porcelain decorated in cobalt blue
Diameter: 12.7 centimeters (5 inches)
Pierced foot rim
Edition size undisclosed, limited by year of issue
Not numbered, without certificate

54-P.62-2.1
1970 *Mare and Foal*
Artist: Gunnar Bratlie
Issue price: $7.50

54-P.62-2.2
1971 *Boy and Geese*
Artist: Gunnar Bratlie
Issue price: $7.50

54-P.62-2.3
1972 *Doe and Fawn*
Artist: Gunnar Bratlie
Issue price: $10.00

54-P.62-2.4
1973 *Cat and Kittens*
Artist: Gunnar Bratlie
Issue price: $10.00

54-P.62-2.5
1974 *Boy and Goats*
Artist: Gunnar Bratlie
Issue price: $10.00

54-P.62-2.6
1975 *Dog and Puppies*
Artist: Gunnar Bratlie
Issue price: $12.50

54-P.62-2.7
1976 *Girl and Calf*
Artist: Gunnar Bratlie
Issue price: $15.00

54-P.62-2.8
1977 *Boy and Chickens*
Artist: Gunnar Bratlie
Issue price: $16.50

54-P.62-2.9
1978 *Girl and Pigs*
Artist: Gunnar Bratlie
Issue price: $17.50

54-P.62-2.10
1979 *Boy and Reindeer*
Artist: Gunnar Bratlie
Issue price: $19.50

54-P.62-2.11
1980 *Girl and Lambs*
Artist: Gunnar Bratlie
Issue price: $21.50

Father's Day Series
Artist: Gunnar Bratlie
Underglaze porcelain decorated in cobalt blue
Diameter: 12.7 centimeters (5 inches)
Pierced foot rim
Edition size undisclosed, limited by year of issue
Not numbered, without certificate

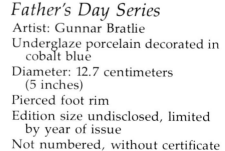

54-P.62-3.1
1971 *Fishing*
Artist: Gunnar Bratlie
Issue price: $10.00

54-P.62-3.2
1972 *Cookout*
Artist: Gunnar Bratlie
Issue price: $10.00

54-P.62-3.3
1973 *Sledding*
Artist: Gunnar Bratlie
Issue price: $10.00

54-P.62-3.4
1974 *Father and Son*
Artist: Gunnar Bratlie
Issue price: $10.00

54-P.62-3.5
1975 *Skating*
Artist: Gunnar Bratlie
Issue price: $12.50

54-P.62-3.6
1976 *Skiing*
Artist: Gunnar Bratlie
Issue price: $15.00

54-P.62-3.7
1977 *Soccer*
Artist: Gunnar Bratlie
Issue price: $16.50

54-P.62-3.8
1978 *Canoeing*
Artist: Gunnar Bratlie
Issue price: $17.50

54-P.62-3.9
1979 *Father and Daughter*
Artist: Gunnar Bratlie
Issue price: $19.50

54-P.62-3.10
1980 *Sailing*
Artist: Gunnar Bratlie
Issue price: $21.50

NORWAY
PORSGRUND
(Porsgrunn, Telemark County)

Traditional Norwegian Christmas Series

Artist: Gunnar Bratlie. Artist's
  initials appear on back

Underglaze porcelain decorated in
  cobalt blue

Diameter: 17.8 centimeters
  (7 inches)

Pierced foot rim

Edition size undisclosed, limited
  by year of issue

Not numbered, without certificate

54-P.62-5.1
1978 *Guests Are Coming for
Christmas Eve*
Artist: Gunnar Bratlie
Issue price: $27.00

54-P.62-5.2
1979 *Home for Christmas*
Artist: Gunnar Bratlie
Issue price: $30.00

54-P.62-5.3
1980 *Preparing for Christmas*
Artist: Gunnar Bratlie
Issue price: $34.00

LLADRÓ

The Lladró Porcelain factory was established in the 1950s by three Lladró brothers — Juan, Jose, and Vincente, sons of a peasant. At night, they studied porcelain designing, modeling, and firing and built their first kiln while in their teens. By 1970 their factory was one of the best-equipped in Europe and had become known for its vases and figurines.

Lladró initiated both its limited-edition *Christmas Series* and *Mother's Day Series* in 1971.

Artist for both series is Juan Lladró, who developed the distinctive "Lladró look" — traditional subjects in a contemporary bas-relief treatment.

Christmas Series

Artist: Undisclosed
White bisque center in bas-relief
  with underglaze porcelain
  border and banded in 14k gold
  rim
Diameter: 20.3 centimeters
  (8 inches)
No hanger
Edition size undisclosed, limited
  by year of issue
Not numbered, without certificate

72-L.41-1.1
1971 *Caroling*
Artist: Undisclosed
Issue price: $27.50

72-L.41-1.2
1972 *Carolers*
Artist: Undisclosed
Issue price: $35.00

72-L.41-1.3
1973 *Boy and Girl*
Artist: Undisclosed
Issue price: $45.00

72-L.41-1.4
1974 *Carolers*
Artist: Undisclosed
Issue price: $55.00

72-L.41-1.5
1975 *Cherubs*
Artist: Undisclosed
Issue price: $60.00

72-L.41-1.6
1976 *Christ Child*
Artist: Undisclosed
Issue price: $60.00

72-L.41-1.7
1977 *Nativity Scene*
Artist: Undisclosed
Issue price: $80.00

Maker had
no photo at
press time

72-L.41-1.8
1978 *Caroling Child*
Artist: Undisclosed
Issue price: $80.00

Maker had
no photo at
press time

72-L.41-1.9
1979 *Snow Dance*
Artist: Undisclosed
Issue price: $90.00

72-L.41-1.10
No information available
at press time

Mother's Day Series
Artist: Undisclosed
White bisque center in bas-relief
with underglaze porcelain
border and banded in gold
Diameter: 20.3 centimeters
(8 inches)
No hanger
Edition size undisclosed, limited
by year of issue
Not numbered, without certificate

72-L.41-2.1
1971 *Kiss of the Child*
Artist: Undisclosed
Issue price: $27.50

72-L.41-2.2
1972 *Bird and Chicks*
Artist: Undisclosed
Issue price: $27.50

72-L.41-2.3
1973 *Mother and Children*
Artist: Undisclosed
Issue price: $35.00

72-L.41-2.4
1974 *Mother Nursing*
Artist: Undisclosed
Issue price: $45.00

72-L.41-2.5
1975 *Mother and Child*
Artist: Undisclosed
Issue price: $60.00

72-L.41-2.6
1976 *Tender Vigil*
Artist: Undisclosed
Issue price: $60.00

72-L.41-2.7
1977 *Mother and Daughter*
Artist: Undisclosed
Issue price: $67.50

72-L.41-2.8
1978 *The New Arrival*
Artist: Undisclosed
Issue price: $80.00

Maker had
no photo at
press time

72-L.41-2.9
1979 *Off to School*
Artist: Undisclosed
Issue price: $90.00

72-L.41-2.10
No information available
at press time

Santa Clara porcelain is made in the Alvarez porcelain factory in Spain. The Santa Clara *Christmas Series* began in 1970.

Artists for Santa Clara plates are not disclosed.

SPAIN
SANTA CLARA
(undisclosed)

Christmas Series

Artist: Undisclosed
Underglaze porcelain decorated in
  14k gold
Diameter: 20.3 centimeters
  (8 inches)
Pierced foot rim
Edition size: As indicated
Numbered since 1971, without
  certificate

72-S.6-1.1
1970 *Christmas Message*
Artist: Undisclosed
Issue price: $18.00. Edition size limited
to announced quantity of 10,000

72-S.6-1.2
1971 *Three Wise Men*
Artist: Undisclosed
Issue price: $18.00
Edition size limited to 10,000

72-S.6-1.3
1972 *Children in the Woods*
Artist: Undisclosed
Issue price: $20.00
Edition size limited to 10,000

72-S.6-1.4
1973 *Archangel*
Artist: Undisclosed
Issue price: $25.00
Edition size limited to 5,000

72-S.6-1.5
1974 *Spirit of Christmas*
Artist: Undisclosed
Issue price: $25.00
Edition size limited to 10,000

72-S.6-1.6
1975 *Christmas Eve in the Country*
Artist: Undisclosed
Issue price: $27.50
Edition size limited to 10,000

72-S.6-1.7
1976 *Madonna and Child*
Artist: Undisclosed
Issue price: $25.00
Edition size limited to 5,000

72-S.6-1.8
1977 *Mother and Child*
Artist: Undisclosed
Issue price: $27.50
Edition size limited to 10,000

72-S.6-1.9
1978 *Angel with Flowers*
Artist: Undisclosed
Issue price: $32.00

72-S.6-1.10
1979 Untitled at press time
Artist: Undisclosed
Issue price: $34.50

Orrefors was originally established in 1726 as an ironworks. In 1898 they began manufacturing glass ink bottles and window glass. Although the ironworks was no longer profitable, Johan Ekman purchased the property in 1913. He was interested in improving the facilities for glassmaking and recognized the importance of the valuable forest land of the area as fuel for glass furnaces. He eventually built an entire community around the glassworks.

Orrefors crystal is made from a mixture of seashore sand and potash, plus a heavy lead content. The ornamentation is created by master blowers who apply liquid molten glass in desired shapes.

In 1970 Orrefors began its *Annual Cathedral Series*, made in untinted crystal, depicting famous places of worship. This series ended in 1978. The *Mother's Day Series*, made in cobalt crystal, started in 1971. These plates are handmade with the designs engraved in the crystal and filled with 24k gold.

John Selbing, Chief Designer for Orrefors plates, developed the technique which allowed production of inlaid-gold crystal plates.

SWEDEN
ORREFORS

(Orrefors, Smaland)

76-O.74-1.1

Annual Cathedral Series
Artist: John Selbing
Leaded crystal with engraved
 designs inlaid in 24k gold
Diameter: 25.4 centimeters
 (10 inches)
No hanger
Edition size: As indicated
Numbered since 1975, without
 certificate

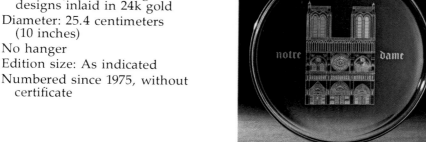

76-O.74-1.1
1970 *Notre Dame Cathedral*
Artist: John Selbing
Issue price: $50.00. Edition size limited
to announced quantity of 5,000

76-O.74-1.2
1971 *Westminster Abbey*
Artist: John Selbing
Issue price: $50.00. Edition size limited
to announced quantity of 5,000

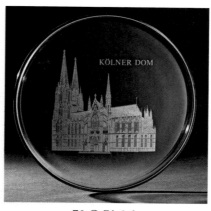

76-O.74-1.3
1972 *Basilica di San Marco*
Artist: John Selbing
Issue price: $50.00. Edition size limited
to announced quantity of 5,000

76-O.74-1.4
1973 *Cologne Cathedral*
Artist: John Selbing
Issue price: $50.00. Edition size limited
to announced quantity of 5,000

76-O.74-1.5
1974 *Temple Rue de la Victoire, Paris*
Artist: John Selbing
Issue price: $60.00. Edition size limited
to announced quantity of 5,000

76-O.74-1.6
1975 *Basilica di San Pietro, Rome*
Artist: John Selbing
Issue price: $85.00
Edition size limited to 5,000

76-O.74-1.7
1976 *Christ Church, Philadelphia*
Artist: John Selbing
Issue price: $85.00
Edition size limited to 3,000

76-O.74-1.8
1977 *Masjid-E-Shah*
Artist: John Selbing
Issue price: $90.00
Edition size limited to 3,000

76-O.74-1.9
1978 *Santiago de Compostela*
Artist: John Selbing
Issue price: $95.00
Edition size limited to 3,000

Mother's Day Series

Artist: John Selbing
Leaded cobalt crystal with
engraved designs inlaid in 24k
gold
Diameter: 20.3 centimeters
(8 inches)
Attached back hanger since 1973
Edition size: As indicated
Numbered since 1975, without
certificate

76-O.74-2.1
1971 *Flowers for Mother*
Artist: John Selbing
Issue price: $45.00. Edition size limited
to announced quantity of 2,500

76-O.74-2.2
1972 *Mother and Children*
Artist: John Selbing
Issue price: $45.00. Edition size limited
to announced quantity of 2,500

76-O.74-2.3
1973 *Mother and Child*
Artist: John Selbing
Issue price: $50.00. Edition size limited
to announced quantity of 2,500

76-O.74-2.4
1974 *Mother and Child*
Artist: John Selbing
Issue price: $50.00. Edition size limited
to announced quantity of 5,000

76-O.74-2.5
1975 *Mother and Child*
Artist: John Selbing
Issue price: $60.00
Edition size limited to 2,500

SWEDEN
ORREFORS
(Orrefors, Smaland)

76-O.74-2.6
1976 *Children and Puppy*
Artist: John Selbing
Issue price: $75.00
Edition size limited to 2,500

76-O.74-2.7
1977 *Child and Dove*
Artist: John Selbing
Issue price: $85.00
Edition size limited to 1,500

76-O.74-2.8
1978 *Mother and Child*
Artist: John Selbing
Issue price: $90.00
Edition size limited to 1,500

The Rorstrand Porcelain factory is Sweden's oldest pottery and the second oldest in Europe. Originally founded in Stockholm in 1726 under government patronage, the plant was later moved inland to Lidkoping for safety during World War II.

In addition to ceramics made of stoneware and high-fired earthenware, Rorstrand produces dinnerware, kitchenware, wall plaques, and other decorative art, including collector's plates. In 1968 Rorstrand began its series of square *Christmas* plates with designs derived from Swedish folk tales and traditions.

Rorstrand artist Gunnar Nylund has exhibited at the Swedish National Museum and is widely known for his monumental ceramic reliefs.

Christmas Series

Artist: Gunnar Nylund

Underglaze porcelain decorated in Scandia blue

Diameter: 19 centimeters
(7½ inches square)

Pierced foot rim

Edition size undisclosed, limited by year of issue

Not numbered, without certificate

76-R.54-1.1
1968 *Bringing Home the Tree*
Artist: Gunnar Nylund
Issue price: $12.00

76-R.54-1.2
1969 *Fisherman Sailing Home*
Artist: Gunnar Nylund
Issue price: $13.50

76-R.54-1.3
1970 *Nils with His Geese*
Artist: Gunnar Nylund
Issue price: $13.50

76-R.54-1.4
1971 *Nils in Lapland*
Artist: Gunnar Nylund
Issue price: $15.00

76-R.54-1.5
1972 *Dalecarlian Fiddler*
Artist: Gunnar Nylund
Issue price: $15.00

76-R.54-1.6
1973 *Farm in Smaland*
Artist: Gunnar Nylund
Issue price: $16.00

76-R.54-1.7
1974 *Vadstena*
Artist: Gunnar Nylund
Issue price: $19.00

76-R.54-1.8
1975 *Nils in Vastmanland*
Artist: Gunnar Nylund
Issue price: $20.00

76-R.54-1.9
1976 *Nils in Uppland*
Artist: Gunnar Nylund
Issue price: $20.00

76-R.54-1.10
1977 *Nils in Värmland*
Artist: Gunnar Nylund
Issue price: $29.50

76-R.54-1.11
1978 *Nils in Fjallbacka*
Artist: Gunnar Nylund
Issue price: $32.50

76-R.54-1.12
1979 *Nils in Vaestergoetland*
Artist: Gunnar Nylund
Issue price: $38.50

76-R.54-1.13
1980 *Nils in Sweden*
Artist: Gunnar Nylund
Issue price: $47.50

Initially organized as DeGrazia of Scottsdale, the company was founded by James LaFond to represent Arizona artist Ted DeGrazia. The present name, Artists of the World, was adopted in 1977 when the company's scope was enlarged to include additional artists.

Children of Aberdeen, a proprietary series with artwork by Kee Fung Ng, began in 1979 and depicts the children who live on boats anchored at the fishing village of Aberdeen near Hong Kong.

Born in Canton, China, and educated at its Fu San Art School, artist Kee Fung Ng is highly regarded for the harmonic balancing of extremes in the ancient Chinese tradition.

UNITED STATES
ARTISTS OF THE WORLD
(Scottsdale, Arizona)

Children of Aberdeen Series
Artist: Kee Fung Ng
China banded in gold
Diameter: 25.4 centimeters
(10 inches)
No hanger
Edition size unannounced
Numbered with certificate

84-A.72-1.1
1979 *Girl with Little Brother*
Artist: Kee Fung Ng
Issue price: $50.00

84-A.72-1.2
1980 *Sampan Girl*
Artist: Kee Fung Ng
Issue price: $50.00

Fairmont

Perfect Porcelain

Fairmont China was established in 1976 to produce limited-edition plates. Three series were begun that year: the *Holiday Series* with artwork by Ted DeGrazia, the *Famous Clowns Series* by comedian Red Skelton, and the *Ruffin Annual Series* by Don Ruffin. In 1977, they issued the third plate in the *Irene Spencer Annual Series* and in 1978 the third plate in the *DeGrazia Children Series*, both originally started by Gorham. (See United States, GORHAM). The two-plate *Irene Spencer's Special Requests Series* was started by Fairmont in 1978.

Ted DeGrazia, one-time apprentice to the great Mexican muralist Diego Rivera, first came to international attention in 1970 when his work was featured on a UNICEF card. Since then, his stylized re-creations of Southwestern subjects and themes have made him one of the most instantly recognizable of American artists. Irene Spencer received her training at the Academy of Art and the Chicago Art Institute, where she developed her distinctive style, reminiscent of the Old Masters. In addition to her accomplishments as a fine artist, she has written and illustrated children's books and worked as a newspaper cartoonist and a commercial artist. Red Skelton, a comedian widely known for his film, stage and television characterizations, has also earned a devoted following for his paintings.

Holiday Series

Artist: Ted DeGrazia. Artist's signature appears on front; first 500 autographed on back

China banded in gold

Diameter: 26 centimeters (10¼ inches)

No hanger

Edition size limited to 10,000

Numbered since 1977, without certificate

84-F.4-1.1
1976 *The Festival of Lights*
Artist: Ted DeGrazia
Issue price: $45.00
autographed: $100.00

84-F.4-1.2
1977 *The Bell of Hope*
Artist: Ted DeGrazia
Issue price: $45.00
autographed: $100.00

84-F.4-1.3
1978 *Little Madonna*
Artist: Ted DeGrazia
Issue price: $45.00
autographed: $100.00

84-F.4-1.4
1979 *The Nativity*
Artist: Ted DeGrazia
Issue price: $50.00
autographed: $100.00

Maker had
no photo at
press time

84-F.4-1.5
1980 *Little Pima Indian Drummer Boy*
Artist: Ted DeGrazia
Issue price: $50.00
autographed: $100.00

Famous Clowns Series

Artist: Red Skelton. Artist's signature appears on front

China banded in gold

Diameter: 21.6 centimeters (8½ inches)

No hanger

Edition size limited to 10,000

Numbered without certificate

84-F.4-2.1
1976 *Freddie the Freeloader*
Artist: Red Skelton
Issue price: $55.00

84-F.4-2.2
1977 *W. C. Fields*
Artist: Red Skelton
Issue price: $55.00

84-F.4-2.3
1978 *Happy*
Artist: Red Skelton
Issue price: $55.00

84-F.4-2.4
1979 *The Pledge*
Artist: Red Skelton
Issue price: $55.00

Irene Spencer Annual Series

Artist: Irene Spencer. Artist's
  signature appears on front
  and back
China banded in gold
Diameter: 21.6 centimeters
  (8½ inches)
No hanger
Edition size limited to 10,000
Numbered without certificate

84-F.4-3.1
1977 *Patient Ones*
Artist: Irene Spencer
Issue price: $42.50

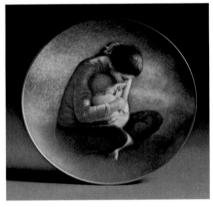

84-F.4-3.2
1978 *Yesterday, Today and Tomorrow*
Artist: Irene Spencer
Issue price: $47.50

DeGrazia Children Series

Artist: Ted DeGrazia. Artist's
  signature appears on front; first
  500 autographed on back
China banded in gold
Diameter: 26 centimeters
  (10¼ inches)
No hanger
Edition size limited to 10,000
Numbered without certificate

84-F.4-4.1
1978 *Flower Girl*
Artist: Ted DeGrazia
Issue price: $45.00
autographed: $100.00

84-F.4-4.2
1979 *Flower Boy*
Artist: Ted DeGrazia
Issue price: $45.00
autographed: $100.00

(Pasadena, California)

84-F.4-4.3
1980 *Little Cocopah Indian Girl*
Artist: Ted DeGrazia
Issue price: $50.00
autographed: $100.00

Irene Spencer's Special Requests

Artist: Irene Spencer. Artist's
signature appears on front
China with gold design on border
Diameter: 26 centimeters
(10¼ inches)
No hanger
Edition size limited to 10,000
Numbered without certificate

84-F.4-7.1
1978 *Hug Me*
Artist: Irene Spencer
Issue price: $55.00

84-F.4-7.2
1978 *Sleep Little Baby*
Artist: Irene Spencer
Issue price: $65.00

Classical American Beauties

Artist: Vincent
China banded in gold
Diameter: 26 centimeters
(10¼ inches)
No hanger
Edition size limited to 7,500
Numbered without certificate

84-F.4-8.1
1979 *Colleen*
Artist: Vincent
Issue price: $60.00

84-F.4-8.2
1979 *Heather*
Artist: Vincent
Issue price: $60.00

84-F.4-8.3
No information available
at press time

Ruffin Annual Series
Artist: Don Ruffin
China banded in gold
Diameter: 26 centimeters
(10¼ inches)
No hanger
Edition size: As indicated
Numbered without certificate

84-F.4-9.1
1976 *Navajo Lullaby*
Artist: Don Ruffin
Issue price: $40.00
Edition size limited to 10,000

84-F.4-9.2
1977 *Through the Years*
Artist: Don Ruffin
Issue price: $45.00
Edition size limited to 5,000

84-F.4-9.3
1978 *Child of the Pueblo*
Artist: Don Ruffin
Issue price: $50.00
Edition size limited to 5,000

84-F.4-9.4
1979 *Colima Madonna*
Artist: Don Ruffin
Issue price: $50.00
Edition size limited to 5,000

84-F.4-9.5
1980 *The Sun Kachina*
Artist: Don Ruffin
Issue price: $50.00
Edition size limited to 5,000

UNITED STATES
FRANKLIN MINT
(Franklin Center, Pennsylvania)

The Franklin Mint, the world's largest private mint, was established in Philadelphia in 1965 by Joseph Segal. The firm specializes in medallic art forms, minting coins for foreign governments, and has several international subsidiaries and branches.

The Franklin Mint entered the limited-edition plate field in 1970 with the six-plate *Rockwell Christmas Series*, made in sterling silver. This series ended in 1975. The Franklin Mint *Mother's Day Series*, designed by Irene Spencer and also in sterling silver, began in 1972 and ended in 1976.

The *Rockwell Christmas Series* is the first and only one to be designed especially for the collector's plate market by the artist, Norman Rockwell. One of the most successful twentieth-century artists, Rockwell created well over 3,000 works, among them the "Four Freedoms," which were widely circulated during World War II to build morale. His NASA-commissioned moonshot canvases hang in the Smithsonian Institution, and he is represented in many of the nation's major collections, including New York's Metropolitan Museum of Art. Irene Spencer received her training at the Academy of Art and the Chicago Art Institute, where she developed her distinctive style, reminiscent of the Old Masters. In addition to her accomplishments as a fine artist, she has written and illustrated children's books and worked as a newspaper cartoonist and commercial artist.

Rockwell Christmas Series
Artist: Norman Rockwell. Artist's
 signature appears on front
Etched sterling silver
Diameter: 20.3 centimeters
 (8 inches)
No hanger
Edition size: As indicated
Numbered, with certificate
 since 1972

84-F.64-1.1
1970 Bringing Home the Tree
Artist: Norman Rockwell
Issue price: $100.00
Edition size limited to 18,321

84-F.64-1.2
1971 Under the Mistletoe
Artist: Norman Rockwell
Issue price: $100.00
Edition size limited to 24,792

84-F.64-1.3
1972 The Carolers
Artist: Norman Rockwell
Issue price: $125.00
Edition size limited to 29,074

84-F.64-1.4
1973 Trimming the Tree
Artist: Norman Rockwell
Issue price: $125.00
Edition size limited to 18,010

84-F.64-1.5
1974 Hanging the Wreath
Artist: Norman Rockwell
Issue price: $175.00
Edition size limited to 12,822

84-F.64-1.6
1975 Home for Christmas
Artist: Norman Rockwell
Issue price: $180.00
Edition size limited to 11,059

Mother's Day Series

Artist: Irene Spencer. Artist's
  signature appears on front
Etched sterling silver
Diameter: 20.3 centimeters
  (8 inches)
No hanger
Edition size: As indicated
Numbered without certificate

84-F.64-2.1
1972 *Mother and Child*
Artist: Irene Spencer
Issue price: $125.00
Edition size limited to 21,987

84-F.64-2.2
1973 *Mother and Child*
Artist: Irene Spencer
Issue price: $125.00
Edition size limited to 6,154

84-F.64-2.3
1974 *Mother and Child*
Artist: Irene Spencer
Issue price: $150.00
Edition size limited to 5,116

84-F.64-2.4
1975 *Mother and Child*
Artist: Irene Spencer
Issue price: $175.00
Edition size limited to 2,704

84-F.64-2.5
1976 *Mother and Child*
Artist: Irene Spencer
Issue price: $180.00
Edition size limited to 1,858

In 1831, Jabez Gorham, a silversmith, established the Gorham Corporation. Today a division of Textron, the firm is one of the world's largest producers of sterling silver and manufactures silverware and holloware, figurines and ornaments.

Gorham Corporation acquired crystal and china manufacturing companies in 1970, enabling it to produce limited-edition plates in china as well as silver.

Gorham's *Rockwell Four Seasons Series*, which began in 1971, creates four plates (spring, summer, fall and winter) each year. A *Christmas Series*, also with artwork by Norman Rockwell, was started in 1974. The *Irene Spencer Annual Series* began in 1974. The *DeGrazia Children Series* and the *Sugar and Spice Series* began in 1976. The *Prince Tatters Series* was started in 1977.

Since 1977, Fairmont China has made the *Irene Spencer Annual* plates and in 1978 they also began making the *DeGrazia Children* plates. (See United States, FAIRMONT). The *Sugar and Spice* and *Prince Tatters Series* are produced for Kern Collectibles by Gorham. (See United States, KERN COLLECTIBLES).

Norman Rockwell is best-known for his *Saturday Evening Post* covers, which he created on a regular basis for six decades. Among the most outstanding of the more than 3,000 works he completed during his career are the "Four Freedoms," which were widely circulated during World War II to build morale. Rockwell's NASA-commissioned moonshot canvases now hang in the Smithsonian Institution, and he is represented in many of the nation's major collections, including the Metropolitan Museum of Art in New York. Irene Spencer received her training at the Academy of Art and the Chicago Art Institute, where she developed her distinctive style, reminiscent of the Old Masters. In addition to her accomplishments as a fine artist, she has written and illustrated children's books and worked as a newspaper cartoonist. Ted DeGrazia, one-time apprentice to the great Mexican muralist Diego Rivera, first came to international attention in 1960 when his work was featured on a UNICEF card. Since then, his stylized re-creations of Southwestern subjects and themes have made him one of the most instantly recognizable of American artists. Dutch artist Leo Jansen is well-known on both sides of the Atlantic for his wistful, evocative portraits.

UNITED STATES
GORHAM
(Providence, Rhode Island)

*Rockwell Four
Seasons Series*
Artist: Norman Rockwell. Artist's
   signature appears on front
China banded in 24k gold
Diameter: 26.7 centimeters
   (10½ inches)
No hanger
Edition size undisclosed, limited
   by year of issue
Not numbered, without certificate
Issued in sets of four

84-G.58-1.1-1
1971 *A Boy and His Dog*
A Boy Meets His Dog
Artist: Norman Rockwell
Issue price: $50.00 the set

84-G.58-1.1-2
1971 *Adventurers Between Adventures*

84-G.58-1.1-3
1971 *A Mysterious Malady*

84-G.58-1.1-4
1971 *Price of Parenthood*

84-G.58-1.2-1
1972 *Young Love; Flying Colors*
Artist: Norman Rockwell
Issue price: $60.00 the set

84-G.58-1.2-2
1972 *Beguiling Buttercup*

84-G.58-1.2-3
1972 *A Scholarly Pace*

84-G.58-1.2-4
1972 *Downhill Daring*

84-G.58-1.3-1
1973 *The Ages of Love*
Sweet Song So Young
Artist: Norman Rockwell
Issue price: $60.00 the set

84-G.58-1.3-2
1973 *Flowers in Tender Bloom*

84-G.58-1.3-3
1973 *Fondly Do We Remember*

84-G.58-1.3-4
1973 *Gaily Sharing Vintage*

84-G.58-1.4-1
1974 *Grandpa and Me; Day Dreamers*
Artist: Norman Rockwell
Issue price: $60.00 the set

84-G.58-1.4-2
1974 *Goin' Fishin'*

84-G.58-1.4-3
1974 *Pensive Pals*

84-G.58-1.4-4
1974 *Gay Blades*

84-G.58-1.5-1
1975 *Me and My Pal;*
Young Man's Fancy
Artist: Norman Rockwell
Issue price: $70.00 the set

84-G.58-1.5-2
1975 *Fisherman's Paradise*

84-G.58-1.5-3
1975 *Disastrous Daring*

84-G.58-1.5-4
1975 *A Lickin' Good Bath*

84-G.58-1.6-1
1976 *Grand Pals; Soaring Spirits*
Artist: Norman Rockwell
Issue price: $70.00 the set

84-G.58-1.6-2
1976 *Fish Finders*

84-G.58-1.6-3
1976 *Ghostly Gourds*

84-G.58-1.6-4
1976 *Snow Sculpture*

84-G.58-1.7-1
1977 *Going on Sixteen; Sweet Serenade*
Artist: Norman Rockwell
Issue price: $75.00 the set

84-G.58-1.7-2
1977 *Sheer Agony*

84-G.58-1.7-3
1977 *Pilgrimage*

84-G.58-1.7-4
1977 *Chilling Chore*

84-G.58-1.8-1
1978 *The Tender Years; Spring Tonic*
Artist: Norman Rockwell
Issue price: $100.00 the set

84-G.58-1.8-2
1978 *Cool Aid*

84-G.58-1.8-3
1978 *Chilly Reception*

84-G.58-1.8-4
1978 *New Year Look*

84-G.58-1.9-1
1979 *A Helping Hand*
Closed for Business
Artist: Norman Rockwell
Issue price: $100.00 the set

84-G.58-1.9-2
1979 *Swatters Rights*

84-G.58-1.9-3
1979 *The Coal Season's Coming*

GORHAM

(Providence, Rhode Island)

84-G.58-1.9-4
1979 Year End Count

84-G.58-1.10-1
1980 Dad's Boy; In His Spirit
Artist: Norman Rockwell
Issue price: $135.00 the set

84-G.58-1.10-2
1980 Trout Dinner

84-G.58-1.10-3
1980 Careful Aim

84-G.58-1.10-4
1980 Ski Skills

Rockwell Christmas Series

Artist: Norman Rockwell. Artist's
  signature appears on front
China banded in 24k gold
Diameter: 21.6 centimeters
  (8½ inches)
No hanger
Edition size undisclosed, limited
  by year of issue
Not numbered, without certificate

84-G.58-3.1
1974 Tiny Tim
Artist: Norman Rockwell
Issue price: $12.50

84-G.58-3.2
1975 Good Deeds
Artist: Norman Rockwell
Issue price: $17.50

84-G.58-3.3
1976 *Christmas Trio*
Artist: Norman Rockwell
Issue price: $19.50

84-G.58-3.4
1977 *Yuletide Reckoning*
Artist: Norman Rockwell
Issue price: $19.50

84-G.58-3.5
1978 *Planning Christmas Visits*
Artist: Norman Rockwell
Issue price: $24.50

84-G.58-3.6
1979 *Santa's Helpers*
Artist: Norman Rockwell
Issue price: $24.50

84-G.58-3.7
1980 *Letter to Santa*
Artist: Norman Rockwell
Issue price: $27.50

Irene Spencer Annual

Artist: Irene Spencer. Artist's
  signature appears on front
China banded in 24k gold
Diameter: 21.6 centimeters
  (8½ inches)
No hanger
Edition size limited to announced
  quantity of 10,000
Not numbered, without certificate

84-G.58-4.1
1974 *Dear Child*
Artist: Irene Spencer
Issue price: $37.50

84-G.58-4.2
1975 *Promises to Keep*
Artist: Irene Spencer
Issue price: $40.00

DeGrazia Children Series
Artist: Ted DeGrazia. Artist's
  signature appears on front
China banded in 24k gold
Diameter: 26.7 centimeters
  (10½ inches)
No hanger
Edition size: As indicated
Not numbered, without certificate

84-G.58-5.1
1976 *Los Niños*
Issue price: $35.00
Edition size limited to announced
quantity of 5,000

84-G.58-5.2
1977 *The White Dove*
Issue price: $40.00
Edition size limited to announced
quantity of 10,000

Sugar and Spice Series
Artist: Leo Jansen. Artist's
  signature appears on front
China banded in 24k gold
Diameter: 21.6 centimeters
  (8½ inches)
No hanger
Edition size limited to 7,500
Numbered without certificate

84-G.58-6.1
1976 *Dana and Debbie*
Artist: Leo Jansen
Issue price: $40.00

84-G.58-6.2
1977 *Becky and Baby*
Artist: Leo Jansen
Issue price: $42.50

84-G.58-6.3
1978 *Jeanette and Julie*
Artist: Leo Jansen
Issue price: $47.50

84-G.58-6.4
1979 *Ramona and Rachel*
Artist: Leo Jansen
Issue price: $50.00

Prince Tatters Series

Artist: Leo Jansen. Artist's
  signature appears on front
China banded in 24k gold
Diameter: 21.6 centimeters
  (8½ inches)
No hanger
Edition size limited to 7,500
Numbered without certificate

84-G.58-8.1
1977 *Johnny and Duke*
Artist: Leo Jansen
Issue price: $40.00

84-G.58-8.2
1978 *Randy and Rex*
Artist: Leo Jansen
Issue price: $42.50

84-G.58-8.3
1979 *Furry Friends*
Artist: Leo Jansen
Issue price: $47.50

84-G.58-8.4
1980 *Benji's Burro*
Artist: Leo Jansen
Issue price: $50.00

**Incolay Studios
of California**

Incolay Studios has been creating cameo *objets d'art* in Incolay stone since 1969. The manufacturing process by which Incolay stone is created is a closely guarded secret, but it is acknowledged that the process includes the addition of a range of quartz-based minerals to the stone to replicate the coloring of precious-stone cameos of the past.

Incolay Studios began its first series of collector's plates, *The Romantic Poets Collection*, in 1977. The series is inspired by the poetry of early nineteenth-century poets. In 1979, a second series of cameo plates, *The Great Romances of History Collection*, began.

Gayle Bright Appleby, designer of the *Romantic Poets Collection*, is widely known for the intricate detail of her sculptures in Incolay stone and in bronze, silver and gold. Carl Romanelli, sculptor of *The Great Romances of History Collection*, has works on display throughout the world. One of the most famous is his bust of John Henry, Cardinal Newman, which is on permanent display at the Vatican.

UNITED STATES
INCOLAY
(San Fernando, California)

Romantic Poets Collection
Artist: Gayle Bright Appleby
  Artist's signature appears on
  front
Incolay stone with high relief
  cameos
Diameter: 26 centimeters
  (10¼ inches)
Attached back hanger
Edition size undisclosed, limited
  by announced period of issue
Numbered with certificate

84-I.31-1.1
1977 *She Walks in Beauty*
Artist: Gayle Bright Appleby
Issue price: $60.00

84-I.31-1.2
1978 *A Thing of Beauty Is a Joy Forever*
Artist: Gayle Bright Appleby
Issue price: $60.00

84-I.31-1.3
1979 *To A Skylark*
Artist: Gayle Bright Appleby
Issue price: $65.00

84-I.31-1.4
No information available
at press time

Great Romances
of History Collection
Artist: Carl Romanelli
  Artist's signature appears on
  front
Incolay stone with high relief
  cameos
Diameter: 26 centimeters
  (10¼ inches)
Attached back hanger
Edition size undisclosed, limited
  by announced period of issue
Numbered with certificate

84-I.31-3.1
1979 *Antony and Cleopatra*
Artist: Carl Romanelli
Issue price: $65.00

84-I.31-3.2
1980 *The Taj Mahal Lovers*
Artist: Carl Romanelli
Issue price: $65.00

International Silver Company, one of the world's largest manufacturers of silver and silver-plated ware, traces its origin to a pewter shop established by Ashbil Griswold in Meriden in 1808. Rogers Brothers, developers of a silver electroplating process, became affiliated with the firm in 1862, and International Silver was incorporated in 1898.

The firm introduced limited-edition pewter plates in 1972 with its six-plate United States Bicentennial *We Are One Series*. The *Christmas Series* began in 1974.

Sculptor Manuel de Oliveiro, Portuguese-born creator of the *We Are One* series, received widespread recognition for his bicentennial creation. The collection has been acquired by the Smithsonian Institution in Washington, D.C.

We Are One

Bicentennial Series

Artist: Manuel de Oliveiro (after works by Carl Sundberg)

Artist's signature appears on back

Pewter with sculpted designs in high relief

Diameter: 22.2 centimeters (8¾ inches)

Attached back hanger

Edition size limited to 7,500

Numbered with certificate

84-I.61-1.1
1972 *Declaration of Independence*
Artist: Manuel de Oliveiro
Issue price: $40.00

84-I.61-1.2
1973 *The Midnight Ride of Paul Revere*
Artist: Manuel de Oliveiro
Issue price: $40.00

84-I.61-1.3
1973 *Stand at Concord Bridge*
Artist: Manuel de Oliveiro
Issue price: $40.00

84-I.61-1.4
1974 *Crossing the Delaware*
Artist: Manuel de Oliveiro
Issue price: $50.00

84-I.61-1.5
1974 *Battle of Valley Forge*
Artist: Manuel de Oliveiro
Issue price: $50.00

84-I.61-1.6
1975 *Surrender at Yorktown*
Artist: Manuel de Oliveiro
Issue price: $50.00

84-I.61-2.1

Christmas Series

Artist: As indicated. Artist's signature appears on back

Pewter with sculpted designs in high relief

Diameter: 23.8 centimeters (9⅜ inches)

Attached back hanger

Edition size limited to 7,500

Numbered with certificate

84-I.61-2.1
1974 *Tiny Tim*
Artist: Carl Sundberg
Issue price: $75.00

84-I.61-2.2
1975 *Caught*
Artist: Beverly Chase (after a work by Thomas Nast)
Issue price: $75.00

84-I.61-2.3
1976 *Bringing Home the Tree*
Artist: Albert Petitto (after a work by Emilie Mary Osborn)
Issue price: $75.00

84-I.61-2.4
1977 *Fezziwig's Christmas Ball*
Artist: Albert Petitto (after a work by John Leech)
Issue price: $75.00

84-I.61-2.5
1978 *Alleluia*
Artist: Albert Petitto (after a work by Uldis Klavina)
Issue price: $75.00

84-I.61-2.6
1979 *Rejoice*
Artist: Albert Pettito (after an Old World engraving c. 1800)
Issue price: $100.00

84-I.61-2.7
No information available at press time

UNITED STATES
KERN COLLECTIBLES
(Stillwater, Minnesota)

The story of Kern Collectibles began in 1969 when Oscar L. Kern founded Commemorative Imports, a distributor of limited-edition collectibles. Mr. Kern expanded his business one step further in 1972 with the establishment of Kern Collectibles. Kern Collectibles issues limited-edition plates produced especially for the company by several of the world's fine china manufacturers.

The *Runci Mother's Day Series* started in 1977.

Artist for the series is Italian-born Edward Runci, a leading contemporary exponent of Impressionism.

UNITED STATES
KERN COLLECTIBLES
(Stillwater, Minnesota)

Runci Mother's Day Series
Artist: Edward Runci
Overglaze porcelain banded
  in gold
Diameter: 19 centimeters
  (7½ inches)
Attached back hanger
Edition size limited to 5,000
Numbered without certificate

84-K.20-6.1
1977 *Darcy*
Artist: Edward Runci
Issue price: $50.00

84-K.20-6.2
1978 *A Moment to Reflect*
Artist: Edward Runci
Issue price: $55.00

84-K.20-6.3
1979 *Fulfillment*
Artist: Edward Runci
Issue price: $45.00

84-K.20-6.4
1980 *A Renewal of Faith*
Artist: Edward Runci
Issue price: $45.00

The Knowles heritage of fine china can be traced to the early nineteenth century when Isaac Knowles, father of Edwin established the family firm — Knowles, Taylor and Knowles — in East Liverpool, Ohio. The site was chosen for its proximity to deposits of high-quality kaolin clay. The firm became well known for its production of Lotus Ware.

After apprenticing with Knowles, Taylor and Knowles, Edwin established his own company in Newell, West Virginia. By the late 1880s, Edwin M. Knowles had become a preeminent force in American china. He was honored by election to the presidency of the United States Potters Association.

After his death, the company ceased operations for a period of time until entering into an affiliation with the Bradford Exchange in order to preserve its time-honored name.

Since 1975 the Edwin M. Knowles name has appeared on issues certified by the Rockwell Society of America (see United States, ROCKWELL SOCIETY). The *Wizard of Oz*, first proprietary series to bear the name of Knowles, began in 1977 and ends in 1980. The *Americana Holidays Series* and the *Gone With the Wind Series*, which is endorsed by Metro-Goldwyn-Mayer, began in 1978. Knowles' latest series is the *Csatari Grandparent Series*, which begins in 1980.

Knowles has commissioned a number of important contemporary artists to create its plates, including: James Auckland, whose stylistic blend of fantasy and realism is uniquely suited to the *Wizard of Oz Collection*; Raymond Kursár, twice recipient of the Award of Merit from the Society of Illustrators and well-known for his prize-winning Broadway show posters; Don Spaulding, Norman Rockwell protege and a leading exponent of authentic historical detail in painting; and Joseph Csatari, winner of the Gold Medal from the Society of Illustrators of New York and designer of a commemorative stamp which took his work to an audience of more than 100 countries.

Wizard of Oz Series

Artist: James Auckland. Artist's
signature appears on front
China
Diameter: 21.6 centimeters
(8½ inches)
No hanger
Edition size undisclosed, limited
by announced period of issue
Numbered with certificate

84-K.41-1.1
1977 *Over the Rainbow*
Artist: James Auckland
Issue price: $19.00

84-K.41-1.2
1978 *If I Only Had a Brain*
Artist: James Auckland
Issue price: $19.00

84-K.41-1.3
1978 *If I Only Had a Heart*
Artist: James Auckland
Issue price: $19.00

84-K.41-1.4
1978 *If I Were King of the Forest*
Artist: James Auckland
Issue price: $19.00

84-K.41-1.5
1979 *The Wicked Witch of the West*
Artist: James Auckland
Issue price: $19.00

84-K.41-1.6
1979 *Follow the Yellow Brick Road*
Artist: James Auckland
Issue price: $19.00

84-K.41-1.7
1979 *Wonderful Wizard of Oz*
Artist: James Auckland
Issue price: $19.00

84-K.41-1.8
1980 *The Grand Finale*
(We're Off to See The Wizard)
Artist: James Auckland
Issue price: $24.00

Americana Holidays Series

Artist: Don Spaulding
China
Diameter: 21.6 centimeters
  (8½ inches)
No hanger
Edition size undisclosed, limited
  by period of issue
Numbered with certificate

84-K.41-2.1
1978 *Fourth of July*
Artist: Don Spaulding
Issue price: $26.00

84-K.41-2.2
1979 *Thanksgiving*
Artist: Don Spaulding
Issue price: $26.00

84-K.41-2.3
1980 *Easter*
Artist: Don Spaulding
Issue price: $26.00

Gone With the Wind Series

Artist: Raymond Kursár
China
Diameter: 21.6 centimeters
  (8½ inches)
No hanger
Edition size undisclosed, limited
  by period of issue
Numbered with certificate

84-K.41-3.1
1978 *Scarlett*
Artist: Raymond Kursár
Issue price: $21.50

84-K.41-3.2
1979 *Ashley*
Artist: Raymond Kursár
Issue price: $21.50

Maker had
no photo at
press time

84-K.41-3.3
1980 *Melanie*
Artist: Raymond Kursár
Issue price: $21.50

Csatari Grandparent Series
Artist: Joseph Csatari
China
Diameter: 21.6 centimeters
  (8½ inches)
No hanger
Edition size undisclosed,
  limited by period of issue
Numbered with certificate

84-K.41-4.1
1980 *Bedtime Story*
Artist: Joseph Csatari
Issue price: Undetermined at
press time

LENOX

Walter Scott Lenox and his partner, Jonathan Coxon, Sr., established the Ceramic Art Company in Trenton, New Jersey, in 1889. In 1895 Lenox bought out Coxon and operated the business alone until it was reorganized in 1906 as Lenox, Inc. The plant later moved to Pomona. The firm's early products were bowls, vases, figurines, and later, tableware. All were made in "American Belleek," named for the town in Ireland where this creamy, ivory-tinted ware was first produced.

During World War I, Lenox was commissioned to supply President Wilson with a complete 1,700 piece dinner service, the first wholly American china ever used in the White House. Later, both Presidents Franklin Roosevelt and Harry Truman commissioned Lenox to make sets of dinnerware. The etched gold and green Truman service is still in use at the White House.

In 1970 Lenox introduced its *Lenox-Boehm Bird Series* using paintings by Lenox artist, Edward Marshall Boehm. The *Lenox-Boehm Woodland Wildlife Series* began in 1973 with artwork adapted from original Boehm sculptures.

Edward Marshall Boehm, who died in 1969, was one of America's greatest wildlife artists. His works appeared in the collections of Queen Elizabeth II and Presidents Eisenhower, Kennedy and Johnson, as well as in numerous museums and galleries, including the Smithsonian Institution.

LENOX

(Lawrenceville, New Jersey)

Lenox/Boehm Bird Series
Artist: Edward Marshall Boehm
  Artist's name appears on back
China with 24k gold design
  on border
Diameter: 26.7 centimeters
  (10½ inches)
No hanger
Edition size undisclosed
Not numbered, without certificate

84-L.18-1.1
1970 *Wood Thrush*
Artist: Edward Marshall Boehm
Issue price: $35.00

84-L.18-1.2
1971 *Goldfinch*
Artist: Edward Marshall Boehm
Issue price: $35.00

84-L.18-1.3
1972 *Mountain Bluebird*
Artist: Edward Marshall Boehm
Issue price: $37.50

84-L.18-1.4
1973 *Meadowlark*
Artist: Edward Marshall Boehm
Issue price: $41.00

84-L.18-1.5
1974 *Rufous Hummingbird*
Artist: Edward Marshall Boehm
Issue price: $45.00

84-L.18-1.6
1975 *American Redstart*
Artist: Edward Marshall Boehm
Issue price: $50.00

84-L.18-1.7
1976 *Cardinal*
Artist: Edward Marshall Boehm
Issue price: $53.00

84-L.18-1.8
1977 *Robins*
Artist: Edward Marshall Boehm
Issue price: $55.00

84-L.18-1.9
1978 Mockingbirds
Artist: Edward Marshall Boehm
Issue price: $58.00

84-L.18-1.10
1979 Golden-Crowned Kinglets
Artist: Edward Marshall Boehm
Issue price: $65.00

84-L.18-1.11
No information available
at press time

Lenox/Boehm Woodland Wildlife Series

Artist: Edward Marshall Boehm
  Artist's name appears on back
China with 24k gold design
  on border
Diameter: 26.7 centimeters
  (10½ inches)
No hanger
Edition size undisclosed
Not numbered, without certificate

84-L.18-3.1
1973 Raccoons
Artist: Edward Marshall Boehm
Issue price: $50.00

84-L.18-3.2
1974 Red Foxes
Artist: Edward Marshall Boehm
Issue price: $52.50

84-L.18-3.3
1975 Cottontail Rabbits
Artist: Edward Marshall Boehm
Issue price: $58.50

84-L.18-3.4
1976 Eastern Chipmunks
Artist: Edward Marshall Boehm
Issue price: $62.50

84-L.18-3.5
1977 Beaver
Artist: Edward Marshall Boehm
Issue price: $67.50

UNITED STATES
LENOX
(Lawrenceville, New Jersey)

84-L.18-3.6
1978 *Whitetail Deer*
Artist: Edward Marshall Boehm
Issue price: $70.00

84-L.18-3.7
1979 *Squirrels*
Artist: Edward Marshall Boehm
Issue price: $76.00

84-L.18-3.8
1980 *Bobcats*
Artist: Edward Marshall Boehm
Issue price: $92.50

UNITED STATES
PICKARD
(Antioch, Illinois)

Pickard was established in Edgerton, Wisconsin, in 1894 by Wilder Austin Pickard, then moved to Chicago in 1897. For some forty years the Pickard China Studio, as the firm was then known, was a decorating company employing artists to hand paint white blanks of bowls, pitchers and other items obtained from factories in Europe.

In 1920 Pickard was incorporated and in 1938 moved to Antioch, Illinois, the site of the present pottery. Here the firm began making its own fine china. Today Pickard, Inc. is headed by Henry Pickard, a third generation descendant of the founder, making it the only American china company in the hands of the founding family.

In 1970 Pickard introduced its *Lockhart Wildlife Series*. These plates were issued in pairs during the first four years of the series, but from 1974 individual plates were issued. The *Christmas Series* began in 1976, and in 1978 Pickard began the *Children of Renoir Series*.

James Lockhart, an ardent naturalist and conservationist, is widely known for his realistic portrayals of wild animals in their natural habitats. The designs for Pickard's *Christmas* and *Children of Renoir* series are reproductions of works by the Masters.

UNITED STATES
PICKARD
(Antioch, Illinois)

Lockhart Wildlife Series
Artist: James Lockhart. Artist's
  signature appears on front
China with 23k gold design
  on border
Diameter: As indicated
No hanger
Edition size: As indicated
Numbered with certificate

84-P.29-1.1-1
1970 *Woodcock*
Artist: James Lockhart
Diameter: 10½ inches
Issue price: $150.00 (pair)
Edition size limited to 2,000

84-P.29-1.1-2
1970 *Ruffed Grouse*

84-P.29-1.2-1
1971 *Green-Winged Teal*
Artist: James Lockhart
Diameter: 10½ inches
Issue price: $150.00 (pair)
Edition size limited to 2,000

84-P.29-1.2-2
1971 *Mallard*

84-P.29-1.3-1
1972 *Mockingbird*
Artist: James Lockhart
Diameter: 10½ inches
Issue price: $162.50 (pair)
Edition size limited to 2,000

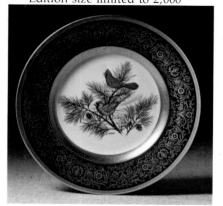

84-P.29-1.3-2
1972 *Cardinal*

84-P.29-1.4-1
1973 *Wild Turkey*
Artist: James Lockhart
Diameter: 10½ inches
Issue price: $162.50 (pair)
Edition size limited to 2,000

84-P.29-1.4-2
1973 *Ring-Necked Pheasant*

84-P.29-1.5
1974 *American Bald Eagle*
Artist: James Lockhart
Diameter: 13 inches
Issue price: $150.00
Edition size limited to 2,000

84-P.29-1.6
1975 *White-Tailed Deer*
Artist: James Lockhart
Diameter: 11 inches
Issue price: $100.00
Edition size limited to 2,500

84-P.29-1.7
1976 *American Buffalo*
Artist: James Lockhart
Diameter: 13 inches
Issue price: $165.00
Edition size limited to 2,500

84-P.29-1.8
1977 *Great Horned Owl*
Artist: James Lockhart
Diameter: 11 inches
Issue price: $100.00
Edition size limited to 2,500

84-P.29-1.9
1978 *American Panther*
Artist: James Lockhart
Diameter: 13 inches
Issue price: $175.00
Edition size limited to 2,000

84-P.29-1.10
1979 *The Red Fox*
Artist: James Lockhart
Diameter: 11 inches
Issue price: $120.00
Edition size limited to 2,500

84-P.29-1.11
No information available
at press time

UNITED STATES
PICKARD
(Antioch, Illinois)

Christmas Series
Artist: As indicated
China with 23k gold design
    on border
Diameter: 21.3 centimeters
    (8⅜ inches)
No hanger
Edition size: As indicated
Numbered without certificate

84-P.29-2.1
1976 *The Alba Madonna*
Artist: Raphael
Issue price: $60.00
Edition size limited to 7,500

84-P.29-2.2
1977 *The Nativity*
Artist: Lorenzo Lotto
Issue price: $65.00
Edition size limited to 7,500

84-P.29-2.3
1978 *The Rest on the Flight into Egypt*
Artist: Gerard David
Issue price: $65.00
Edition size limited to 10,000

84-P.29-2.4
1979 *Adoration of the Magi*
Artist: Botticelli
Issue price: $70.00
Edition size limited to 10,000

84-P.29-2.5
No information available
at press time

The Children of Renoir Series
Artist: Auguste Renoir. Artist's
    name appears on back
China banded in 23k gold
Diameter: 20.9 centimeters
    (8¼ inches)
No hanger
Edition size limited to 5,000.
    Two annual issues
Numbered without certificate

84-P.29-4.1
1978 *A Girl with a Watering Can*
Artist: Auguste Renoir
Issue price: $50.00

84-P.29-4.2
1978 *Child in White*
Artist: Auguste Renoir
Issue price: $50.00

84-P.29-4.3
1974 *Girl with Hoop*
Artist: Auguste Renoir
Issue price: $55.00

84-P.29-4.4
1979 *At the Piano*
Artist: Auguste Renoir
Issue price: $55.00

84-P.29-4.5
1980 *Two Little Circus Girls*
Artist: Auguste Renoir
Issue price: $60.00

84-P.29-4.6
No information available
at press time

UNITED STATES
RECO INTERNATIONAL
(Port Washington, New York)

Reco International was founded in 1967 by Heio W. Reich who continues as its president. From the beginning the firm has been an importer and maker of limited-edition plates.

World of Children, Reco International's first proprietary series, was introduced in 1977. A second series also with artwork by John McClelland, the *Mother Goose Series,* was introduced in 1979.

John McClelland is the author of definitive books on flower and portrait painting and is particularly noted for his portraiture of personages in politics and the arts.

RECO INTERNATIONAL

(Port Washington, New York)

The World of Children Series

Artist: John McClelland. Artist's
  signature appears on front
China banded in 24k gold
Diameter: 26.7 centimeters
  (10½ inches)
No hanger
Edition size: As indicated
Numbered with certificate since
  1978

84-R.17-1.1
1977 *Rainy Day Fun*
Artist: John McClelland
Issue price: $50.00
Edition size limited to 10,000

84-R.17-1.2
1978 *When I Grow Up*
Artist: John McClelland
Issue price: $50.00
Edition size limited to 15,000

84-R.17-1.3
1979 *You're Invited*
Artist: John McClelland
Issue price: $50.00
Edition size limited to 15,000

84-R.17-1.4
1980 *Kittens for Sale*
Artist: John McClelland
Issue price: $50.00
Edition size limited to 15,000

John McClelland's Mother Goose Series

Artist: John McClelland
China
Diameter: 21.6 centimeters
  (8½ inches)
No hanger
Edition size unannounced
Numbered with certificate

84-R.17-2.1
1979 *Mary, Mary*
Artist: John McClelland
Issue price: $22.50

84-R.17-2.2
1980 *Little Boy Blue*
Artist: John McClelland
Issue price: $22.50

Reed & Barton Silversmiths traces its origin to a factory established by Isaac Babbitt in the early nineteenth century. In 1824 Babbitt developed an alloy, harder and more lustrous than pewter, which he named Britannia metal. Henry G. Reed and Charles E. Barton, artists working for Babbitt, acquired the firm in the 1830s and continued to manufacture Britannia ware. In the late 1840s, the factory began to produce plated silverware. Reed & Barton was incorporated in 1888 and started producing solid silver services. Sterling flatware and holloware soon replaced plated ware as their largest line. In 1903 the firm began reproducing colonial pewter ware.

Artist Robert Johnson, whose works are in private collections throughout the United States, Europe and the Far East, developed the patented electroplating process used in the creation of the two Reed & Barton *Christmas Series*. The medium, known as Damascene, combines silver, gold, copper and bronze, and the electroplating process is derived from a hand-done method perfected at Damascus in the middle ages. Maxwell Mays specializes in Americana, and his art has appeared in such magazines as *Colliers*, *Yankee*, *Cosmopolitan* and *New England*.

In 1970 Reed & Barton began their *Christmas Series* which changes theme every three years. The first three plates are based on Christmas carols; the second three are based on fifteenth-century altar art; the next are based on American Christmas scenes; and the next depict nineteenth-century American illustrations.

Christmas Series

Artist: As indicated
Damascene silver
Diameter: 27.9 centimeters
(11 inches) through 1978;
thereafter, 20.3 centimeters
(8 inches)
No hanger
Edition size: As indicated
Numbered without certificate
through 1978, thereafter not
numbered accompanied with
numbered certificate

84-R.18-2.1
1970 *A Partridge in a Pear Tree*
Artist: Robert Johnson
Issue price: $55.00
Edition size limited to 2,500

84-R.18-2.2
1971 *We Three Kings of Orient Are*
Artist: Robert Johnson
Issue price: $60.00
Edition size limited to 7,500

84-R.18-2.3
1972 *Hark! The Herald Angels Sing*
Artist: Robert Johnson
Issue price: $60.00
Edition size limited to 7,500

84-R.18-2.4
1973 *Adoration of the Kings*
Artist: Rogier van der Weyden
Issue price: $60.00
Edition size limited to 7,500

84-R.18-2.5
1974 *The Adoration of the Magi*
Artist: Fra Angelico and Fra Lippi
Issue price: $65.00
Edition size limited to 7,500

84-R.18-2.6
1975 *Adoration of the Kings*
Artist: Steven Lochner
Issue price: $65.00
Edition size limited to 7,500

84-R.18-2.7
1976 *Morning Train*
Artist: Maxwell Mays
Issue price: $65.00
Edition size limited to 7,500

84-R.18-2.8
1977 *Decorating the Church*
Artist: Maxwell Mays
Issue price: $65.00
Edition size limited to 7,500

84-R.18-2.9
1978 *The General Store at
Christmas Time*
Artist: Maxwell Mays
Issue price: $65.00
Edition size limited to 7,500

84-R.18-2.10
1979 *Merry Old Santa Claus*
Artist: Thomas Nast
Issue price: $55.00
Edition size limited to 2,500

84-R.18-2.11
1980 *Gathering Christmas Greens*
Artist: Unknown
Issue price: Undetermined at press
time. Edition size limited to 2,500

84-R.69-0.0

River Shore, Ltd.®

Creators of Museum Quality Limited Editions

RiverShore Productions was established in 1975 to distribute limited-edition creations.

In 1976 RiverShore began its *Famous Americans* series, the first collector's plates crafted in copper, based on artwork by Norman Rockwell.

The series is sculpted by Roger Brown, a member of the National Sculpture Society. Brown's works appear in museums throughout the United States, including the Lyndon Baines Johnson Memorial Library and the Teterboro Aviation Museum.

UNITED STATES

RIVERSHORE, LTD.

(Caledonia, Michigan)

Famous Americans Series

Artist: Roger Brown (after works by Norman Rockwell). Artist's signature appears on front along with name of Norman Rockwell

Copper

Diameter: 20.3 centimeters (8 inches)

No hanger

Edition size limited to 9,500

Numbered with certificate

84-R.69-1.1
1976 Lincoln
Artist: Roger Brown
Issue price: $40.00

84-R.69-1.2
1977 Rockwell
Artist: Roger Brown
Issue price: $45.00

84-R.69-1.3
1978 Peace Corps
Artist: Roger Brown
Issue price: $45.00

84-R.69-1.4
1979 Spirit of Lindbergh
Artist: Roger Brown
Issue price: $50.00

UNITED STATES
ROCKWELL SOCIETY
(Stony Brook, New York)

The Rockwell Society of America is a chartered non-profit organization devoted to the study and appreciation of the works of Norman Rockwell. The Society's *Christmas Series* began in 1974, with the first issue manufactured by Ridgewood. Subsequent issues have been made by the Edwin M. Knowles China Company (see United States, KNOWLES). The *Mother's Day Series* started in 1976 and in 1977 the *Rockwell Heritage Series* began.

Norman Rockwell is best known for his *Saturday Evening Post* covers, which he created on a regular basis for six decades. Among the most outstanding of his more than 3,000 works are the "Four Freedoms," which were widely circulated during World War II to build morale. His NASA-commissioned moonshot canvases now hang in the Smithsonian Institution, and he is represented in many of the nation's major collections, including New York's Metropolitan Museum of Art.

UNITED STATES
ROCKWELL SOCIETY
(Stony Brook, New York)

Christmas Series

Artist: Norman Rockwell. Artist's
  signature appears on front
China
Diameter: 21.6 centimeters
  (8½ inches)
Attached back hanger
Edition size undisclosed, limited
  by announced period of issue
Numbered with certificate

84-R.70-1.1
1974 *Scotty Gets His Tree*
Artist: Norman Rockwell
Issue price: $24.50

84-R.70-1.2
1975 *Angel with a Black Eye*
Artist: Norman Rockwell
Issue price: $24.50

84-R.70-1.3
1976 *Golden Christmas*
Artist: Norman Rockwell
Issue price: $24.50

84-R.70-1.4
1977 *Toy Shop Window*
Artist: Norman Rockwell
Issue price: $24.50

84-R.70-1.5
1978 *Christmas Dream*
Artist: Norman Rockwell
Issue price: $24.50

84-R.70-1.6
1979 *Somebody's Up There*
Artist: Norman Rockwell
Issue price: $24.50

Maker had
no photo at
press time

84-R.70-1.7
1980 *Scotty Plays Santa*
Artist: Norman Rockwell
Issue price: Undetermined at
press time

Mother's Day Series

Artist: Norman Rockwell. Artist's
  signature appears on front

China

Diameter: 21.6 centimeters
  (8½ inches)

Attached back hanger

Edition size undisclosed, limited
  by announced period of issue

Numbered with certificate

84-R.70-2.1
1976 *A Mother's Love*
Artist: Norman Rockwell
Issue price: $24.50

84-R.70-2.2
1977 *Faith*
Artist: Norman Rockwell
Issue price: $24.50

84-R.70-2.3
1978 *Bedtime*
Artist: Norman Rockwell
Issue price: $24.50

84-R.70-2.4
1979 *Reflections*
Artist: Norman Rockwell
Issue price: $24.50

84-R.70-2.5
1980 *A Mother's Pride*
Artist: Norman Rockwell
Issue price: $24.50

UNITED STATES
ROCKWELL SOCIETY
(Stony Brook, New York)

Rockwell Heritage Series
Artist: Norman Rockwell. Artist's
  signature appears on front
China
Diameter: 21.6 centimeters
  (8½ inches)
Attached back hanger
Edition size undisclosed, limited
  by announced period of issue
Numbered with certificate

84-R.70-3.1
1977 *The Toy Maker*
Artist: Norman Rockwell
Issue price: $14.50

84-R.70-3.2
1978 *The Cobbler*
Artist: Norman Rockwell
Issue price: $19.50

84-R.70-3.3
1979 *The Lighthouse Keeper's Daughter*
Artist: Norman Rockwell
Issue price: $19.50

84-R.70-3.4
1980 *The Ship Builder*
Artist: Norman Rockwell
Issue price: $19.50

Royal Devon plates are manufactured by the Gorham Company (see United States, GORHAM). Both the *Christmas Series* and *Mother's Day Series*, bearing artwork by Norman Rockwell, began in 1975.

Norman Rockwell is best known for his *Saturday Evening Post* covers, which he created on a regular basis for six decades. Among the most outstanding of his more than 3,000 works are the "Four Freedoms," which were widely circulated during World War II to build morale. His NASA-commissioned moonshot canvases now hang in the Smithsonian Institution, and he is represented in many of the nation's major collections, including New York's Metropolitan Museum of Art.

Christmas Series

Artist: Norman Rockwell. Artist's
  signature appears on front
China banded in gold
Diameter: 21.6 centimeters
  (8½ inches)
No hanger
Edition size undisclosed, limited
  by year of issue
Not numbered, without certificate

84-R.60-1.1
1975 *Downhill Daring*
Artist: Norman Rockwell
Issue price: $24.50

84-R.60-1.2
1976 *The Christmas Gift*
Artist: Norman Rockwell
Issue price: $24.50

84-R.60-1.3
1977 *The Big Moment*
Artist: Norman Rockwell
Issue price: $27.50

84-R.60-1.4
1978 *Puppets for Christmas*
Artist: Norman Rockwell
Issue price: $27.50

84-R.60-1.5
1979 *One Present Too Many*
Artist: Norman Rockwell
Issue price: $31.50

84-R.60-1.6
No information available
at press time

Mother's Day Series

Artist: Norman Rockwell. Artist's
   signature appears on front

China banded in gold

Diameter: 21.6 centimeters
   (8½ inches)

No hanger

Edition size undisclosed, limited
   by year of issue

Not numbered, without certificate

84-R.60-2.1
1975 *Doctor and the Doll*
Artist: Norman Rockwell
Issue price: $23.50

84-R.60-2.2
1976 *Puppy Love*
Artist: Norman Rockwell
Issue price: $24.50

84-R.60-2.3
1977 *The Family*
Artist: Norman Rockwell
Issue price: $24.50

84-R.60-2.4
1978 *Mother's Day Off*
Artist: Norman Rockwell
Issue price: $27.00

84-R.60-2.5
1979 *Mother's Evening Out*
Artist: Norman Rockwell
Issue price: $30.00

84-R.60-2.6
1980 *Mother's Treat*
Artist: Norman Rockwell
Issue price: $30.00

Royal Worcester is the American subsidiary of the English company of the same name. (See England, ROYAL WORCESTER). The firm was established in the United States after World War II.

In 1972 Royal Worcester initiated the *Birth of a Nation Series* of five annual pewter plates to commemorate the Bicentennial of the United States.

Massachusetts-born sculptor Prescott Baston was commissioned to design all plates in the series.

UNITED STATES
ROYAL WORCESTER
(Hudson, Massachusetts)

Birth of a Nation Series
Artist: Prescott Baston
Pewter with designs in bas-relief
Diameter: 26 centimeters
   (10¼ inches)
No hanger
Edition size limited to 10,000
Numbered without certificate

84-R.76-1.1
1972 *Boston Tea Party*
Artist: Prescott Baston
Issue price: $45.00

84-R.76-1.2
1973 *The Ride of Paul Revere*
Artist: Prescott Baston
Issue price: $45.00

84-R.76-1.3
1974 *Incident at Concord Bridge*
Artist: Prescott Baston
Issue price: $50.00

84-R.76-1.4
1975 *Signing of the Declaration of
Independence*
Artist: Prescott Baston
Issue price: $65.00

84-R.76-1.5
1976 *Washington Crossing the Delaware*
Artist: Prescott Baston
Issue price: $65.00

UNITED STATES
VILETTA
(Houston, Texas)

Viletta China Company was started in 1959 in Roseberg, Oregon, by Viletta West who hand painted china and sold it through stores in the Pacific Northwest. The firm is involved in many areas of the giftware and fine china field, including commemorative china items and limited-edition collector's plates.

In 1978 Viletta China moved from Roseberg to Houston, Texas.

The *Zolan's Children Series* and the *Nutcracker Ballet Plate Collection* began in 1978.

Shell Fisher, a noted contemporary artist who works in oils, received his formal training at the Art Institute of Chicago, the University of Illinois and Northwestern University. Donald Zolan also studied at the Art Institute of Chicago and won a scholarship to the American Academy of Art. His works, created in the representational style, hang in numerous galleries throughout the United States and in private collections in Mexico, Australia, France, Italy, South Korea and Colombia.

UNITED STATES
VILETTA

(Houston, Texas)

Zolan's Children Series

Artist: Donald Zolan
China
Diameter: 21.6 centimeters
　(8½ inches)
No hanger
Edition size undisclosed, limited
　by period of issue
Numbered with certificate

84-V.36-1.1
1978 *Erik and Dandelion*
Artist: Donald Zolan
Issue price: $19.00

84-V.36-1.2
1979 *Sabina in the Grass*
Artist: Donald Zolan
Issue price: $22.00

84-V.36-1.3
1980 *By Myself*
Artist: Donald Zolan
Issue price: $24.00

Nutcracker Ballet Plate Collection

Artist: Shell Fisher
China
Diameter: 21.6 centimeters
　(8½ inches)
No hanger
Edition size undisclosed, limited
　by year of issue
Numbered with certificate

84-V.36-2.1
1978 *Clara and Nutcracker*
Artist: Shell Fisher
Issue price: $19.50

84-V.36-2.2
1979 *Gift From Godfather*
Artist: Shell Fisher
Issue price: $19.50

84-V.36-2.3
1979 *The Sugarplum Fairy*
Artist: Shell Fisher
Issue price: $19.50

84-V.36-2.4
1979 *The Snow King and Queen*
Artist: Shell Fisher
Issue price: $19.50

84-V.36-2.5
1980 *The Waltz of the Flowers*
Artist: Shell Fisher
Issue price: $19.50

GUIDE TO MAKERS AND SPONSORS
OF OVER-THE-COUNTER ISSUES

Abbey Press *(Viletta)*
Accent on Art
Addams Family
American Archives *(International Silver)*
American Arts Services *(Viletta)*
American Commemorative *(Gorham)*
American Express *(Gorham)*
American Express *(Lenox)*
American Preservation Guild *(Gorham)*
American Rose Society *(Gorham)*
Anna-Perenna
Anri
Antique Trader
Arabia
Arizona Artisan
Arlington Mint
Armstrong
Arta
Artists of the World
Audubon Crystal Ltd.
Aynsley

Bareuther
Bayel of France
Bengough
Berlin Design
Betourne Studios
Bing & Grondahl
Blue Delft *(Schoonhaven)*
Boehm Studios
Boehm Studios *(Hamilton Collection)*
Bohemia
Bonita Silver Co.
Borsato
Brantwood Collection
John Brindle Fine Arts
Brown & Bigelow *(Gorham)*

Caithness Glass, Ltd.
Calhoun's Collectors Society
California Porcelain and Bronze
Capo Di Monte
Carlo Monti
Carson Mint *(Viletta)*
Cartier
Castleton *(American Historical)*
Castleton *(Shenango)*
Castleton China
Certified Rarities
Chateau Tyr
Chilmark
Cleveland Mint
Coalport
Collector Creations *(Reed & Barton)*
Collector's Heirlooms *(Viletta)*
Collectors Weekly
Continental Mint
Count Agazzi
Creative World
Cristal D'Albret
Crown Delft
Crown Parian

Danbury Mint
Daum
Dave Grossman Designs
De Pauw Studios
De Pauw Studios *(Pickard)*

R. J. Ernst Enterprises *(Viletta)*

Fairmont
Fenton
First International *(Viletta)*
Fleetwood Collection *(Gorham)*
Fostoria
Franklin Crystal
Franklin Mint

Franklin Porcelain
Frankoma
Furstenberg

George Washington Mint
Ghent Collection
Ghent Collection *(Bing & Grondahl)*
Ghent Collection *(Caverswall)*
Ghent Collection *(Fairmont)*
Ghent Collection *(Gorham)*
Ghent Collection *(Kaiser)*
Gnomes United
Goebel
Golf Digest
Gorham
Gourinat-Dolan Co.
Grafburg
Grande Copenhagen
Grande Danica
Greentree Potteries

Hackett American Collector
Hamilton Collection *(Viletta)*
Hamilton Mint
Haviland
Haviland-Parlon
Heinrich
Historic Providence Mint
Hudson Pewter
Hutschenreuther
Hutschenreuther *(Edna Hibel Corp.)*

Imperial
Incolay
International Silver
Interpace

J M Company
Jensen, Georg
Josair
Joys *(Viletta)*
Judaic Heritage Society
Judaic Heritage Society *(Avondale)*
Judaic Heritage Society *(Viletta)*

K P M-Royal Berlin
Kaiser
Keller & George *(Reed & Barton)*
Kera
Kern Collectibles
Kern Collectibles *(Pickard)*
Kern Collectibles *(Sango)*
Kilkelly
Kings
Kirk, Jodi
Koscherak Bros.
Kosta
Kurz *(Shuler International)*

Lake Shore Prints
Lapsys
Lenox
Lihs-Lindner
Lincoln Mint
Lincoln Mint *(Gorham)*
Litt
Lund & Clausen
Lynell Studios

Mallek
Manjundo
Marmot
Mason
Master Engravers of America
Metal Arts Co.
Metawa
Metropolitan Museum of Art
Mingolla
Moser
Moussalli
Mueller
Museums Editions *(Viletta)*

North Dakota Auto Club

Palisander
Paramount Classics *(Pickard)*
Pickard
Poole Pottery
Porsgrund
Puiforcat

Ram
Reco International
Reed & Barton
Renaud-Limoges
Ridgwood
RiverShore Ltd.
Rockwell Collectors Club
Rockwell Museum
Roman Cermica
Rorstrand
Rosenthal
Royal Bayreuth
Royal Copenhagen
Royal Cornwall
Royal Delft
Royal Doulton
Royal Grafton
Royal Limoges
Royal Tettau
Royal Worcester
Royale
Royale Germania
Royalwood
Russel, E. Ward *(Imperial)*
Ruthven, John A.

Sabino
Sango
Santa Clara
Sarna
Schmid Design
Schmid Pewter
Schumann
Schumann *(Calhouns)*
Sebastian
Seven Seas
Smith Glass
Spode
Sterling America
Stieff
Stumar
Syracuse China

Tirschenreuth
Toleware
Trester *(Gorham)*
Trester *(Kaiser)*
Trester *(Ridgwood)*

Vague Shadows
Val St. Lambert
Veneto Flair
Vernonware *(Metlox)*
Villeroy & Boch
Viletta
Viletta *(Homan)*
Viletta *(McCalla Enterprises)*
Viletta *(Westbury)*
Viletta *(Weston)*
Volair *(Gorham)*

Warwick *(Viletta)*
Wedgwood
Wendell August Forge
Westminster Collectibles
Wheaton
White House of The Confederacy *(Lenox)*
Whitehall China

Zenith Delftware

OVER-THE-COUNTER ISSUES

Over-the-counter plates may be traded but are not listed on the Bradford Exchange with "Bradex" plates, which generally trade with greater regularity and frequency. They are, nonetheless, true collector's plates issued in editions usually limited either to an announced number or to the year of issue as indicated. With the exception of the *Jubilee Christmas* plates of Bing & Grøndahl (Denmark), any editions considered repetitious of previous editions are excluded.

Over-the-counter issues are arranged alphabetically by country, then alphabetically by maker or maker/sponsor, then chronologically by series. Each entry includes the series name, the year and name of the plate, the edition limit, and the U.S. issue price wherever available.

	EDITION LIMIT	ISSUE PRICE (US)
AUSTRIA		
Arta		
Mother's Day		
1973 Family With Puppy	1,500	$ 50.00
Christmas		
1973 Nativity — In Manger	1,500	50.00
BELGIUM		
Val St. Lambert		
American Heritage		
1969 Pilgrim Fathers	500	200.00
1970 Paul Revere's Ride	500	200.00
1971 Washington on Delaware	500	200.00
Annual Old Masters		
1969 Rubens & Rembrandt (Pair)	5,000	50.00
1969 Van Gogh & Van Dyck (Pair)	5,000	50.00
1970 Da Vinci & Michelangelo (Pair)	5,000	50.00
1971 El Greco & Goya (Pair)	5,000	50.00
1972 Reynolds & Gainsborough (Pair)	5,000	50.00
(Single issue)		
1970 Rembrandt	Year	25.00
CANADA		
Bengough		
Christmas		
1972 Charles Dickens Christmas Carol	490	125.00
Northwest Mounted Police		
1972 1898 Dress Uniform	1,000	140.00
1972 First Uniform	1,000	140.00
Royal Canadian Police		
1972 Order Dress	1,000	140.00
CHINA (TAIWAN)		
Royal Cornwall		
The Five Perceptions of Weo Cho		
1979 Sense of Touch	19,500	55.00
1979 Sense of Sight	19,500	55.00
1979 Sense of Taste	19,500	55.00
1979 Sense of Hearing	19,500	55.00
1979 Sense of Smell	19,500	55.00
CZECHOSLOVAKIA		
Bohemia		
Mother's Day		
1974 Mother's Day	500	130.00
1975 Mother's Day	500	140.00
1976 Mother's Day	500	150.00
Koschevak Bros.		
Mary Gregory Christmas		
1973 Christmas	1,000	55.00
1974 Christmas	1,000	60.00
1975 Christmas	1,000	60.00
1976 Christmas	500	65.00
Mary Gregory Mother's Day		
1973 Mother's Day	500	55.00
1974 Mother's Day	300	60.00
1975 Mother's Day	300	60.00
1976 Mother's Day	500	65.00
Moser		
Christmas (Vanoce)		
1970 Hradcany Castle	400	75.00
1971 Karlstein Castle	1,365	75.00
1972 Old Town Hall	1,000	85.00
1973 Karlovy Vary Castle	500	90.00
Mother's Day (Den Matek)		
1971 Peacocks	350	75.00
1972 Butterflies	750	85.00
1973 Squirrels	200	90.00
DENMARK		
Bing & Grøndahl		
Jubilee Christmas		
1915 First Frozen Window	Year	3.00
1920 Crows Enjoying Christmas	Year	4.00
1925 Dog Outside Window	Year	5.00

	EDITION LIMIT	ISSUE PRICE (US)
1930 Old Organist	Year	$ 5.00
1935 Little Match Girl	Year	6.00
1940 Three Wise Men	Year	10.00
1945 Royal Guard Amalienborg Castle	Year	10.00
1950 Eskimos	Year	15.00
1955 Dybbol Mill	Year	20.00
1960 Kronborg Castle	Year	25.00
1965 Churchgoers	Year	25.00
1970 Amalienborg Castle	Year	30.00
1975 Horses Enjoying Meal	Year	40.00
1980 Happiness Over Yule Tree	Year	60.00
Olympic Games		
1972 Olympiade — Munich	Year	20.00
1976 Olympic Montreal	Year	29.50
1980 Moscow By Night	Year	43.00
Bicentennial		
1976 E Pluribus Unum	Year	50.00
Heritage		
1976 Norseman	5,000	30.00
1977 Navigators	5,000	30.00
1978 Discovery	5,000	39.50
1979 Exploration	5,000	39.50
Carl Larsson (Sets of four)		
1977 Flowers on Windowsill		
1977 Breakfast Under Big Birch		
1977 Yard & Warehouse		
1977 Kitchen	7,500	150.00
1978 Working in Woods		
1978 Fishing		
1978 Harvest		
1978 Potato Harvest	7,500	170.00
(Single issue)		
1977 Madonna	10,000	45.00
(Single issue)		
1978 Seagull	7,500	75.00
Mother's Day Jubilee		
1979 Mother's Day Jubilee	Year	55.00
Grande Copenhagen		
Bicentennial (Single issue)		
1976 Great Seal	Year	35.00
Grande Danica		
Mother's Day		
1977 Dog with Puppies	10,000	25.00
1978 Storks	10,000	25.00
1979 Badgers	10,000	25.00
Georg Jensen		
Christmas		
1972 Doves	Year	15.00
1973 Christmas Eve	Year	15.00
1974 Christmas Story	Year	17.50
1975 Winter Scene	Year	22.50
1976 Christmas in Country	Year	22.50
Mother's Day		
1973 Mother & Child	Year	15.00
1974 Sweet Dreams	Year	17.50
1975 Mother's World	Year	22.50
Kera		
Christmas		
1967 Kobenhavn	Year	6.00
1968 Forste	Year	6.00
1969 Andersen's House	Year	6.00
1970 Langelinie	Year	6.00
1971 Lille Peter	Year	6.00
Moon		
1969 Apollo 11	Year	6.00
1970 Apollo 13	Year	6.00
Mother's Day		
1970 Mother's Day	Year	6.00
1971 Mother's Day	Year	6.00

	EDITION LIMIT	ISSUE PRICE (US)
Lund & Clausen		
Moon		
1969 Moon Landing — Apollo 11	Year	$ 10.00
1971 Apollo 13	Year	15.00
Mother's Day		
1970 Rose	Year	10.00
1971 Forget-Me-Nots	Year	10.00
1972 Bluebell	Year	15.00
1973 Lily of the Valley	Year	16.00
Christmas		
1971 Animal Garden	Year	13.50
1972 Stave Church	Year	13.50
1973 Christmas Scene	Year	13.50
Palisander		
Christmas		
1971 Red Robin on Holly	1,200	50.00
1972 Flying Geese	1,200	50.00
1973 Christmas	1,200	50.00
Presidential		
1971 George Washington	1,000	50.00
1972 Thomas Jefferson	1,000	50.00
1973 John Adams	1,000	50.00
(Single issue)		
1973 Bicentennial	250	50.00
Royal Copenhagen		
National Parks of America		
1978 Yellowstone	5,000	75.00
1979 Shenandoah	5,000	75.00
1980 Yosemite	5,000	75.00
FINLAND		
Arabia		
Christmas 100 Years Ago		
1978 Inland Village Scene	Year	49.00
1979 Forest Village Scene	Year	72.00
1980 Seaside Village Scene	Year	79.00
FRANCE		
Bayel of France		
Flowers		
1972 Rose	300	50.00
1973 Lillies	300	50.00
1973 Orchid	300	50.00
Bicentennial		
1974 Liberty Bell	500	50.00
1975 Independence Hall	500	60.00
1976 Spread Eagle	500	60.00
Eagles		
1974 Eagle Head	300	50.00
1974 Eagle in Flight	300	50.00
Betourne Studios		
Jean-Paul Loup Christmas		
1971 Noel	300	125.00
1972 Noel	300	150.00
1973 Noel	300	175.00
1974 Noel	400	200.00
1975 Noel	250	250.00
1976 Noel	150	300.00
Mother's Day (Champleve)		
1974 Mother & Child	500	250.00
Mother's Day (Enamel)		
1975 Mother's Day	400	285.00
1976 Mother & Child	250	300.00
Cartier		
Cathedral		
1972 Chartres Cathedral	12,500	50.00
1974 Chartres, Millous	500	130.00
Cristal D'Albret		
Four Seasons		
1972 Summer	1,000	75.00
1973 Autumn	648	75.00
1973 Spring	312	75.00
1974 Winter	1,000	88.00
(Single issue)		
1972 Bird of Peace	3,700	64.00

	EDITION LIMIT	ISSUE PRICE (US)
Daum		
Four Seasons		
1969 Autumn (Amethyst)	2,000	$150.00
1970 Winter (Aquamarine)	2,000	150.00
1970 Spring (Emerald)	2,000	150.00
1970 Summer (Topaz)	2,000	150.00
Famous Musicians		
1970 Bach (Emerald)	2,000	60.00
1970 Beethoven (Amethyst)	2,000	60.00
1971 Mozart (Tourmaline)	2,000	60.00
1971 Wagner (Peridot)	2,000	60.00
1972 Debussy (Topaz)	2,000	60.00
1972 Gershwin (Sapphire)	2,000	60.00
Dali		
1971 Ceci N'est Pas Une Assiette	2,000	200.00
1971 Triomphale	2,000	200.00
Nymphea		
1979 Waterlillies	4,000	125.00
1980 Lily Pond	4,000	150.00
Gourinat-Dolan Co.		
(Single issue)		
1978 Doves of Peace	3,000	60.00
Haviland		
Presidential		
1968 Martha Washington	2,500	35.00
1969 Lincoln	2,500	100.00
1970 Grant	3,000	100.00
1971 Hayes	2,500	110.00
Theatre Des Saisons		
1979 Spring	5,000	120.00
1979 Summer	5,000	120.00
1979 Autumn	5,000	120.00
1979 Winter	5,000	120.00
Mother's Day		
1980 Child and His Animals	Year	55.00
Christmas		
1980 Twas the Night Before Christmas	Year	55.00
Haviland-Parlon		
Nan Lee (Single issue)		
1973 Peaceable Kingdom	5,000	30.00
King Tut (Single issue)		
1977 Scarab	2,500	80.00
Zodiac (Single issue)		
1977 Astrological Man	5,000	50.00
Josair		
Bicentennial		
1972 American Eagle	400	250.00
1973 American Flag	400	250.00
1974 Abraham Lincoln	400	250.00
1975 George Washington	400	250.00
1976 Declaration of Independence	400	250.00
Poillerat		
Christmas		
1972 Three Kings	500	350.00
1973 Rose	250	350.00
Puiforcat		
Cartes a Jouer		
1972 (Set of five)	2,000	300.00
(Single issue)		
1973 Exodus (Silver)	2,000	200.00
Raynaud-Limoges		
Castles		
1979 Bodiam Castle	5,000	48.00
1979 Glamis Castle	5,000	48.00
1979 Tower of London	5,000	48.00
Wildlife Collection		
1978 Tiger Bouquet	Year	50.00
Royal Limoges		
Christmas		
1972 Nativity	5,000	25.00
1973 Three Wise Men	5,000	27.50

	EDITION LIMIT	ISSUE PRICE (US)
Sabino		
Annual Crystal		
1970 King Henry IV & Maria De Medici	1,500	$ 65.00
1971 Milo & Beasts	1,500	65.00
WEST GERMANY		
Anna-Perenna		
Birds of Fancy		
1978 Firebird	5,000	110.00
Floral Fantasies		
1978 Empress Gold	5,000	110.00
Enchanted Gardens		
1978 June Dream	5,000	75.00
1979 Summer Day	5,000	95.00
Oriental Tranquility		
1978 Chun Li at Pond	5,000	100.00
1979 Ming Tao on Path of Faith	5,000	110.00
Bareuther		
Mother's Day		
1969 Mother & Children	5,000	12.00
1970 Mother & Children	5,000	12.00
1971 Mother & Children	5,000	13.50
1972 Mother & Children	5,000	15.00
1973 Mother & Children	5,000	15.00
1974 Musical Children	5,000	19.00
1975 Spring Outing	5,000	21.50
1976 Rocking the Cradle	5,000	23.00
1977 Noon Feeding	5,000	24.50
1978 Blind Man's Buff	5,000	27.50
1979 Mother's Love	5,000	35.00
1980 First Cherries	5,000	37.50
Barthmann		
Christmas		
1977 Mary with Child	300	236.00
1978 Adoration of Child	500	326.00
1979 Holy Mother of Kasanskaja	500	361.00
Berlin Design		
Father's Day (Historical)		
1971 Brooklyn Bridge on Opening Day	12,000	14.50
1972 Continent Spanned	3,000	15.00
1973 Landing of Columbus	2,000	18.00
1974 Adorn's Balloon	Year	25.00
1975 Washington Crossing the Delaware	Year	30.00
1976 Tom Thumb	Year	32.00
1977 Zeppelin	Year	32.00
1978 Carl Benz	Year	36.00
1979 Johannes Gutenberg at Mainz	Year	47.50
Furstenberg		
Easter		
1971 Sheep	3,500	15.00
1972 Chicks	4,000	15.00
1973 Bunnies	4,000	6.00
1974 Pussywillow	4,000	20.00
1975 Village Church	4,000	24.00
1976 Country Watermill	4,000	25.00
Christmas		
1971 Rabbits	7,500	14.00
1972 Snowy Village	6,000	15.00
1973 Christmas Eve	3,000	18.00
1974 Sparrows	4,000	20.00
1975 Deer Family	4,000	24.00
1976 Winter Birds	4,000	25.00
Deluxe Christmas		
1971 Wise Men	1,500	45.00
1972 Holy Family	2,000	45.00
1973 Christmas Eve	2,000	60.00
Mother's Day		
1972 Hummingbird	5,000	15.00
1973 Hedgehogs	5,000	16.00
1974 Doe with Fawn	4,000	20.00
1975 Swan Family	4,000	24.00
1976 Koala Bear	4,000	25.00
Olympic		
1972 Olympics — Munich	5,000	20.00
1976 Olympics — Montreal	5,000	37.50
Goebel		
Charlot Byj		
1973 Santa at Tree	Year	16.50
1974 Santa and Girl	Year	22.00
1975 Up and Away	Year	25.00
1976 Boy with Teddy Bear	Year	25.00
1977 Joy to World	Year	25.00
Robson Christmas		
1975 Flight to Egypt (Porcelain)	Year	50.00
1975 Flight to Egypt (Pewter)	Year	45.00
American Heritage		
1978 Freedom & Justice Soaring	Year	100.00
1979 Wild & Free	10,000	100.00
Old Testament Themes		
1978 12 Tribes of Israel	10,000	125.00
1979 Ten Commandments	10,000	175.00
(Single issue)		
1979 Christmas	200	5,000.00

	EDITION LIMIT	ISSUE PRICE (US)
Bratsoff		
1979 Star Steed	15,000	$ 125.00
Grafburg		
Christmas		
1975 Black-Capped Chickadee	5,000	20.00
1976 Squirrels	5,000	22.00
Marmot		
Father's Day		
1970 Stag	3,500	12.00
1971 Horse	3,500	12.50
Christmas		
1970 Polar Bear	5,000	13.00
1971 Buffalo	5,000	14.00
1972 Boy & Grandfather	5,000	20.00
1973 Snowman	3,000	20.00
1974 Dancing Children	2,000	24.00
1975 Covey of Quail	2,000	30.00
1976 Windmill	2,000	30.00
Presidents		
1971 Washington	1,500	25.00
1972 Jefferson	1,500	25.00
1973 John Adams	1,500	25.00
Mother's Day		
1972 Seal	6,000	16.00
1973 Polar Bear	2,000	20.00
1974 Penguins	2,000	24.00
1975 Raccoons	2,000	30.00
1976 Ducks	2,000	40.00
Heinrich		
UNICEF Children in the World		
1977 Europe	Year	30.00
1978 Asia	Year	30.00
1979 Africa	Year	30.00
1980 America	Year	30.00
(Single issue)		
1979 International Year of The Child	Year	35.00
The Flower Fairies Collection		
1979 Lavendar Fairy	21 Days	35.00
1980 Sweet Pea Fairy	21 Days	35.00
1980 Candytuft Fairy	21 Days	35.00
1981 Heliotrope Fairy	21 Days	35.00
1981 Black Thorne Fairy	21 Days	35.00
1982 Apple Blossom Fairy	21 Days	35.00
Hutschenreuther		
Songbirds of America		
1972 Eastern Bluebirds Goldfinch (Pair)	5,000	100.00
1973 Mockingbird/Robins (Pair)	5,000	100.00
*Christmas**		
1972 On the Way to Egypt	5,000	N/A
1973 The Adoration	5,000	N/A
1974 The Annunciation	5,000	N/A
*Series not available in U.S.		
Canada Christmas		
1973 Parliament Building	N/A	15.00
1974 Moose	N/A	16.00
1975 Basilica	N/A	21.00
1976 Winter on the Prairies	N/A	23.00
1977 Bluenose	N/A	23.00
1978 Lost Lagoon	N/A	27.00
1979 Yukon Highway Bridge	N/A	33.00
Bicentennial		
1976 Freedom in Flight	5,000	100.00
1976 Freedom in Flight (Gold)	200	200.00
Plates of the Month (Set of 12)		
1977 January — December	5,000	780.00
Annual		
1978 Mother and Child	Year	55.00
1979 Mother and Child	Year	65.00
1980 Mother and Child	Year	87.50
Birthday Annual		
1978 Birthday Plate	10,000	165.00
Winther Christmas		
1978 Christmas	2,000	260.00
1979 Christmas	2,500	295.00
Friendship Annual		
1978 Friendship Plate	Year	80.00
Dolores Valenza		
1978 Princess Snowflake	5,000	50.00
1979 Blossom Queen	5,000	62.50
1980 Princess Marina	5,000	87.50
Wedding Annual		
1978 Wedding Plate	10,000	210.00
Zodiac Collection (Set of 12)		
1978 Aries — Pisces	1,500	1,500.00
Hans Achtziger		
1979 Heading South	4,000	150.00
1980 Playful Flight	5,000	187.50
Arzberg Christmas		
1979 Christmas	2,500	60.00
(Single issue)		
1979 Celebration Plate	Year	67.50
(Single issue)		
1979 Anniversary Plate	Year	120.00
(Single issue)		
1977 Allegro Ensemble	7,500	120.00

	EDITION LIMIT	ISSUE PRICE (US)
Hibel Museum (Single issue)		
1977 Flower Girl of Provence	12,750	$ 175.00
Floral Heirlooms		
1977 Zinnias in Sugar Bowl	5,000	65.00
1978 Pansies in Antique Tin	5,000	65.00
1979 Primroses in Staffordshire Pitcher	5,000	65.00
Kaiser		
Passion Play		
1970 Oberammergau	Year	18.00
Great Yachts		
1971 Cetonia	1,000	50.00
1971 Westward	1,000	50.00
Feathered Friends		
1978 Blue Jays	10,000	70.00
1979 Cardinals	10,000	80.00
King Tut		
1978 Golden Mask	15,000	65.00
People of the Midnight Sun		
1978 Northern Lullaby	15,000	70.00
1979 Ilaga, My Friend	15,000	75.00
1980 Motherhood	15,000	85.00
Yesterday's World		
1978 Time for Dreaming	5,000	70.00
1979 Summer is Forever	5,000	75.00
KPM — Royal Berlin		
Christmas		
1969 Christmas Star	5,000	28.00
1970 Three Kings	5,000	28.00
1971 Christmas Tree	5,000	28.00
1972 Christmas Angel	5,000	31.00
1973 Christchild on Sled	5,000	33.00
1974 Angel & Horn	5,000	35.00
1975 Shepherds	5,000	40.00
1976 Star of Bethlehem	5,000	43.00
1977 Mary at Crib	5,000	46.00
1978 Three Wise Men	5,000	49.00
1979 At Manger	5,000	55.00
Lihs-Lindner		
Mother's Day		
1972 Mother and Child	1,000	25.00
1973 Mother and Child	2,000	25.00
1974 Bouquet for Mother	2,000	25.00
1975 We Wish You Happiness	2,000	28.00
Union Pacific Railroad		
1972 Union Pacific	1,500	25.00
1973 Union Pacific Big Boy	1,500	25.00
History		
1973 Tribute to Flag	3,000	60.00
1974 Golden Spike Centennial	1,500	40.00
Easter		
1973 Happy Easter	1,500	25.00
1974 Springtime	1,500	25.00
1975 With Love to You at Easter	1,500	28.00
America the Beautiful		
1975 Independence Hall	1,500	42.00
1975 Statue of Liberty	1,500	42.00
1975 Niagara Falls	1,500	42.00
1975 Grand Canyon	1,500	42.00
1975 Golden State	1,500	42.00
1975 Capitol	1,500	42.00
Bicentennial		
1976 Freedom Train	1,500	45.00
1976 Spirit of America	3,500	45.00
Playmates		
1976 Timmy and His Pal	5,000	45.00
1977 Heidi and Playmate	5,000	45.00
Meissen		
Annual		
1973 Winter Countryside by Sleigh	5,000	71.00
1974 Sleeping Beauty	5,000	75.00
1975 Archway to Albrecht's Castle	5,500	92.00
1976 Doge's Palace in Venice	5,000	92.00
1977 Fra Holle	5,000	114.00
1978 Ice Crystal with Children	7,000	123.00
1979 Winter Fairy Tale	7,000	151.00
Mueller		
Christmas		
1971 Christmas in Tyrol	Year	20.00
1972 Christmas Messenger	Year	15.00
1973 Bringing Home Tree	Year	20.00
1974 Trimming Tree	Year	25.00
1975 Family on Christmas Morning	Year	27.50
1976 Christmas Fire	Year	28.50
1977 Ice Skating	Year	28.50
Father's Day		
1973 Three Generations	N/A	17.50
1974 Fishing	N/A	20.00
1975 Hiking	N/A	27.50
Rosenthal		
Annual (Porcelain)		
1971 Tapio Wirkkala	3,000	N/A
1972 Natale Sapone	3,000	N/A
1973 Otto Piene	3,000	N/A
1974 Gunther Fruhtrunk	3,000	N/A
1975 Srivastava Narendra	3,000	N/A

	EDITION LIMIT	ISSUE PRICE (US)
1976 Salvador Dali	3,000	N/A
1977 Victor Vasarely	3,000	N/A
1978 E. Paolozzi	3,000	N/A
1979 Arnold Leissler	3,000	N/A
*Artist Plates **		
1973 NR 1 Gunter Grass	5,000	N/A
1974 NR 2 Jean Cocteau	5,000	N/A
1974 NR 3 Eugen Gomringer	5,000	N/A
1974 NR 4 Otto Piene	5,000	N/A
1975 NR 5 Max Bill	5,000	N/A
1975 NR 6 Hans-Werner Henze	5,000	N/A
1975 NR 7 Bjorn Wiinblad	5,000	N/A
1975 NR 8 Kriwet	5,000	N/A
1976 NR 9 Hildegard Knef	5,000	N/A
1977 NR10 Yehudi Menuhin	5,000	N/A
1977 NR11 Emilio Pucci	5,000	N/A
1978 NR12 Salvador Dali	5,000	N/A
1978 NR13 Victor Vasarely	5,000	N/A
1978 NR14 Almir Mazignier	5,000	N/A
1979 NR15 Ivan Rapuzin	5,000	N/A
*Series not available in U.S.		
*Satire Plates **		
NR1 Konrad Adenauer	5,000	N/A
NR2 Willy Brandt	5,000	N/A
NR3 Theodor Heuss	5,000	N/A
NR4 Walter Scheel	5,000	N/A
NR5 Helmut Schmidt	5,000	N/A
NR6 Franz-Josef Strauss	5,000	N/A
NR7 Helmut Kohl	5,000	N/A
NR8 Heinz Ruhmann	5,000	N/A
NR9 Herbert Von Karajan	5,000	N/A
NR10 Marlene Dietrich	5,000	N/A
NR11 Mao-Tse-Tung	5,000	N/A
NR12 Bruno Kreisky	5,000	N/A
*Series not available in U.S.		
Annual (Crystal)		
1974 Otto Piene (Clear)	3,000	200.0
1974 Otto Piene (Gold Inlaid)	3,000	250.0
1974 Otto Piene (Platinum Inlaid)	3,000	250.0
1975 G. Uecker	3,000	200.0
1976 Bjorn Wiinblad	3,000	N/A
1977 Gunter F. Ris	3,000	N/A
1978 Ivan Rapuzin	3,000	600.0
1979 Salvador Dali	3,000	N/A
Wiinblad Studio-Linie		
1976 Madonna	2,000	150.0
1977 Annunciation	2,000	195.0
1978 Three Kings	2,000	225.0
Aladdin		
1978 Aladdin and Lamp	N/A	65.0
1979 Aladdin and Street Urchins	N/A	65.0
1979 Aladdin and Genie	N/A	65.0
1979 Aladdin in Magic Garden	N/A	65.0
1980 Aladdin and Spirits	N/A	85.0
1980 Aladdin and Princess	N/A	85.0
Rosenthal (Trester)		
Lorraine Trester		
1975 Once Upon a Summertime	5,000	60.0
1976 One Lovely Yesterday	5,000	70.0
Rosenthal (Kern)		
John Falter Harvest Time		
1976 Gathering Pumpkins	5,000	70.0
1977 Honest Day's Work	4,000	70.0
Runci Classic		
1977 Summertime	5,000	95.0
1978 Springtime	5,000	95.0
Royal Bayreuth (Kern)		
Sunbonnet Babies (Set of seven)		
1974 Monday (Washing Day)		
1974 Tuesday (Ironing Day)		
1974 Wednesday (Mending Day)		
1974 Thursday (Scrubbing Day)		
1974 Friday (Sweeping Day)		
1974 Saturday (Baking Day)		
1974 Sunday (Fishing Day)	15,000	120.
(Single issue)		
1976 Sunbonnet Babies Composite	15,000	75.
L. Henry		
1976 Just Friends	5,000	50.
1977 Interruption	4,000	55.
Anniversary		
1980 Young Americans	5,000	125.
Royal Tettau		
Papal Plates		
1971 Pope Paul VI	5,000	100.
1972 Pope John XXIII	5,000	100.
1973 Pope Pius XII	5,000	100.
Royale		
Mother's Day		
1970 Swan and Brood	6,000	12.
1971 Doe and Fawn	9,000	13.
1972 Rabbit Family	9,000	16
1973 Owl Family	6,000	18
1974 Duck Family	5,000	22.

	EDITION LIMIT	ISSUE PRICE (US)
1975 Lynx Family	5,000	$ 26.00
1976 Woodcock and Young	5,000	27.50
1977 Koala Bear	5,000	30.00
Father's Day		
1970 U.S. Frigate Constitution	5,000	13.00
1971 Man Fishing	5,000	13.00
1972 Mountain Climber	6,000	16.00
1973 Camping	4,000	18.00
1974 Eagel	2,500	22.00
1975 Regatta	2,500	26.00
1976 Hunting Scene	2,500	27.50
1977 Fishing	5,000	30.00
Game		
1972 Setters Pointing Quail	500	180.00
1973 Fox	500	200.00
1974 Osprey	250	250.00
1975 California Quail	250	265.00
Royale Germania		
Annual		
1970 Orchid (blue)	600	200.00
1971 Cyclamen (red)	1,000	200.00
1972 Silver Thistle (green)	1,000	250.00
1973 Tulips (lilac)	600	275.00
1974 Sunflowers (topaz)	500	300.00
1975 Snowdrops (amber)	350	450.00
1976 Flaming Heart (red)	350	450.00
Mother's Day		
1971 Roses (red)	250	135.00
1972 Elephant (green)	750	180.00
1973 Koala Bear (lilac)	600	200.00
1974 Squirrels (topaz)	500	240.00
1975 Swan Family (amber)	350	250.00
Schmid		
Bavarian Christmas		
1971 Family Portrait	5,000	26.50
1972 On Horseback	5,000	26.50
1973 Bringing Home Tree	5,000	26.50
1974 Decorating Tree	5,000	26.50
1975 Opening Presents	5,000	26.50
1976 By Fireside	5,000	26.50
1977 Skating	5,000	28.50
1978 Family Picking Tree	5,000	36.00
1979 Breakfast by Tree	5,000	45.00
Ferrandiz Christmas		
1972 Christ in Manger	Year	30.00
1973 Christmas	Year	30.00
Golden Moments		
1978 Tranquility	15,000	250.00
Schumann		
Composers		
1970 Beethoven	N/A	8.00
1972 Mozart	N/A	13.00
Christmas		
1971 Snow Scene	10,000	12.00
1972 Deer in Snow	15,000	12.00
1973 Weihnachten	5,000	12.00
1974 Church in Snow	5,000	12.00
1975 Fountain	5,000	12.00
Schumann (Calhouns)		
Imperial Christmas		
1979 Liebling	10,000	65.00
Stumar		
Christmas		
1970 Angel	10,000	8.00
1971 Old Canal	10,000	8.00
1972 Countryside	10,000	8.00
1973 Friendship	10,000	10.00
1974 Making Fancy	10,000	10.00
1975 Preparation	10,000	10.00
1976 Drummer Boy	10,000	10.00
1977 Joyful Expectations	10,000	15.00
1978 Christmas	10,000	19.50
Mother's Day		
1971 Amish Mother & Daughter	10,000	8.00
1972 Children	10,000	8.00
1973 Mother Sewing	10,000	10.00
1974 Mother Cradle	10,000	10.00
1975 Baking	10,000	10.00
1976 Reading to Children	10,000	15.00
1977 Comforting Child	10,000	15.00
1978 Tranquility	10,000	19.50
Egyptian		
1977 Ancient Egyptian Trilogy	5,000	45.00
1978 Charioteer	5,000	54.00
Tirschenreuth		
Christmas		
1969 Homestead	3,500	12.00
1970 Church	3,500	12.00
1971 Star of Bethlehem	3,500	12.00
1972 Elk Silhouette	2,000	13.00
1973 Christmas	Year	14.00
Villeroy & Boch		
Christmas		
1977 Holy Family	10,000	175.00
1978 Three Holy Kings	20,000	175.00
1979 Mary with Child	10,000	198.00

GREAT BRITAIN

	EDITION LIMIT	ISSUE PRICE (US)
Aynsley		
Christmas Carol		
1979 Mr. Fezziwig's Ball	Year	$ 30.00
1980 Marley's Ghost	Year	36.00
Boehm Studios		
European Bird Plates		
1973 Swallow	5,000	48.75
1973 Chaffinch	5,000	48.75
1973 Coal Tit	5,000	48.75
1973 Tree Sparrow	5,000	48.75
1973 King Fisher	5,000	48.75
1973 Gold Crest	5,000	48.75
1973 Blue Tit	5,000	48.75
1973 Linnet	5,000	48.75
Honor America		
1974 American Bald Eagle	12,000	85.00
Butterfly		
1975 Blue Mountain Swallowtails	100	450.00
1975 Jezabels	100	450.00
1976 Comma with Loops	100	450.00
1976 African Butterflies	100	450.00
1976 Solandras Maxima	100	450.00
Hard Fruit		
1975 Plums	100	450.00
1975 Pears	100	450.00
1976 Peaches	100	450.00
1976 Apples	100	450.00
Oriental Birds		
1975 Bluebacked Fairy Bluebirds	100	400.00
1975 Azure-Winged Magpies	100	400.00
1976 Golden-Fronted Leafbird	100	400.00
1976 Golden-Throated Barbet	100	400.00
Seashell		
1975 Violet Spider Conch	100	450.00
1975 Rooster Tail Conch	100	450.00
1976 Orange Spider Conch	100	450.00
1976 Cheragra Spider Conch	100	450.00
Soft Fruit		
1975 Loganberries	100	450.00
1975 Cherries	100	450.00
1976 Strawberries	100	450.00
1976 Grapes	100	450.00
Butterflies of the World		
1978 Monarch and Daisy	5,000	62.00
1978 Red Admiral & Thistle	5,000	62.00
Flower		
1975 Lillies	100	450.00
1975 Passion Flowers	100	450.00
1976 Double Clematis	100	450.00
Favorite Floral		
1978 Clematis	5,000	62.00
1978 Rhododendron	5,000	62.00
Boehm Studios (Hamilton Collection)		
Rose Collection		
1979 Peace Rose	15,000	45.00
1979 Queen Elizabeth Rose	15,000	45.00
1979 White Masterpiece Rose	15,000	45.00
1979 Angel Face Rose	15,000	45.00
1979 Tropicana Rose	15,000	45.00
1979 Elegance Rose	15,000	45.00
1979 Royal Highness Rose	15,000	45.00
1979 Mister Lincoln Rose	15,000	45.00
Boehm Owl Collection		
1980 Boreal Owl	15,000	45.00
1980 Snowy Owl	15,000	45.00
1980 Barn Owl	15,000	45.00
1980 Saw Whet Owl	15,000	45.00
1980 Great Horned Owl	15,000	45.00
1980 Screech Owl	15,000	45.00
1980 Short Eared Owl	15,000	45.00
1980 Barred Owl	15,000	45.00
Caithness Glass, Ltd.		
America's Favorite Birds		
1979 Crystal Wren	5,000	79.50
Coalport		
*Christmas**		
1976 Christmas Eve	Year	12.00
1977 Dangerous Skating	Year	16.00
1978 Alas! Poor Bruin	Year	18.00
1979 Christmas Morning	Year	22.00
1980 Blind Man's Bluff	Year	N/A
*Series not available in U.S.		
Mother's Day		
1978 Clematis	Year	16.00
1979 Orchid	Year	21.00
(Single issue)		
1972 Indy 500	2,000	49.95
Hornsea		
Christmas		
1979 'c' — Nativity	10,000	21.00
Mason		
Christmas		
1975 Windsor Castle	Year	75.00
1976 Holyrood House	Year	75.00
1977 Buckingham Palace	Year	75.00
1978 Balmoral Castle	Year	75.00
1979 Hampton House	Year	75.00

	EDITION LIMIT	ISSUE PRICE (US)
1980 Sandring Space Han.	Year	$ 75.00
Poole Pottery		
Medieval Calendar		
1972 Drinking Wine by Fire (January)	1,000	100.00
1972 Chopping Wood (February)	1,000	100.00
1973 Digging in Fields and Setting Seeds (March)	1,000	125.00
1973 Carrying Flowering Branch (April)	1,000	125.00
1974 Hawking (May)	1,000	125.00
1974 Mowing the Hay (June)	1,000	125.00
1975 Cutting Corn With Sickle (July)	1,000	125.00
1975 Threshing With Flail (August)	1,000	125.00
1976 Picking Grapes (September)	1,000	125.00
1976 Sowing Winter Corn (October)	1,000	125.00
1977 Gathering Acorns to Feed the Pigs (November)	1,000	125.00
1977 Pig Killing (December)	1,000	125.00
Cathedral		
1973 Christ on Cross	11,000	125.00
Christmas		
1973 Adoration of Magi	1,000	125.00
1973 Flight Into Egypt	1,000	125.00
Home at Christmas		
1978 Santa's Helpers	10,000	37.50
1979 Three Wisemen	10,000	37.50
Birds of North America		
1979 Great Horned Owl	10,000	37.50
Mother's Day		
1979 Tenderness	10,000	37.50
Royal Doulton		
Ports of Call		
1975 San Francisco	15,000	60.00
1976 New Orleans	15,000	65.00
1977 Venice	15,000	70.00
1978 Montmartre	15,000	70.00
I Remember America		
1977 Pennsylvania Pastorale	15,000	70.00
1978 Lovejoy Bridge	15,000	70.00
1979 Four Corners	15,000	75.00
Victorian Christmas		
1977 The Skater	Year	25.00
1978 Victorian Girl	Year	27.50
1979 Sleigh Ride	Year	29.95
All God's Children		
1978 Brighter Day	10,000	60.00
1979 Village Children	10,000	65.00
American Tapestries		
1978 Sleigh Bells	10,000	70.00
1979 Pumpkin Patch	10,000	70.00
Jungle Fantasy		
1979 Ark	10,000	75.00
1980 Compassion	10,000	75.00
Royal Grafton		
Twelve Days of Christmas		
1976 Partridge in Pear Tree	3,000	17.50
1977 Two Turtle Doves	3,000	17.50
1978 Three French Hens	3,000	21.50
1979 Four Colly Birds	3,000	26.50
1980 Five Gold Rings	3,000	35.00
Royal Worcester (Porcelain)		
Bicentennial		
1976 Independence	10,000	150.00
Fabulous Birds		
1976 Peacocks I	10,000	65.00
1977 Peacocks II	10,000	65.00
Audubon Birds		
1977 Warbler & Jay	5,000	150.00
1978 Kingbird & Sparrow	10,000	150.00
Chinoiserie		
1977 Bishop Sumner	Year	65.00
English Christmas		
1979 Christmas Eve	Year	60.00
Scenes of the English Countryside		
1980 Woodlands in April	*	55.00
1980 June In Country Garden	*	55.00
1980 July Beside River	*	55.00
1980 Wheatfields in August	*	55.00
1980 September on the Moors	*	55.00
1980 Country Lane in December	*	55.00
*Subscription period		
Spode		
Ray Harm Birds (Set of 12)		
1970 Rufus-Sided Towhee		
1970 Winter Wren		
1971 Eastern Bluebird		
1971 Stellar's Jay		
1971 Eastern Mockingbird		
1971 Barn Swallow		
1971 Rose-Breasted Grosbeak		
1971 Cardinal		
1972 Western Tanager		
1972 Woodpecker		
1972 Chickadee		

	EDITION LIMIT	ISSUE PRICE (US)
1972 American Goldfinch	5,000	$ 300.00
Wedgwood		
Calendar		
1971 Zodiac Sign	Year	12.00
1972 Carousel	Year	12.95
1973 Bountiful Butterfly	Year	12.95
1974 Knights of Camelot	Year	14.00
1975 Children's Game	Year	15.00
1976 Robin	Year	25.00
1977 Tonateuk — The Aztec Sun	Year	30.00
1978 Samurai	Year	30.00
1979 Sacred Scarab	Year	35.00
1980 Safari	Year	35.00
Children's Story		
1971 Sandman	Year	30.00
1972 Tinder Box	Year	30.00
1973 Emperor's New Clothes	Year	30.00
1974 Ugly Duckling	Year	10.00
1975 Little Mermaid	Year	14.00
1976 Hansel & Gretel	Year	17.00
1977 Rumpelstiltskin	Year	17.00
1978 Frog Prince	Year	15.00
1979 Golden Goose	Year	15.00
1980 Rapunzel	Year	16.00
(Single issue)		
1978 Tri-Color Decade Christmas	10,000	325.00
(Single issue)		
1978 Anniversary Christmas	Year	130.00
Trophy		
1978 Tutankhamun	500	1,000.00
1978 Ankhesenamum	500	1,000.00
Child's Christmas		
1979 Snowman	Year	35.00

INDIA

	EDITION LIMIT	ISSUE PRICE (US)
Sarna		
Christmas		
1975 Holy Family	4,000	17.50

ITALY

	EDITION LIMIT	ISSUE PRICE (US)
Anri		
Mother's Day		
1972 Alpine Mother & Children	5,000	35.00
1973 Alpine Mother & Children	5,000	40.00
1974 Alpine Mother & Children	5,000	50.00
1975 Alpine Stroll	5,000	60.00
1976 Knitting	5,000	60.00
Father's Day		
1972 Alpine Father & Children	5,000	35.00
1973 Alpine Father & Children	5,000	40.00
1974 Cliff Gazing	5,000	50.00
1975 Sailing	5,000	60.00
Ferrandiz Birthday		
1972 Birthday Girl	Year	15.00
1972 Birthday Boy	Year	15.00
1973 Birthday	Year	20.00
1974 Birthday Girl	Year	22.00
1974 Birthday Boy	Year	22.00
1975 Birthday Girl	Year	35.00
Ferrandiz Mother's Day		
1972 Mother Sewing	2,500	35.00
1973 Mother & Child	1,500	40.00
1974 Mother & Child	1,500	50.00
1975 Mother Holding Dove	1,500	60.00
1976 Mother and Child	1,500	60.00
1977 Girl With Flowers	1,500	65.00
1978 Beginning	3,000	77.50
1979 All Hearts	3,000	120.00
Ferrandiz Christmas		
1972 Finishing Cradle	2,500	35.00
1973 Boy With Lamb	Year	40.00
1974 Nativity	Year	40.00
1975 Flight Into Egypt	Year	40.00
1976 Mary & Joseph Pray	Year	40.00
1977 Girl with Tree	4,000	65.00
1978 Leading the Way	4,000	77.50
1979 Drummer Boy	4,000	120.00
Ferrandiz Wedding Day		
1972 Wedding	Year	40.00
1973 Wedding	Year	40.00
1974 Wedding	Year	48.00
1975 Wedding	Year	60.00
1976 Wedding	Year	60.00
Jubilee (Single issue)		
1978 Spring Dance	2,500	500.00
Capo Di Monte		
Christmas		
1972 Cherubs	500	55.00
1973 Bells & Holly	500	55.00
1974 Christmas	1,000	60.00
1975 Christmas	1,000	60.00
1976 Christmas	250	65.00
Mother's Day		
1973 Mother's Day	500	55.00
1974 Mother's Day	500	60.00

	EDITION LIMIT	ISSUE PRICE (US)
1975 Mother's Day	500	$ 60.00
1976 Mother's Day	500	65.00
Carlo Monti		
Mother's Day		
1973 Madonna & Child	2,000	35.00
Count Agazzi		
Famous Personalities		
1968 Famous Personalities	600	8.00
1970 Famous Personalities	1,000	12.50
1973 Famous Personalities	600	15.00
(Single issue)		
1969 Apollo II	1,000	17.00
Children's Hour		
1970 Owl	2,000	12.50
1971 Cat	2,000	12.50
1972 Pony	2,000	12.50
1973 Panda	2,000	12.50
Easter		
1971 Playing the Violin	600	12.50
1972 At Prayer	600	12.50
1973 Winged Cherub	600	12.50
Mother's Day		
1972 Mother's Day	144	35.00
1973 Mother's Day	720	19.50
Father's Day		
1972 Father's Day	144	35.00
1973 Father's Day	288	19.50
Christmas		
1973 Christmas	1,000	19.50
(Single issue)		
1973 Peace	720	12.50
Kings		
Mother's Day		
1973 Dancing Girl	1,500	100.00
1974 Dancing Boy	1,500	115.00
1975 Motherly Love	1,500	140.00
1976 Maiden	1,500	180.00
Christmas		
1973 Adoration	1,500	150.00
1974 Madonna	1,500	150.00
1975 Heavenly Choir	1,500	160.00
1976 Girl and Brother	1,500	200.00
Veneto Flair		
Christmas		
1971 Three Kings	1,500	45.00
1972 Shepherds	2,000	45.00
1973 Christ Child	2,000	55.00
1974 Angel	2,000	55.00
Wildlife		
1971 Deer	500	37.50
1972 Elephant	1,000	37.50
1973 Puma	2,000	37.50
1974 Tiger	2,000	40.00
Birds		
1972 Owl	2,000	37.50
1973 Falcon	2,000	27.50
1974 Mallard Duck	2,000	45.00
Mother's Day		
1972 Madonna and Child	2,000	55.00
1973 Madonna and Child	2,000	55.00
1974 Mother and Son	2,000	55.00
1975 Daughter and Doll	2,000	45.00
1976 Son and Daughter	2,000	55.00
1977 Mother and Child	2,000	50.00
1977 Crib Scene	2,000	50.00
Easter		
1973 Rabbits	2,000	50.00
1974 Chicks	2,000	50.00
1975 Lamb	2,000	50.00
1976 Composite	2,000	55.00
Goddess		
1973 Pomona	1,500	75.00
1974 Diana	1,500	75.00
Cats		
1974 Persian	2,000	40.00
1975 Siamese	2,000	45.00
1976 Tabby	2,000	45.00
Valentine's Day		
1977 Valentine Boy	3,000	45.00
1978 Valentine Girl	3,000	45.00
Flower Children		
1978 Rose	3,000	45.00
1979 Orchid	3,000	60.00
1980 Camillia	3,000	65.00
La Belle Femme		
1978 Lily	9,500	70.00
1978 Gigi	9,500	76.50
1980 Dominique	9,500	76.50
1980 Gabrielle	9,500	76.50
American Landscape		
1979 Hudson Valley	7,500	75.00
1980 Northwest Cascade	7,500	75.00
Children's Christmas		
1979 Carolers	7,500	60.00
1980 Heading Home	7,500	70.00

JAPAN

	EDITION LIMIT	ISSUE PRICE (US)
Manjundo		
Chinese Lunar Calendar		
1972 Year of the Rat	5,000	$ 15.00
1973 Year of the Ox	5,000	15.00
Noritake		
Christmas		
1975 Madonna with Child	3,000	42.00
1976 Gratia Hoso Kawa	3,000	54.00
1977 Julia Otaa	3,000	83.00
1978 Amakusa Shiro	3,000	109.00
1979 Munzio Ito	3,000	124.00
Annual		
1977 Paradise Birds	3,000	380.00
1978 Chrysanthemums	3,000	494.00
1979 Cranes	3,000	556.00
Sango		
Christmas		
1974 Spark of Christmas	5,000	25.00
1975 Christmas Eve in Country	5,000	27.50
1976 Madonna & Child	5,000	25.00
1976 Undesired Slumber	7,500	25.00
1977 Togetherness	5,000	25.00
Mother's Day		
1976 Spring Delight	7,500	20.00
1977 Broken Wing	5,000	22.50
Sango (Kern)		
Living American Artist		
1976 Sweathearts (Rockwell)	10,000	30.00
1977 Apache Girl (Perillo)	5,000	35.00
1978 Natural Habitat	5,000	40.00
Great Achievements in Art		
1980 Arabian	3,000	65.00

MEXICO

	EDITION LIMIT	ISSUE PRICE (US)
Bonita Silver Co.		
Mother's Day		
1972 Mother and Baby	4,000	125.00
Roman Ceramica Excelsis		
Masterpiece Collection		
1979 Adoration	5,000	65.00
1980 Madonna of Grapes	5,000	N/A

NETHERLANDS

	EDITION LIMIT	ISSUE PRICE (US)
Blue Delft (Schoonhaven)		
Christmas		
1970 Drawbridge Near Binnehof	Year	12.00
1971 St. Lauren's Church	Year	12.00
1972 Church at Bierkade	Year	12.00
1973 St. Jan's Church	Year	12.00
1974 Dongeradeel	Year	13.00
1975 Maassluis	Year	15.00
1976 Montelbaanstower	Year	15.00
1977 Harbour Tower of Hoorn	Year	19.50
1978 Binnenpoort Gate	Year	21.00
Mother's Day		
1971 Mother & Daughter of The 1600s	Year	12.00
1972 Mother & Daughter of Isle of Urk	Year	12.00
1973 Rembrandt's Mother	Year	12.00
Father's Day		
1971 Francisco Lana's Airship	Year	12.00
1972 Dr. Jonathon's Balloon	Year	12.00
Crown Delft		
Christmas		
1969 Man by Tree	Year	10.00
1970 Two Sleigh Riders	Year	10.00
1971 Christmas Tree on Market Square	Year	10.00
1972 Baking for Christmas	Year	10.00
Mother's Day		
1970 Sheep	Year	10.00
1971 Stork	Year	10.00
1972 Ducks	Year	10.00
1973 Mother's Day	1,000	10.00
Father's Day		
1970 Father's Day	Year	10.00
1971 Father's Day	Year	10.00
1972 Father's Day	1,000	10.00
1973 Father's Day	1,000	10.00
Kurz (Shuler International)		
Christmas		
1972 Christmas	500	60.00
1973 Christmas	500	70.00
1974 Christmas	500	65.00
Mother's Day		
1973 Mother's Day	500	65.00
Metawa		
Christmas		
1972 Skaters	3,000	30.00
1973 One-Horse Sleigh	1,500	30.00
1974 Sailboat	Year	35.00
Royal Delft		
Christmas		
1915 Glory to God, Christmas Bells (10")	Year	N/A
1915 Christmas Star (7")	Year	N/A
1916 Star — Floral Design (10")	Year	N/A
1916 Cradle of Child (10")	Year	N/A
1917 Shepherd With Sheep in Stable (10")	Year	N/A
1917 Christmas Star (10")	Year	N/A
1917 Shepherd With Sheep in Stable (10")	Year	N/A
1918 Christmas Star — Peace on Earth (10")	Year	N/A
1919 Church (10")	Year	N/A
1919 Christmas Star (10")	Year	N/A
1920 Holly Wreath (10")	Year	N/A
1920 Church Tower (10")	Year	N/A
1921 Canal Boatman (10")	Year	N/A
1921 Christmas Star (10")	Year	N/A
1922 Landscape (10")	Year	N/A
1922 Christmas Wreath (10")	Year	N/A
1923 Shepherd (10")	Year	N/A
1923 Christmas Star (10")	Year	N/A
1924 Christmas Star (10")	Year	N/A
1924 Town Gate With Shepherd (10")	Year	N/A
1925 Towngate in Delft (10")	Year	N/A
1925 Christmas Star (10")	Year	N/A
1926 Christmas Star (10")	Year	N/A
1926 Bell Tower (7")	Year	N/A
1926 Windmill Landscape (10")	Year	N/A
1927 Christmas Star (10")	Year	N/A
1927 Sailing Boat (10")	Year	N/A
1928 Christmas Poinsettia (10")	Year	N/A
1927 Church Tower (7")	Year	N/A
1928 Mill Christmas (7")	Year	N/A
1928 Lighthouse Christmas (10")	Year	N/A
1929 Christmas Bell (10")	Year	N/A
1929 Church Spire (7")	Year	N/A
1929 Small Dutch Town (10")	Year	N/A
1930 Church Entrance, Delft (10")	Year	N/A
1930 Christmas Rose (10")	Year	N/A
1930 Sailing Boat (7")	Year	N/A
1931 Christmas Star (10")	Year	N/A
1931 Snow Landscape (10")	Year	N/A
1932 Church Tower (7")	Year	N/A
1932 Bell Tower (7")	Year	N/A
1932 Fireplace (10")	Year	N/A
1932 Christmas Star (10")	Year	N/A
1933 Interior Scene with/Exterior View (10")	Year	N/A
1934 Interior Scene (10")	Year	N/A
1934 Snowy Stable (10")	Year	N/A
1935 Interior Scene with/Exterior View (10")	Year	N/A
1936 Interior Scene with/Exterior View (10")	Year	N/A
1937 Interior Scene with/Exterior View (10")	Year	N/A
1938 Interior Scene with/Exterior View (10")	Year	N/A
1939 Interior Scene with/Well-Staircase (10")	Year	N/A
1940 Interior with/Christmas Tree (10")	Year	N/A
1941 Interior Scene Fireplace & Tree (10")	Year	N/A
1955 Christmas Star (9")	Year	N/A
1955 Church Tower (10")	200	20.00
1956 Two Christmas Bells in Floral (9")	Year	N/A
1956 Landscape (10")	200	20.00
1956 Flower Design (9")	Year	N/A
1957 Christmas Star (9")	Year	N/A
1957 Landscape (10")	225	22.00
1958 Christmas Star (9")	Year	N/A
1958 View of Village at Riverside (10")	225	25.00
1959 View of Village at Riverside (10")	250	25.00
1959 Landscape With Mill (7")	400	10.00
1960 Landscape (7")	400	10.00
1960 Street in Delft (10")	250	25.00
1961 Snow Landscape (7")	500	10.00
1961 Village Scene with/Church Town (10")	260	30.00
1962 Town View (7")	500	10.00
1962 Tower in Leeuwarden (10")	275	30.00
1963 Mill in Zeddam (7")	500	15.00
1963 Tower in Enkhuisen (10")	275	35.00
1964 Tower in Hoorn (10")	300	35.00
1964 Mill in Poelenburg (7")	600	15.00
1965 Towngate in Kampen (7")	600	15.00
1965 Corn-Mill in Rhoon (10")	300	35.00
1966 Towngate in Medemblik (7")	600	20.00
1966 Snuff Mill in Rotterdam (10")	325	40.00
1967 Mill in Hazerswoude (7")	700	20.00
1967 Tower in Amsterdam (10")	350	45.00
1968 Mill in Schiedam (7")	700	25.00
1968 Tower in Amsterdam "Schreierstoren" (10")	350	60.00
1969 Mill Near Gorkum (7")	800	35.00
1969 Church in Utrecht (10")	400	60.00
1970 Mill Near Haarlem (7")	1,500	$ 25.00
1970 Cathedral in Veere (10")	500	60.00
1971 Towngate at Zierikzee (7")	3,500	25.00
1971 "Dom" Tower in Utrecht (10")	550	60.00
1972 Towngate at Elburg (7")	3,500	40.00
1972 Church in Edam (10")	1,500	70.00
1973 Towngate at Amersfoort (7")	4,500	50.00
1973 DeWaag in Alkmaar (10")	1,500	75.00
1974 Watergate at Sneek (7")	4,500	80.00
1974 Kitchen in Hindeloopen (10")	1,500	160.00
1975 Towngate at Amsterdam (7")	1,000	140.00
1975 Farmer in Laren (10")	1,500	250.00
1976 Towngate in Gorinehem (7")	4,500	115.00
1976 Farmer's Wife in Staphorst (10")	1,500	220.00
1977 Dromedaris Tower (7")	4,500	140.00
1977 Farm Family in Spakenburg (10")	1,500	277.00
1978 Winter Skating Scene (10")	1,000	277.00
1978 Christmas Fisherman (7")	1,500	140.00
1978 Christmas Angels (7")	1,500	140.00
Mother's Day		
1971 Mother & Daughter (Volendam)	2,500	50.00
1972 Mother & Daughter (Hindeloopen)	2,500	40.00
1973 Mother & Daughter (Marken)	3,000	50.00
1974 Mother & Daughter (Zuid-Beveland)	Year	80.00
1975 Mother & Daughter (Spakenburg)	Year	100.00
1976 Mother & Daughter (Scheveningen)	Year	115.00
Father's Day		
1972 Father & Son (Volendam)	1,500	40.00
1973 Father & Son (Hindeloopen)	2,000	40.00
1974 Father & Son (Marken)	1,000	80.00
1975 Father & Son (Zuid-Beveland)	Year	80.00
1976 Father & Son (Spakenburg)	Year	140.00
Easter		
1973 Dutch Easter Palm (7")	3,500	75.00
1973 Dutch Easter Palm (10")	3,500	N/A
1974 Dutch Easter Palm	1,000	110.00
1975 Dutch Easter Palm	1,000	125.00
1976 Dutch Easter Palm	1,000	175.00
Valentine		
1973 Enduring Beauty	1,500	75.00
1974 Valentine	1,000	125.00
1975 Valentine	1,000	125.00
1976 Valentine	1,000	175.00
Special Bicentenary		
1976 George Washington	2,500	350.00
1976 Eagle Plate	5,000	150.00
Zenith Delftware		
Hans Brinker		
1972 Skating	500	60.00
1973 Gretel Tending Geese	750	60.00
Anniversary		
1973 Autumn	500	45.00
1973 Spring	500	45.00
1973 Summer	500	45.00
1973 Winter	500	45.00
Birthday Boy		
1973 Monday's Child	3,000	15.00
1973 Tuesday's Child	3,000	15.00
1973 Wednesday's Child	3,000	15.00
1973 Thursday's Child	3,000	15.00
1973 Friday's Child	3,000	15.00
1973 Saturday's Child	3,000	15.00
1973 Sunday's Child	3,000	15.00
Birthday Girl		
1973 Monday's Child	3,000	15.00
1973 Tuesday's Child	3,000	15.00
1973 Wednesday's Child	3,000	15.00
1973 Thursday's Child	3,000	15.00
1973 Friday's Child	3,000	15.00
1973 Saturday's Child	3,000	15.00
1973 Sunday's Child	3,000	15.00

NORWAY

	EDITION LIMIT	ISSUE PRICE (US)
Porsgrund		
Jubilee		
1970 Femboringer	Year	25.00
Easter		
1972 Ducks	Year	7.00
1973 Birds	Year	10.00
1974 Rabbits	Year	11.00
1975 Chicks	Year	16.00
1976 Sheep in Field	Year	18.00
1977 Butterflies	Year	23.00

	EDITION LIMIT	ISSUE PRICE (US)
PORTUGAL		
Calhoun's Collectors Society		
Crystal Maidens		
1979 Spring — Strawberry Season	2,500	N/A
1979 Summer — Sunshine Season	2,500	N/A
1979 Autumn — Scenic Season	2,500	N/A
1979 Winter — Snowflake Season	2,500	N/A
SPAIN		
Santa Clara		
Mother's Day		
1971 Mother and Child	10,000	15.00
1971 Mother and Children	12,000	15.00
SWEDEN		
Kosta		
Annual		
1971 Madonna & Child	Year	30.00
1972 St. George & Dragon	Year	30.00
1973 Viking Ship	Year	40.00
1974 Annual	Year	40.00
Rorstrand		
Mother's Day		
1971 Mother & Child	Year	15.00
1972 Shelling Peas	Year	15.00
1973 Old Fashioned Picnic	Year	16.00
1974 Candle Lighting	Year	18.00
1975 Pontius on Floor	Year	20.00
1976 Apple Picking	Year	20.00
1977 Kitchen	Year	27.50
1978 Azalea	Year	27.50
1979 Studio Idyll	Year	31.50
Father's Day		
1971 Father & Child	Year	15.00
1972 Meal at Home	Year	15.00
1973 Tilling Fields	Year	16.00
1974 Fishing	Year	18.00
1975 Painting	Year	20.00
1976 Plowing	Year	20.00
1977 Sawing	Year	27.50
1978 Self Portrait	Year	27.50
1979 The Bridge	Year	31.50
Annual		
1979 Silent Night, Holy Night	N/A	173.00
UNITED STATES		
Abbey Press (Viletta)		
Mother's Day		
1979 Special Mothers are God's Creation	6,000	37.50
Christmas		
1979 Christmas is a Gentle Season	6,000	37.50
Accent on Art		
Mother Goose		
1978 Jack & Jill	5,000	59.50
Nobility of the Plains		
1978 Commanche	12,500	80.00
1979 Moving Day	3,500	80.00
Addams Family (Schmid)		
Mother's Day		
1972 On Tracks	Year	10.00
Christmas		
1972 Christmas Dinner	Year	10.00
American Archives (International Silver)		
(Single issue)		
1972 Christmas Rose	2,500	100.00
American Arts Services (Viletta)		
Children		
1979 Last of Ninth	5,000	45.00
American Commemorative (Gorham)		
Southern Landmark		
1973 Monticello	9,800	35.00
1973 Williamsburg	9,800	40.00
1974 Beauvoir	9,800	40.00
1974 Cabildo	9,800	40.00
1975 Hermitage	9,800	40.00
1975 Oak Hill	9,800	40.00
1976 Governor Tryon's Palace	9,800	40.00
1976 Montpelier	9,800	40.00
1977 Elmscourt	9,800	40.00
1977 Ashland	9,800	40.00
1978 Mt. Vernon	9,800	40.00
American Express (Gorham)		
Four Freedoms		
1976 Freedom to Worship	Year	37.50
976 Freedom from Want	Year	37.50
976 Freedom from Fear	Year	37.50
976 Freedom of Speech	Year	37.50
Birds of North America		
1978 Saw Whet Owls	9,800	38.00
978 Bobwhite Quail	9,800	38.00
978 October Cardinals	9,800	38.00
978 Long-Eared Owl	9,800	38.00
978 Eastern Bluebirds	9,800	38.00
978 American Woodcock	9,800	38.00
978 Ruffed Grouse	9,800	38.00
978 House Wren	9,800	38.00

	EDITION LIMIT	ISSUE PRICE (US)
American Express (Lenox)		
A: ierican Trees of Christmas		
1976 Douglas Fir	Year	$ 60.00
1977 Scotch Pine	Year	60.00
American Preservation Guild (Gorham)		
Catesby Collection		
1977 Cardinal	9,900	39.00
American Rose Society (Gorham)		
All American Rose		
1975 Oregold	9,800	38.00
1976 America	9,800	38.00
1976 Cathedral	9,800	38.00
1976 Seashell	9,800	38.00
1976 Yankee Doodle	9,800	38.00
1977 Double Delight	9,800	38.00
Antique Trader		
Currier & Ives		
1969 Baseball	2,000	9.00
1969 Franklin Experiment	2,000	9.00
1969 Haying Time	2,000	9.00
1969 Winter in Country	2,000	9.00
Easter		
1971 Child and Lamb	1,500	10.95
1972 Shepherd with Lamb	1,000	10.95
Mother's Day		
1971 Madonna and Child	1,500	10.95
1972 Mother Cat and Kittens	1,000	10.95
Father's Day		
1971 Pilgrim Father	1,500	10.95
1972 Deer Family	1,000	10.95
Thanksgiving		
1971 Pilgrims	1,500	10.95
1972 First Thanksgiving	1,000	10.95
Christmas		
1971 Christ Child	1,500	10.95
1972 Flight Into Egypt	1,000	10.95
C. M. Russell		
1971 Bad One	2,000	11.95
1971 Discovery of Last Chance Gulch	2,000	11.95
1971 Doubtful Visitor	2,000	11.95
1971 Innocent Allies	2,000	11.95
1971 Medicine Man	2,000	11.95
Bible		
1973 David & Goliath	2,000	10.75
1973 Moses and Golden Idol	2,000	10.75
1973 Noah's Ark	2,000	10.75
1973 Samson	2,000	10.75
Arizona Artisan		
Christmas		
1974 Mexican Christmas	Year	20.00
1975 Navajo Christmas	Year	20.00
Thanksgiving		
1975 Navajo Thanksgiving Feast	Year	15.00
Arlington Mint		
Christmas		
1972 Hands in Prayer	Year	125.00
Armstrong		
Bicentennial		
1971 Calm Before Storm	250	250.00
1972 Gaspee Incident	175	250.00
Artists of the World		
World of Game Birds		
1977 Mallards	5,000	45.00
1978 Gambel Quail	5,000	45.00
1979 American Autumn Ring-necked Pheasant	5,000	50.00
Don Ruffin Self-Portrait		
1979 Clown Also Cries	7,500	65.00
Audubon Crystal Ltd.		
Endangered Birds		
1976 Kirtland's Warbler	5,000	195.00
1976 American Eagle	5,000	195.00
1977 Peregrine Falcon	5,000	200.00
Avondale		
Annual		
1978 Melissa	28,050	65.00
1979 First Born	12,000	70.00
1980 Melissa's Brother	Year	70.00
Myths of the Sea		
1979 Poseidon	15,000	70.00
Tribute to Ageless Art		
1979 Court Jesters	10,000	70.00
World of Dance		
1979 Prima Ballerina	15,000	70.00
Brantwood Collection		
Marian Carlsen Mother's Day		
1978 Jennifer and Jenny Fur	Year	45.00
1979 Football Brothers	5,000	45.00
Howe Christmas		
1978 Visit from Santa	Year	45.00
(Single issue)		
1978 Tribute to Rockwell	Year	35.00
John Falter Christmas		
1979 Christmas Morning	5,000	24.50
Rockwell Mother's Day		
1979 Homecoming	20,000	39.50

	EDITION LIMIT	ISSUE PRICE (US)
Little Clown		
1979 Going to Circus	5,000	$ 29.50
John Brindle Fine Arts		
Fantasy in Motion		
1978 Little Blue Norse	3,000	75.00
1979 Horse of a Different Color	3,000	75.00
Moods of the Orient		
1978 Softly, Sun Sets	4,000	75.00
Expressions		
1979 Quiet Eyes	3,000	60.00
Brown & Bigelow (Gorham)		
Grandpa and Me		
1977 Gay Blades	Year	55.00
Clown Series		
1977 Runaway	7,500	45.00
1978 Its Your Move	7,500	45.00
1979 Understudy	7,500	45.00
Traveling Salesman		
1977 Traveling Salesman	7,500	35.00
1978 Country Peddler	7,500	40.00
1978 Horse Trader	7,500	40.00
Wilderness Wings		
1978 Gliding In	5,000	35.00
1979 Taking Off	5,000	40.00
Rockwell Four Seasons (Bronze)		
1979 Adventurers Between Adventures	9,500	55.00
Cowboy Series		
1980 Sharing an Apple	5,000	35.00
1980 Split Decision	5,000	35.00
1980 Hiding Out	5,000	35.00
Mother's Day		
1980 Family Circus	5,000	25.00
California Porcelain and Bronze		
The Best of Sascha		
1979 Flower Bouquet	7,500	65.00
Vanishing Animals		
1979 Asian Monarchs	7,500	40.00
1979 Snow Leopards	7,500	45.00
Carson Mint (Viletta)		
Yesterday's Children		
1978 Lisa and Jumeau Doll	5,000	60.00
1979 Adrianne and Bye-Lo Baby	5,000	60.00
The Hollywood Squares		
1979 Peter Marshall	100 Days	28.50
1980 George Gobel	100 Days	28.50
Moment in Time		
1979 Freedom Flight	5,000	55.00
Old Fashioned Mother's Day		
1979 Daisies from Mary-Beth	20 Days	37.50
1980 Daisies from Jimmy	20 Days	37.50
America Has Heart		
1980 My Heart's Desire	Year	24.50
Magic Afternoon		
1980 Enchanted Garden	5,000	39.50
Castleton China		
Natural History		
1973 Painted Lady	1,500	40.00
1973 Roseate Spoonbill	1,500	40.00
(Single issue)		
1976 Gen. Douglas MacArthur	1,000	30.00
Castleton (American Historical)		
Aviation		
1972 Amelia Earhart	3,500	40.00
1972 Charles Lindberg	3,500	40.00
Castleton (Shenango)		
Bicentennial		
1972 New Dawn	7,600	60.00
1972 Turning Point	7,600	60.00
1973 Valley Forge	7,600	60.00
1973 Declaration	7,600	60.00
1973 Star Spangled Banner	7,600	60.00
1973 U.S.S. Constitution	7,600	60.00
1974 One Nation	7,600	60.00
1974 Westward Ho	7,600	60.00
Certified Rarities		
Postal Artists		
1978 Colias Eurydice	15,000	60.00
1979 Euphydryas Phaeton	7,500	60.00
Chilmark		
Family Christmas		
1978 Trimming Tree	10,000	65.00
In Appreciation		
1979 Flowers of Field	10,000	65.00
Holy Night		
1979 Wisemen	10,000	65.00
The Twelve Days of Christmas		
1979 Partridge in Pear Tree	10,000	89.50
Cleveland Mint		
Da Vinci		
1972 Last Supper	5,000	125.00
Collector Creations (Reed & Barton)		
Thomas Nast Christmas		
1973 Christmas	750	100.00

	EDITION LIMIT	ISSUE PRICE (US)
(Single issue)		
1973 Alice in Wonderland	750	$ 100.00
Collector's Heirlooms (Viletta)		
Childhood Memories		
1978 Jennifer by Candlelight	5,000	60.00
Joys of Motherhood		
1978 Crystal's Joy	7,500	60.00
Children at Play		
1979 Maple Leaf Noses	7,500	60.00
Passing of Plains Indians		
1979 Cheyenne Chieftain	7,500	65.00
Collectors Weekly		
American		
1971 Miss Liberty	500	12.50
1972 Miss Liberty	900	12.50
1973 Eagle	900	9.75
Continental Mint		
Tom Sawyer		
1976 Taking His Medicine	5,000	60.00
1977 Painting Fence	5,000	60.00
1978 Lost in Cave	5,000	60.00
1979 Smoking Pipe	5,000	60.00
(Single issue)		
1979 Butter Girl	7,000	60.00
Creative World		
Pearl Buck (Single issue)		
1972 Good Earth	10,000	N/A
Four Seasons		
1972 Fall (Silverplate)	2,000	75.00
1972 Fall (Sterling)	2,000	125.00
1973 Winter (Silverplate)	2,000	75.00
1973 Winter (Sterling)	250	125.00
1973 Spring (Silverplate)	300	75.00
1973 Spring (Sterling)	750	125.00
1974 Summer (Silverplate)	300	75.00
1974 Summer (Sterling)	750	125.00
Brown's Rockwells		
1977 Looking Out to Sea	15,000	50.00
1978 Yankee Doodle	15,000	50.00
1979 Girl at Mirror	15,000	55.00
Immortals of Early American Literature		
1978 Village Smithy	15,000	50.00
1979 Rip Van Winkle	15,000	50.00
Aesop's Fables		
1979 Fox & Grapes	9,750	85.00
Crown Parian		
Rosemary Calder		
1978 Affection	7,500	60.00
James Daly		
1978 Sweet Dreams	7,500	55.00
Beautiful Cats of the World		
1979 Sheena	5,000	60.00
1980 Sheena and Sheena's Cubs	5,000	60.00
Penni Anne Cross		
1979 Crow Baby	7,500	55.00
Julian Ritter		
1979 Reve de Ballet	7,500	55.00
Red Skelton		
1979 Freddie in Bathtub	10,000	55.00
Wells Fargo Collection		
1979 Under Surveillance	10,000	65.00
1979 Promised Land	10,000	65.00
1979 Winter Song	10,000	65.00
1979 Turning Lead	10,000	65.00
Danbury Mint		
Currier & Ives		
1972 Christmas	7,500	125.00
1973 Christmas	7,500	125.00
Old Masters		
1972 Adam	7,500	150.00
1973 Pieta	7,500	150.00
1973 Moses	7,500	150.00
R.J. Ernst Enterprises (Viletta)		
The Performance		
1979 Act I	5,000	65.00
Women of the West		
1979 Expectation	10,000	39.50
1979 Silver Dollar Sal	10,000	39.50
1980 First Day	10,000	39.50
1980 Dolly	10,000	39.50
Love Is		
1980 Rufus and Roxanne	Year	14.95
Fairmont		
Carousel Horses		
1977 (Set of two)	3,000	80.00
Fiddler's People		
1978 Fiddler on Roof	7,500	60.00
1979 Tevya	7,500	60.00
Timeless Moments		
1978 Tenderness	5,000	45.00
1979 Renaissance	5,000	50.00
Olaf Wieghorst		
1978 Sioux Warrior	5,000	65.00
1979 Indian Scout	5,000	65.00
Rural America		
1978 Fence	5,000	45.00
Children of America		
1979 Eskimo Girl	3,000	48.00

	EDITION LIMIT	ISSUE PRICE (US)
Gnomes Christmas		
1979 Christmas Bliss	10,000	$ 24.95
Gnomes Four Seasons		
1980 Little Swinger (Spring)	15,000	29.50
1980 Gnome de Bloom (Summer)	15,000	29.50
1980 Lookouts (Fall)	15,000	29.50
1980 First Skater (Winter)	15,000	29.50
Fenton		
American Craftsman		
1970 Glassmaker	Year	10.00
1971 Printer	Year	10.00
1972 Blacksmith	Year	10.00
1973 Shoemaker	Year	10.00
1974 Cooper	Year	11.00
1975 Silversmith	Year	13.50
1976 Gunsmith	Year	13.50
1977 Potter	Year	15.00
1978 Wheelwright	Year	15.00
1979 Cabinetmaker	Year	15.00
1980 Tanner	Year	16.50
Christmas		
1970 Little Brown Church (Blue Satin)	Year	12.50
1970 Little Brown Church (Carnival)	Year	12.50
1970 Little Brown Church (Brown)	Year	17.50
1971 Old Brick Church (Blue Satin)	Year	12.50
1971 Old Brick Church (Brown)	Year	17.50
1971 Old Brick Church (Carnival)	Year	12.50
1971 Old Brick Church (White Satin)	Year	12.50
1972 Two Horned Church (Blue Satin)	Year	12.50
1972 Two Horned Church (Brown)	Year	17.50
1972 Two Horned Church (Carnival)	Year	12.50
1972 Two Horned Church (White Satin)	Year	12.50
1973 St. Mary's (Blue Satin)	Year	12.50
1973 St. Mary's (Carnival)	Year	12.50
1973 St. Mary's (White Satin)	Year	12.50
1973 St. Mary's (Brown)	Year	17.50
1974 Nation's Church (Blue Satin)	Year	13.50
1974 Nation's Church (Carnival)	Year	13.50
1974 Nation's Church (White Satin)	Year	13.50
1974 Nation's Church (Brown)	Year	18.50
1975 Birthplace of Liberty (Blue Satin)	Year	13.50
1975 Birthplace of Liberty (Carnival)	Year	13.50
1975 Birthplace of Liberty (White Satin)	Year	13.50
1975 Birthplace of Liberty (Brown)	Year	20.00
1976 Old North Church (Blue Satin)	Year	15.00
1976 Old North Church (Carnival)	Year	15.00
1976 Old North Church (White Satin)	Year	15.00
1976 Old North Church (Brown)	Year	25.00
1977 San Carlos (Blue Satin)	Year	15.00
1977 San Carlos (Carnival)	Year	15.00
1977 San Carlos (White Satin)	Year	15.00
Mother's Day		
1971 Madonna, Sleeping Child (Blue Satin)	Year	12.50
1971 Madonna, Sleeping Child (Carnival)	Year	12.50
1972 Madonna of Goldfinch (Blue Satin)	Year	12.50
1972 Madonna of Goldfinch (Carnival)	Year	12.50
1972 Madonna of Goldfinch (White Satin)	Year	12.50
1973 Cowper Madonna (Blue Satin)	Year	12.50
1973 Cowper Madonna (Carnival)	Year	12.50
1973 Cowper Madonna (White Satin)	Year	12.50
1974 Madonna of Grotto (Blue Satin)	Year	12.50
1974 Madonna of Grotto (Carnival)	Year	12.50
1974 Madonna of Grotto (White Satin)	Year	12.50

	EDITION LIMIT	ISSUE PRICE (US)
1975 Taddei Madonna (Blue Satin)	Year	$ 13.50
1975 Taddei Madonna (Carnival)	Year	13.50
1975 Taddei Madonna (White Satin)	Year	13.50
1976 Holy Night (Blue Satin)	Year	13.50
1976 Holy Night (Carnival)	Year	13.50
1976 Holy Night (White Satin)	Year	13.50
1977 Madonna & Child (Blue Satin)	Year	15.00
1977 Madonna & Child (Carnival)	Year	15.00
1977 Madonna & Child (White Satin)	Year	15.00
1978 Madonnina (White Satin)	Year	15.00
1978 Madonnina (Blue Satin)	Year	15.00
1978 Madonnina (Carnival)	Year	15.00
Valentine's Day		
1972 Romeo and Juliet (Blue Satin)	Year	15.00
1972 Romeo and Juliet (Carnival)	Year	15.00
Bicentennial		
1974 Eagle (Blue Satin)	Year	15.00
1975 Eagle (Red Satin)	Year	15.00
1976 Eagle (Chocolate)	Year	17.50
1976 Eagle (White Satin)	Year	15.00
Alliance		
1975 Lafayette and Washington (Blue Satin)	Year	15.00
1975 Lafayette and Washington (Red Satin)	Year	17.50
1975 Lafayette and Washington (White Satin)	Year	15.00
1976 Lafayette and Washington (Blue Satin)	Year	15.00
1976 Lafayette and Washington (Chocolate)	Year	17.50
1976 Lafayette and Washington (White Satin)	Year	15.00
Christmas Classics		
1979 Nature's Christmas	15,000	35.00
Fleetwood Collection (Gorham)		
Birds & Flowers of the Meadow and Garden		
1980 Robin and Crab Apple Blossom	*	39.00
1980 Goldfinch and Bull Thistle	*	39.00
1980 Cardinal and Wild Lupine	*	39.00
1980 Chickadee and New England Aster	*	39.00
1980 Baltimore Oriole and Morning Glory	*	39.00
1980 Blue Bird and Black-Eyed Susan	*	39.00
*Subscription period		
Fostoria		
American Milestones		
1971 Betsy Ross Flag	5,000	12.50
1972 National Anthem	8,000	12.50
1973 Washington Crossing Delaware	Year	12.50
1974 Spirit of '76	Year	13.00
1975 Mount Rushmore	Year	16.00
State Plates		
1971 California	6,000	12.50
1971 New York	12,000	12.50
1971 Ohio	3,000	12.50
1972 Florida	Year	12.50
1972 Hawaii	Year	12.50
1972 Pennsylvania	Year	12.50
1972 Massachusetts	Year	13.00
1972 Texas	Year	13.00
1973 Michigan	Year	13.50
Franklin Crystal		
Historical		
1976 Liberty Tree	10,927	120.00
Seven Seas		
1976 Atlantic Ocean	2,799	120.00
1976 Caribbean	2,799	120.00
1976 Indian Ocean	2,799	120.00
1976 Mediterranean	2,799	120.00
1976 Pacific	2,799	120.00
1976 South China Sea	2,799	120.00
1976 Arctic	2,799	120.00
Annual		
1977 Snowflake	3,428	185.00
1978 Snowbird	798	185.00
Rockwell's American Sweethearts		
1977 Youngsters at Play	1,004	120.00
1977 Teenagers Together	1,004	120.00
1978 Bride and Groom	1,004	120.00
1978 Proud Parents	1,004	120.00
1978 Graduation Day	1,004	120.00
1978 Retirement Kiss	1,004	120.00

	EDITION LIMIT	ISSUE PRICE (US)
Franklin Mint		
American West		
1972 Horizon's West (Silver)	5,860	$ 150.00
1972 Horizon's West (Gold)	67	2200.00
1973 Mountain Man (Silver)	5,860	150.00
1973 Mountain Man (Gold)	67	2200.00
1973 Prospector (Silver)	5,860	150.00
1973 Prospector (Gold)	67	2200.00
1973 Plains Hunter (Silver	5,860	150.00
1973 Plains Hunter (Gold)	67	2200.00
Audubon Society		
1972 Goldfinch	10,193	125.00
1972 Wood Duck	10,193	125.00
1973 Cardinal	10,193	125.00
1973 Ruffed Grouse	10,193	125.00
Presidential		
1972 George Washington	10,304	150.00
1972 John Adams	4,859	150.00
1972 Thomas Jefferson	4,933	150.00
1972 James Madison	3,058	150.00
1972 James Monroe	2,722	150.00
1972 John Quincy Adams	2,501	150.00
1972 Andrew Jackson	2,408	150.00
1973 Martin Van Buren	2,291	150.00
1973 William H. Harrison	2,182	150.00
1973 John Tyler	2,144	150.00
1973 James Polk	2,083	150.00
1973 Zachary Taylor	2,023	150.00
1973 Millard Fillmore	1,967	150.00
1974 Franklin Pierce	1,907	150.00
1974 James Buchanan	1,841	150.00
1974 Abraham Lincoln	2,955	150.00
1974 Andrew Johnson	1,777	150.00
1974 Ulysses S. Grant	1,754	150.00
1975 Rutherford B. Hayes	1,705	150.00
1975 James A. Garfield	1,675	150.00
1975 Chester A. Arthur	1,604	150.00
1975 Grover Cleveland	1,644	150.00
1976 Benjamin Harrison	1,619	150.00
1976 William McKinley	1,571	150.00
1976 Theodore Roosevelt	1,555	150.00
1976 William H. Taft	1,592	150.00
1976 Woodrow Wilson	1,563	150.00
1977 Warren G. Harding	1,544	150.00
1977 Calvin Coolidge	1,527	150.00
1977 Herbert Hoover	1,520	150.00
1977 Franklin D. Roosevelt	1,770	150.00
1977 Harry S. Truman	1,493	150.00
1978 Dwight D. Eisenhower	1,494	150.00
1978 John F. Kennedy	1,494	150.00
1978 Lyndon B. Johnson	1,483	150.00
1978 Richard M. Nixon	1,475	150.00
1978 Gerald R. Ford	N/A	150.00
1978 Jimmy Carter	N/A	150.00
Wyeth, James		
1972 Along Brandywine	19,670	125.00
1973 Winter Fox	10,394	125.00
1974 Riding to Hunt	10,751	150.00
1975 Skating on Brandywine	8,058	175.00
1976 Brandywine Battlefield	6,968	180.00
Younger's Bird		
1972 Cardinal	13,939	125.00
1972 Bobwhite	13,939	125.00
1972 Mallards	13,939	125.00
1972 American Bald Eagle	13,939	125.00
Audubon, John James		
1973 Wood Thrush	5,273	150.00
1973 Bald Eagle	3,005	150.00
1974 Night Heron	3,040	150.00
1974 Audubon's Warbler	3,034	150.00
Bernard Buffet		
1973 Gazelle	570	150.00
1974 Panda	570	150.00
1975 Giraffe	570	150.00
1976 Lion	570	150.00
1977 Rhinoceros	570	150.00
Bicentennial		
1973 Jefferson Drafting Declaration of Independence	8,556	175.00
1974 John Adams Champions Cause of Independence	8,442	175.00
1975 Caesar Rodney Decides Vote on Independence	8,319	175.00
1976 John Hancock Signs Declaration of Independence	10,166	175.00
Easter		
1973 Resurrection	7,116	175.00
1974 He Is Risen	3,719	185.00
1975 Last Supper	2,004	200.00
1976 Crucifixion	3,904	250.00
1977 Resurrection	1,206	250.00
Presidential Inaugural		
1973 Nixon/Agnew	10,483	150.00
1974 Ford (Silver)	1,141	200.00
1974 Ford (Gold)	11	3500.00
1977 Carter	928	225.00

	EDITION LIMIT	ISSUE PRICE (US)
Thanksgiving – by Dohanos		
1972 First Thanksgiving	10,142	$ 125.00
1973 American Wild Turkey	3,547	125.00
1974 Thanksgiving Prayer	5,150	150.00
1975 Family Thanksgiving	3,025	175.00
1976 Home From Hunt	3,474	175.00
Four Seasons		
1975 Spring Blossoms	2,648	240.00
1975 Summer Bouquet	2,648	240.00
1976 Autumn Garland	2,648	240.00
1976 Winter Spray	2,648	240.00
American Revolution Bicentennial		
1976 Boston Tea Party	3,596	75.00
1976 Patrick Henry Urges Armed Resistance	3,596	75.00
1976 Paul Revere's Ride	3,596	75.00
1976 Battle of Concord Bridge	3,596	75.00
1976 Capture of Fort Ticonderoga	3,596	75.00
1976 Battle of Bunker Hill	3,596	75.00
1977 Signing of Declaration	3,596	75.00
1977 Washington Crosses Delaware	3,596	75.00
1977 Burgoyne Defeated at Saratoga	3,596	75.00
1977 Winter at Valley Forge	3,596	75.00
1977 Alliance with France	3,596	75.00
1977 Bonhomme Richard Defeats Serapis	3,596	75.00
1977 Victory at Yorktown	3,596	75.00
Annual		
1977 Tribute to Arts	1,901	280.00
1978 Tribute to Nature	435	280.00
Belskie		
1977 Mother's Day	290	210.00
Freedom		
1977 Lafayette Joins Washington	546	275.00
Rockwell Thanksgiving		
1977 Old Fashioned Thanksgiving	2,361	185.00
Christmas		
1977 Skating Party	908	55.00
Franklin Porcelain		
Hans Christian Andersen		
1976 Princess and Pea	16,875	38.00
1976 Ugly Duckling	16,875	38.00
1976 Little Mermaid	16,875	38.00
1976 Emperor's New Clothes	16,875	38.00
1976 Steadfast Tin Soldier	16,875	38.00
1976 Little Match Girl	16,875	38.00
1977 Snow Queen	16,875	38.00
1977 Red Shoes	16,875	38.00
1977 Tinder Box	16,875	38.00
1977 Nightingale	16,875	38.00
1977 Thumbelina	16,875	38.00
1977 Shepherdess & Chimney Sweep	16,875	38.00
Christmas Annual		
1976 Silent Night	19,286	65.00
1977 Deck Halls	9,185	65.00
Flowers of the Year		
1976 January	27,394	50.00
1976 February	27,394	50.00
1977 March	27,394	50.00
1977 April	27,394	50.00
1977 May	27,394	50.00
1978 June	27,394	50.00
1978 July	27,394	50.00
1978 August	27,394	50.00
1978 September	27,394	50.00
1979 October	27,394	50.00
1979 November	27,394	50.00
1979 December	27,394	50.00
Grimm's Fairy Tales		
1978 Sleeping Beauty	27,006	42.00
1978 Twelve Dancing Princesses	27,006	42.00
1978 Brementown Musicians	27,006	42.00
1979 Golden Goose	27,006	42.00
1979 Hansel and Gretel	27,006	42.00
1979 Rapunzel	27,006	42.00
Songbirds of the World		
1977 Baltimore Oriole	20,225	55.00
1978 Bohemian Waxwing	20,225	55.00
Mark Twain		
1977 Whitewashing Fence	2,645	38.00
1977 Stealing a Kiss	2,645	38.00
1977 Traveling River	2,645	38.00
1977 Trading Lives	2,645	38.00
1977 Rafting Down River	2,645	38.00
1978 Riding Bronc	2,645	38.00
1978 Jumping Frog Race	2,645	38.00
1978 Facing Charging Knight	2,645	38.00
1978 Disguising Huck	2,645	38.00

	EDITION LIMIT	ISSUE PRICE (US)
1978 Living Along River	2,645	$ 38.00
1978 Learning to Smoke	2,645	38.00
1978 Finger Printing Pays Off	2,645	38.00
Frankoma		
Christmas		
1965 Goodwill Toward Man	Year	5.00
1966 Bethlehem Shepherds	Year	5.00
1967 Gifts for Christ Child	Year	5.00
1968 Flight Into Egypt	Year	5.00
1969 Laid In a Manger	Year	5.00
1970 King of Kings	Year	5.00
1971 No Room in Inn	Year	5.00
1972 Seeking Christ Child	Year	5.00
1973 Annunciation	Year	5.00
1974 She Loved & Cared	Year	5.00
1975 Peace on Earth	Year	5.00
1976 The Gift of Love	Year	6.00
1977 Birth of Eternal Life	Year	6.00
1978 All Nature Rejoiced	Year	6.00
1979 The Stay of Hope	Year	6.00
1980 Unto Us a Child is Born	Year	10.00
Bicentennial		
1972 Provocations	Year	6.00
1973 Patriots & Leaders	Year	6.00
1974 Battles, Independence	Year	5.00
1975 Victories for Independence	Year	6.00
1976 Symbols of Freedom	Year	6.00
Teenagers of The Bible		
1973 Jesus and Carpenter	Year	5.00
1974 David the Musician	Year	5.00
1975 Jonathan the Archer	Year	5.00
1976 Dorcas the Seamstress	Year	5.00
1977 Peter the Fisherman	Year	5.00
1978 Martha the Homemaker	Year	7.50
1979 Daniel the Courageous	Year	7.50
Madonnas		
1977 Grace Madonna	Year	12.50
1978 Madonna of Love	Year	12.50
George Washington Mint		
American Indian		
1972 Curley (Gold)	100	2,000.00
1972 Curley (Proof)	100	1,000.00
1972 Curley (Sterling)	7,300	150.00
1973 Two Moons (Gold)	100	2,000.00
1973 Two Moons (Proof)	100	1,000.00
1973 Two Moons (Sterling)	7,300	150.00
Mother's Day		
1972 Whistler's Mother (Sterling)	9,800	150.00
1972 Whistler's Mother (Proof)	100	1,000.00
1972 Whistler's Mother (Gold)	100	2,000.00
1974 Motherhood (Sterling)	2,300	175.00
1974 Motherhood (Proof)	100	1,000.00
1974 Motherhood (Gold)	100	2,000.00
Picasso		
1972 Don Quixote (Gold)	100	2,000.00
1972 Don Quixote (Proof)	100	1,000.00
1972 Don Quixote (Sterling)	9,800	125.00
Remington		
1972 Rattlesnake (Gold)	100	2,000.00
1972 Rattlesnake (Proof)	100	1,000.00
1972 Rattlesnake (Sterling)	800	250.00
Da Vinci		
1972 Last Supper	N/A	125.00
N. C. Wyeth		
1972 Uncle Sam's America (Gold)	100	2,000.00
1972 Uncle Sam's America (Proof)	100	1,000.00
1972 Uncle Sam's America (Sterling)	9,800	150.00
Israel Anniversary (Single issue)		
1973 Struggle	10,000	300.00
N. C. Wyeth		
1973 Massed Flags (Gold)	100	2,000.00
1973 Massed Flags (Proof)	100	1,000.00
1973 Massed Flags (Sterling)	2,300	150.00
Picasso (Single issue)		
1974 Rites of Spring (Sterling)	9,800	125.00
Remington (Single issue)		
1974 Coming Through Rye (Sterling)	2,500	300.00
Ghent Collection		
Christmas Wildlife		
1974 Cardinals in Snow	10,135	20.00
1975 We Three Kings	12,750	29.00
1976 Partridge and Pear Tree	12,750	32.00
1977 Foxes and Evergreen	12,750	32.00
1978 Snowy Owls	12,750	32.00
Mother's Day		
1975 Cotton Tail	12,750	20.00
1976 Mallard Family	12,750	29.00
1977 Chipmunks & Trillium	12,750	32.00
1978 Raccoon Family	12,750	32.00
1979 Maytime	12,750	32.00
The American Bicentennial Wildlife		
1976 American Bald Eagle	2,500	95.00

	EDITION LIMIT	ISSUE PRICE (US)
1976 American White-Tailed Deer	2,500	$ 95.00
1976 American Bison	2,500	95.00
1976 American Wild Turkey	2,500	95.00
Fausett Mural (Single issue)		
1976 From Sea to Shining Sea	1,976	76.00
Ghent Collection		
(Single issue)		
1978 Pilgrim of Peace	15 Days	29.50
Ghent Collection (Bing & Grøndahl)		
Hans Christian Andersen		
1979 Thumbelina	7,500	42.50
1979 Princess and Pea	7,500	42.50
1979 Wild Swans	7,500	42.50
1979 Emperor's New Clothes	7,500	42.50
1980 Little Mermaid	7,500	42.50
1980 Nightingale	7,500	42.50
Ghent Collection (Caverswall)		
Christmas Annual		
1979 Good King Wenceslaus	2,500	350.00
The Country Diary of An Edwardian Lady		
1979 April	10,000	80.00
1979 June	10,000	80.00
Ghent Collection (Fairmont)		
The Legends of Christmas		
1979 Bringing in Tree	5,000	65.00
Memory Annual		
1978 1977 Memory Plate	1,977	77.00
1979 1978 Memory Plate	1,978	78.00
1980 1979 Memory Plate	1,979	78.00
Israeli Commemorative (Single issue)		
1978 Promised Land	5,738	79.00
Spirit of America		
1978 Making of a Nation	1,978	78.00
1979 Growing Years	1,978	78.00
Ghent Collection (Gorham)		
April Fool Annual		
1978 April Fool's Day	10,000	35.00
1979 April Fool's Day	10,000	35.00
1980 April Fool's Day	10,000	37.50
Ghent Collection (Kaiser)		
Treasures of Tutankhamun		
1978 Golden Mask	3,247	90.00
1978 Golden Throne	3,247	90.00
1978 Horus Falcon	3,247	90.00
1978 Ivory Chest	3,247	90.00
Ghent Collection (Viletta)		
(Single issue)		
1979 Official 1980 Olympic Winter Games	13 Days	24.50
Gnomes United		
Gnomes		
1979 Gnome on Range	10,000	23.00
Gnome Patrol		
1979 Dr. Kwik	5,000	45.00
Golf Digest		
Second Hole (Single issue)		
1973 Dorado Beach Club	2,000	45.00
Twelfth Hole (Single issue)		
1973 Spyglass Hill	2,000	45.00
Gorham		
(Single issue)		
1970 American Family Tree	5,000	17.00
Lionel Barrymore		
1971 Quiet Waters	15,000	25.00
1972 San Pedro Harbor	15,000	25.00
1972 Little Boatyard (Silver)	1,000	100.00
1972 Nantucket (Silver)	1,000	100.00
Bicentennial		
1971 Burning of Gaspee (Pewter)	5,000	35.00
1972 Burning of Gaspee (Silver)	750	550.00
1972 1776 (China)	18,500	17.50
1972 1776 (Vermeil)	500	500.00
1972 1776 (Silver)	750	250.00
1972 Boston Tea Party (Pewter)	5,000	35.00
1973 Boston Tea Party (Silver)	750	550.00
Gallery of Masters		
1971 Man in Gilt Helmet	10,000	50.00
1972 Self-Portrait Rembrandt, with Saskia	10,000	50.00
1973 Honorable Mrs. Graham	7,500	50.00
Moppets Mother's Day		
1973 Flowers for Mother	20,000	10.00
1974 Mother's Hat	20,000	12.00
1975 In Mother's Clothes	20,000	13.00
1976 Flowers	20,000	13.00
1977 Gift for Mother	18,500	13.00
1978 Moppet's Mother's Day	18,500	10.00
Moppets Christmas		
1973 Christmas March	20,000	10.00
1974 Trimming Tree	20,000	12.00
1975 Carrying Tree	20,000	13.00
1976 Asleep Under Tree	18,500	13.00
1977 Star for Treetop	18,500	13.00
1978 Presents	18,500	10.00
1979 Moppet's Christmas	18,500	12.00

	EDITION LIMIT	ISSUE PRICE (US)
Remington Western		
1973 Aiding a Comrade	Year	$ 25.00
1973 New Year on Cimarron	Year	25.00
1973 Fight for Waterhole	Year	25.00
1973 Flight	Year	25.00
(Issued as a set)		
1974 Old Ramond	Year	20.00
1974 Breed	Year	20.00
1975 Cavalry Officer	5,000	37.50
1975 Trapper	5,000	37.50
(Single issue)		
1974 Streakers	Year	19.50
1974 Golden Rule	Year	19.50
1974 Big Three	10,000	17.50
1974 Weigh-In	10,000	17.50
1975 Benjamin Franklin	18,500	19.50
Boy Scouts of America		
1975 Our Heritage	18,500	19.50
1976 Scout is Loyal	18,500	19.50
1977 Scoutmaster	18,500	19.50
1977 Good Sign	18,500	19.50
1978 Pointing Way	18,500	19.50
1978 Campfire Story	18,500	19.50
American Artists		
1976 Apache Mother & Child	9,800	25.00
1976 Black Regiment	7,500	25.00
America's Cup Plates (Set of five)		
1976 America, 1861		
1976 Puritan		
1976 Reliance		
1976 Ranger		
1976 Courageous	1,000	200.00
Omnibus Muralis		
1976 200 Years With Old Glory	5,000	60.00
1977 Life of Christ	5,000	65.00
First Lady		
1977 Amy and Rosalynn	Year	24.95
1977 Cherokee Princess	3,000	48.00
Presidential		
1977 John F. Kennedy	9,800	30.00
1977 Eisenhower	9,800	30.00
Julian Ritter Annual		
1977 Christmas Visit	9,800	24.50
1978 Fluttering Heart	9,800	24.50
Ritter's Four Seasons Clowns		
1977 Falling in Love *(Set of four)*	5,000	100.00
1978 To Love a Clown *(Set of four)*	5,000	120.00
Santa Fe Railway Collection		
1977 Navajo Silversmith	7,500	37.50
1978 Turquoise Bead Maker	7,500	37.50
1979 Basketweaver	7,500	42.50
Borsato Masterpiece Collection		
1977 Serenity	5,000	75.00
1978 Titan Madonna	5,000	75.00
1979 Ballerina	5,000	75.00
Moppets Anniversary		
1979 Moppet Couple	20,000	13.00
(Single issue)		
1978 Triple Self-Portrait	Year	37.50
Wild West		
1980 Bronc To Breakfast	9,800	38.00
Greentree Potteries		
Grant Wood		
1971 Studio	2,000	10.00
1972 Antioch School	2,000	10.00
1973 At Stone City	2,000	10.00
1974 Adolescence	2,000	10.00
1975 Birthplace	2,000	10.00
1976 American Gothic	2,000	10.00
Kennedy		
1972 Center for Performing Arts	2,000	20.00
1973 Birthplace, Brookline, Mass.	2,000	12.00
Motorcar		
1972 1929 Packard Dietrich Convertible	2,000	20.00
1973 Model "A" Ford	2,000	20.00
Mississippi River		
1973 Delta Queen	2,000	10.00
1973 Tri-Centennial	2,000	10.00
Dave Grossman Designs		
Margaret Keene		
1976 Balloon Girl	5,000	20.00
1977 My Kitty	5,000	13.00
1978 Bedtime	5,000	25.00
Tom Sawyer		
1975 Whitewashing Fence	10,000	24.00
1976 First Smoke	10,000	24.00
1977 Take Your Medicine	10,000	24.00
1978 Lost in Cave	10,000	25.00
Looney Tunes Mother's Day		
1976 Bugs Bunny	10,000	13.00
Looney Tunes Christmas		
1977 Christmas	10,000	13.00
1978 Christmas	5,000	14.00
Children of the Week		
1978 Monday's Child	5,000	30.00
1979 Tuesday's Child	5,000	30.00

	EDITION LIMIT	ISSUE PRICE (US)
1979 Wednesday's Child	5,000	$ 30.00
1980 Thursday's Child	5,000	30.00
Annual Fall		
1978 Peace	5,000	55.00
1979 Santa	5,000	55.00
Rockwell		
1979 Butter Boy	5,000	40.00
Huckleberry Finn		
1979 Secret	10,000	40.00
1980 Listening	10,000	40.00
(Single issue)		
1980 Norman Rockwell Back to School	10,000	24.00
Rockwell Christmas		
1980 Christmas Trio	Year	75.00
Hackett American Collector		
Annual		
1979 I Love You Very	30,000	19.95
Hamilton Mint		
Picasso Series		
1972 Le Gourmet	5,000	125.00
1972 Tragedy	5,000	125.00
1973 Lovers	5,000	125.00
Kennedy		
1974 (Gold on Pewter)	Year	40.00
1974 (Pewter)	Year	25.00
Man's Best Friend		
1978 Hobo	9,500	40.00
1978 Doctor	9,500	40.00
1979 Making Friends	9,500	40.00
Hamilton Collection (Viletta)		
Coppelia Ballet		
1980 Franz's Fantasy Love	28 Days	25.00
Historic Providence Mint		
(Single issue)		
1979 Children's Year	3,000	95.00
Hudson Pewter		
Mother's Day		
1979 Cherished	10,000	35.00
Songbirds of the Four Seasons		
1979 Hummingbird	7,500	35.00
America's Sailing Ships		
1979 U.S.S. Constitution	5,000	35.00
A Child's Christmas		
1979 Littlest Angels	10,000	35.00
1980 Heaven's Christmas Tree	10,000	42.50
Imperial		
Christmas		
1970 Partridge (Carnival)	Year	12.00
1970 Partridge (Crystal)	Year	15.00
1971 Two Turtle Doves (Carnival)	Year	12.00
1971 Two Turtle Doves (Crystal)	Year	16.50
1972 Three French Hens (Carnival)	Year	12.00
1972 Three French Hens (Crystal)	Year	16.50
1973 Four Colly Birds (Carnival)	Year	12.00
1973 Four Colly Birds (Crystal)	Year	16.50
1974 Five Golden Rings (Carnival)	Year	12.00
1974 Five Golden Rings (Crystal)	Year	16.50
1975 Six Geese A-Laying (Carnival)	Year	14.00
1975 Six Geese A-Laying (Crystal)	Year	19.00
1976 Seven Swans (Carnival)	Year	16.00
1976 Seven Swans (Crystal)	Year	21.00
1977 Eight Maids A-Milking (Carnival)	Year	18.00
1977 Eight Maids A-Milking (Crystal)	Year	23.00
1978 Nine Drummers Drumming (Carnival)	Year	20.00
1978 Nine Drummers Drumming (Crystal)	Year	25.00
1979 Ten Pipers Piping (Carnival)	Year	22.00
1979 Ten Pipers Piping (Crystal)	Year	27.00
Coin Crystal		
1971 1964 Kennedy Half Dollar	Year	15.00
1972 Eisenhower Dollar	Year	15.00
(Single issue)		
1976 Bicentennial	Year	20.00
Incolay Studios		
Life's Interludes		
1979 Uncertain Beginning	Year	95.00
International Silver		
Presidential		
1975 Washington	7,500	75.00
1976 Jefferson	7,500	75.00

	EDITION LIMIT	ISSUE PRICE (US)
1976 Lincoln	7,500	$ 75.00
1976 F. Roosevelt	7,500	75.00
1977 Eisenhower	7,500	75.00
1977 Kennedy	7,500	75.00
Seasons American Past		
1976 Autumn	7,500	60.00
1976 Spring	7,500	60.00
1976 Summer	7,500	60.00
1976 Winter	7,500	60.00
Interpace		
Modigliani (Single issue)		
1972 Caryatid	10,000	60.00
Georg Jensen		
Chagall (Single issue)		
1972 Lovers	12,500	50.00
JM Company		
Competitive Sports		
1979 Downhill Racing Slalom	10,000	25.00
Oriental Birds		
1979 Window at Tiger Spring Temple	10,000	39.00
Love		
1980 Love's Serenade	5,000	50.00
Joys (Viletta)		
Precious Moments		
1979 Friend in Sky	28 Days	21.50
1980 Sand in Her Shoe	28 Days	21.50
Alice in Wonderland		
1980 Alice and White Rabbit	28 Days	25.00
Judaic Heritage Society		
Jewish Holidays		
1972 Chanukah (Silver)	2,000	150.00
1972 Chanukah (Gold)	25	1,900.00
1972 Pesach (Silver)	2,000	150.00
1972 Pesach (Gold)	25	1,900.00
1972 Purim (Silver)	2,000	150.00
1974 Purim (Silver)		
(Single issue)		
1974 Purim (Silver)	1,000	150.00
Great Jewish Women		
1976 Golda Mier	4,000	35.00
1976 Henrietta Szold	4,000	35.00
1976 Emma Lazarus	4,000	35.00
The Heritage Plates		
1976 Rabbi	4,000	35.00
1976 Hasidim	4,000	35.00
1976 Shtetl	4,000	35.00
(Single issue)		
1977 Jacob and Angel	5,000	45.00
1977 Hatikvah (Copper)	5,000	55.00
1977 Hatikvah (Gold Plated)	1,000	75.00
1977 Hatikvah (Sterling Silver)	500	180.00
Jewish Holidays		
1979 Chanukah	2,500	50.00
1979 Purim	2,500	50.00
1979 Shavouth	2,500	50.00
1979 Rosh Hashanah	2,500	50.00
1979 Simchat Torah	2,500	50.00
1979 Pesach	2,500	50.00
Jerusalem Wedding		
1979 Bride of Jerusalem	6,000	65.00
1979 Hasidic Dancers	6,000	65.00
Judaic Heritage Society (Avondale)		
(Single issue)		
1980 Shalom — Peace	6,000	95.00
Judaic Heritage Society (Viletta)		
Israel's 30th Anniversary (Single issue)		
1979 L'Chayim To Israel	10,000	59.50
1979 Prophecy of Isaiah's	4,000	59.50
Keller & George (Reed & Barton)		
Bicentennial		
1972 Monticello (Damascene)	1,000	75.00
1972 Monticello (Silver Plate)	200	200.00
1973 Mt. Vernon (Damascene)	Year	75.00
Kern Collectibles		
Linda's Little Loveables		
1977 Blessing	7,500	30.00
1978 Appreciation	7,500	37.50
1979 Adopted Burro	7,500	42.50
Christmas of Yesterday		
1978 Christmas Call	5,000	45.00
1979 Woodcutter's Christmas	5,000	50.00
Kern Collectibles (Pickard)		
Cowboy Artists Sets of Two		
1976 Out There		
1976 Cutting Out a Stray	3,000	130.00
1977 Broken Cinch		
1977 No Place to Cross	1,000	130.00
Companions		
1977 Cubs	5,000	40.00
1978 Mighty Sioux	5,000	40.00
1979 Nature Girl	5,000	50.00
1980 Buffalo Boy	5,000	50.00

	EDITION LIMIT	ISSUE PRICE (US)
Kilkelly		
St. Patrick's Day		
1975 Pipe and Shamrock	Year	$ 16.50
1976 Third Look in Logan	Year	20.00
Kirk, Jodi		
DeGrazia		
1972 Heavenly Blessing	200	75.00
Kirk		
Mother's Day		
1972 Mother and Child	3,500	75.00
1973 Mother and Child	2,500	80.00
Bicentennial		
1972 U.S.S. Constellation	825	75.00
1972 Washington	5,000	75.00
Thanksgiving		
1972 Thanksgiving Ways and Means	3,500	150.00
Christmas		
1972 Flight Into Egypt	3,500	150.00
Lake Shore Prints		
Rockwell		
1973 Butter Girl	9,433	14.95
1974 Truth About Santa	15,141	19.50
1975 Home From Fields	8,500	24.50
1976 A President's Wife	2,500	70.00
Lapsys		
Crystal Christmas		
1977 Snowflake	5,000	47.50
1978 Peace on Earth	5,000	47.50
Lenox		
Boehm Birds		
1972 Bird of Peace (Mute Swan)	5,000	150.00
1973 Young America, 1776 (Eaglet)	6,000	175.00
Lincoln Mint		
Great Artists (Dali)		
1971 Unicorn Dyonisiaque (Gold)	100	1,500.00
1971 Unicorn Dyonisiaque (Silver)	5,000	100.00
1972 Dyonisiaque et Pallas Athens (Gold)	300	2,000.00
1972 Dyonisiaque et Pallas Athens (Gold Plate)	2,500	150.00
1972 Dyonisiaque et Pallas Athens (Silver)	7,500	125.00
Easter		
1972 Christ (Silver)	20,000	150.00
1972 Christ (Gold Plate)	10,000	200.00
1974 Christ (Pewter)	Year	45.00
Mother's Day		
1972 Collies (Silver)	3,000	125.00
Christmas		
1972 Madonna Della Seggiola (Gold Plate)	125	150.00
1972 Madonna Della Seggiola (Silver)	3,000	125.00
Dali Cross Plate		
1977 Gold Cross	5,000	225.00
1977 Silver Cross	10,000	175.00
Lincoln Mint (Gorham)		
Christmas		
1978 Santa Belongs to All Children	7,500	29.50
Litt		
Christmas		
1978 Madonna & Child	1,000	200.00
1979 O Holy Night	1,000	200.00
Annual		
1979 Apache Sunset	1,250	275.00
Lynell Studios		
Little Traveler		
1978 On His Way	4,000	45.00
1979 On Her Way	4,000	45.00
American Adventure		
1979 Whaler	7,500	50.00
1979 Trapper	7,500	50.00
All American Soap Box Derby		
1979 Last Minute Changes	Year	24.50
Norman Rockwell Collection of Legendary Art		
Christmas		
1979 Snow Queen	60 Days	24.50
John Wayne		
1979 Man of The Golden West	Year	45.00
RCA Victor Nipper Plate		
1980 His Master's Voice	N/A	24.50
Norman Rockwell Collection of Legendary Art Annual		
1980 Artist's Daughter	Year	65.00
Norman Rockwell Collection of Legendary Art		
Mother's Day		
1980 Cradle of Love	60 Days	29.50
Popeye's 50th Anniversary (Single issue)		
1980 Happy Birthday Popeye	Year	22.50
Mallek		
Navajo Christmas		
1971 Indian Wise Men	1,000	15.00

	EDITION LIMIT	ISSUE PRICE (US)
1972 On The Reservation	2,000	$ 17.00
1973 Hoke Denetsosie	2,000	17.00
1974 Monument Valley	2,000	18.00
1975 Coming Home for Christmas	2,000	18.00
1976 Deer With Rainbow	2,000	20.00
1977 Goat Herders	2,000	20.00
1978 Hogan Christmas	2,000	20.00
Chinese Lunar Calendar		
1972 Year of the Rat	1,000	15.00
1973 Year of the Ox	1,000	15.00
1974 Year of the Rabbit	1,000	15.00
Christmas Game Birds		
1972 Gambel Quail	1,000	15.00
1973 Partridge	1,000	15.00
1974 Owl and Cactus	1,000	15.00
1975 Chinese Wood Duck	1,000	15.00
1976 Wild Turkey	1,000	15.00
1977 Mallard	1,000	15.00
1978 Canadian Geese	1,000	15.00
Mexican Christmas		
1972 Christmas	1,000	15.00
1973 Christmas	1,000	15.00
1974 Christmas	1,000	18.00
1975 Christmas	1,000	18.00
1976 Christmas	1,000	20.00
1977 Christmas	1,000	20.00
Navidad (Single issue)		
1972 Navidad en Mexico	500	15.00
(Single issue)		
1972 Amish Harvest	1,000	17.00
A.B.C.'s		
1974 A.B.C. Rabbit	1,000	15.00
1975 A.B.C. Mice	1,000	15.00
(Single issue)		
1976 Kewpie Doll	1,000	15.00
Master Engravers of America		
Indian Dancers		
1979 Eagle Dancer	2,500	300.00
1980 Hoop Dancer	2,500	300.00
Metal Arts Co.		
America's First Family (Single issue)		
1977 Carters	9,500	40.00
Freedom (Single issue)		
1977 Washington at Valley Forge (Sterling)	500	225.00
1977 Washington at Valley Forge (Pewter)	1,000	95.00
Winslow Homer's The Sea		
1977 Breezing Up	9,500	29.95
Rockwell Copper Christmas		
1978 Christmas Gift	Year	48.00
1979 Big Moment	Year	48.00
Metropolitan Museum of Art		
Treasures of Tutankhamun		
1977 King Tut	2,500	150.00
Mingolla		
Christmas (Enamel on Copper)		
1973 Christmas	1,000	95.00
1974 Christmas	1,000	110.00
1975 Christmas	1,000	125.00
1976 Christmas	1,000	125.00
1977 Scene From Childhood	2,000	200.00
Christmas (Porcelain)		
1974 Christmas	5,000	35.00
1975 Christmas	5,000	35.00
1976 Christmas	5,000	35.00
1977 Winter Wonderland	7,000	45.00
Four Seasons (Enamel on Copper)		
1978 Dashing Thru Snow	2,000	150.00
1979 Spring Flowers	2,000	150.00
1980 Beach Fun	2,000	150.00
1981 Balloon Breeze	2,000	150.00
Moussalli		
Birds of Four Seasons		
1978 Cardinal (Winter)	1,000	375.00
1979 Indigo Bunting (Fall)	1,000	375.00
1979 Hummingbird (Summer)	1,000	375.00
1980 Wren (Spring)	1,000	375.00
Museum Editions (Viletta)		
Christmas Annual		
1978 Expression of Faith	7,400	49.95
1979 Skating Lesson	7,400	49.95
Colonial Heritage		
1980 Mulberry Plantation	Year	99.00
Ohio Arts		
Norman Rockwell		
1979 Looking Out to Sea	20,000	19.50
Paramount Classics (Pickard)		
Jubilee		
1977 Queen Elizabeth	5,000	375.00
(Single issue)		
1977 Coronation Plate	5,000	95.00
(Single issue)		
1977 Queen Victoria	5,000	95.00
Queen's Jubilee		
1977 Queens of England	5,000	95.00

	EDITION LIMIT	ISSUE PRICE (US)
(Single issue)		
1977 King George III	5,000	$ 95.0
Pickard		
Presidential		
1971 Truman	3,000	35.0
1973 Lincoln	5,000	35.0
Ram		
Boston 500		
1973 Easter	500	30.0
1973 Mother's Day	500	30.0
1973 Father's Day	500	30.0
1973 Christmas	500	30.0
Great Bird Heroes		
1973 Cher Ami	1,000	7.9
1973 Mocker	1,000	7.9
Reco International		
Americana (Single issue)		
1972 Gaspee	1,000	130.0
Four Seasons (Set of four)		
1973 Fall		
1973 Spring		
1973 Summer		
1973 Winter	2,500	200.0
Western (Single issue)		
1974 Mountain Man	1,000	165.0
Christmas (Single issue)		
1977 Old Mill in Valley	5,000	28.0
Games Children Play		
1979 Me First	10,000	45.0
Reed & Barton		
Audubon		
1970 Pine Siskin	5,000	60.0
1971 Red-Shouldered Hawk	5,000	60.0
1972 Stilt Sandpiper	5,000	60.0
1973 Red Cardinal	5,000	60.0
1974 Boreal Chickadee	5,000	60.0
1975 Yellow-Breasted Chat	5,000	65.0
1976 Bay-Breasted Warbler	5,000	65.0
1977 Purple Finch	5,000	65.0
(Single issue)		
1970 Zodiac	1,500	75.0
California Missions		
1971 San Diego	1,500	75.0
1972 Carmel	1,500	75.0
1973 Santa Barbara	1,500	60.0
1974 Santa Clara	1,500	60.0
1976 San Gabriel	1,500	65.0
Annual		
1972 Free Trapper	2,500	65.0
1973 Outpost	2,500	65.0
1974 Toll Collector	2,500	65.0
1975 Indians Discovering Lewis & Clark	2,500	65.0
Currier & Ives		
1972 Village Blacksmith	1,500	85.0
1972 Western Migration	1,500	85.0
1973 Oaken Bucket	1,500	85.0
1973 Winter in the Country	1,500	85.0
1974 Preparing for Market	1,500	85.0
Kentucky Derby		
1972 Nearing the Finish	1,000	75.0
1973 Riva Ridge	1,500	75.0
1974 100th Running	1,500	75.0
(Single issue)		
1972 Delta Queen	2,500	75.
(Single issue)		
1972 Road Runner	1,500	65.0
Founding Father		
1973 Ben Franklin	2,500	65.0
1974 George Washington	2,500	65.
1975 Thomas Jefferson	2,500	65.0
1976 Patrick Henry	2,500	65.0
1976 John Hancock	2,500	65.0
1976 John Adams	2,500	65.0
(Single issue)		
1973 Chicago Fire	Year	60.
(Single issue)		
1975 Mississippi Queen	2,500	75.
Ridgewood		
Bicentennial		
1974 First in War	12,500	40.
Tom Sawyer (Set of four)		
1974 Trying a Pipe		
1974 Lost in Cave		
1974 Painting Fence		
1974 Taking Medicine	3,000	39.
Wild West		
1975 Discovery of Last Chance Gulch		
1975 Doubtful Visitor		
1975 Bad One		
1975 Cattleman	15,000	65.
Leyendecker Christmas		
1975 Christmas Morning	10,000	24.
1976 Christmas Surprise	10,000	24.
Leyendecker Mother's Day		
1976 Grandma's Apple Pie	5,000	24.

	EDITION LIMIT	ISSUE PRICE (US)
RiverShore Ltd.		
Baby Animals Collection		
1979 Akiku	20,000	$ 65.00
Della Robbia Annual		
1979 Adoration	5,000	550.00
1980 Virgin and Child	5,000	450.00
Remington Bronze		
1977 Bronco Buster	15,000	55.00
1978 Coming Thru Rye	15,000	60.00
(Single issue)		
1979 Spring Flowers	17,000	75.00
Rockwell Collectors Club		
Christmas		
1978 Christmas Story	15,000	24.50
Rockwell Museum		
American Family		
1978 Baby's First Step	9,900	28.50
1978 Happy Birthday Dear Mother	9,900	28.50
1978 Sweet Sixteen	9,900	28.50
1978 First Haircut	9,900	28.50
1979 First Prom	9,900	28.50
1979 Student	9,900	28.50
1979 Wrapping Christmas Presents	9,900	28.50
1979 Birthday Party	9,900	28.50
1979 Little Mother	9,900	28.50
1980 Washing Our Dog	9,900	28.50
1980 Mother's Little Helper	9,900	28.50
1980 Bride & Groom	9,900	28.50
American Family II		
1980 New Arrival	22,500	35.00
Christmas		
1979 Day After Christmas	25,000	75.00
(Single issue)		
1979 Norman Rockwell Remembered	Year	45.00
Royal Cornwall		
Bethlehem Christmas		
1977 First Christmas Eve	10,000	29.95
1978 Glad Tidings	10,000	34.50
1979 Gift Bearers	10,000	34.50
The Creation		
1977 In Beginning	19,500	45.00
1977 In His Image	19,500	45.00
1977 Adam's Rib	19,500	45.00
1977 Banished From Eden	19,500	45.00
1977 Noah and Ark	19,500	45.00
1977 Tower of Babel	19,500	45.00
1978 Sodom & Gomorrah	19,500	45.00
1978 Jacob's Wedding	19,500	45.00
1978 Rebekah at Well	19,500	45.00
1978 Jacob's Ladder	19,500	45.00
1978 Joseph's Coat of Many Colors	19,500	45.00
1978 Joseph Interprets Pharaoh's Dream	19,500	45.00
Classic Christmas		
1978 Child of Peace	17,500	55.00
1978 Silent Night	17,500	55.00
1978 Most Precious Gift	17,500	55.00
1978 We Three Kings	17,500	55.00
Four Seasons		
1978 Warmth	17,500	60.00
1978 Voices of Spring	17,500	60.00
1978 Fledgling	17,500	60.00
1978 We Survive	17,500	60.00
Golden Age of Cinema		
1978 King & His Ladies	22,500	45.00
1978 Fred & Ginger	22,500	45.00
1978 Judy & Mickey	22,500	45.00
1979 Philadelphia Story	22,500	45.00
1979 Thin Man	22,500	45.00
1979 Gigi	22,500	45.00
Mother's Day		
1978 God Bless Mommy	10,000	35.00
Alice in Wonderland		
1979 Alice and White Rabbit	27,500	45.00
1979 Advice From Caterpillar	27,500	45.00
1979 Cheshire Cat's Grin	27,500	45.00
1979 Mad Hatter's Tea Party	27,500	45.00
1979 Queen's Croquet Match	27,500	45.00
1979 Who Stole Tarts?	27,500	45.00
Kitten's World		
1979 Just Curious	27,500	45.00
1979 Hello, World	27,500	45.00
1979 Are You a Flower?	27,500	45.00
1979 Talk To Me	27,500	45.00
1979 My Favorite Toy	27,500	45.00
1979 Purr-Fect Pleasure	27,500	45.00
The Promised Land		
1979 Pharaoh's Daughter Finds Moses	24,500	45.00
1979 Burning Bush	24,500	45.00
1979 Let My People Go	24,500	45.00
1979 Parting of Red Sea	24,500	45.00

	EDITION LIMIT	ISSUE PRICE (US)
1979 Miriam's Song of Thanksgiving	24,500	$ 45.00
1979 Manna From Heaven	24,500	45.00
1979 Water From Rock	24,500	45.00
1979 Battle of Amalek	24,500	45.00
1979 Ten Commandments	24,500	45.00
1979 Golden Calf	24,500	45.00
1979 Moses Smashes Tablets	24,500	45.00
1979 Glorious Tabernacle	24,500	45.00
Treasures of Childhood		
1979 My Cuddlies Collection	19,500	45.00
1979 My Coin Collection	19,500	45.00
1979 My Shell Collection	19,500	45.00
1979 My Stamp Collection	19,500	45.00
1979 My Doll Collection	19,500	45.00
1979 My Rock Collection	19,500	45.00
The Beauty of Bouguereau		
1980 Lucie	19,500	35.00
1980 Madelaine	19,500	35.00
1980 Frere et Soeur	19,500	35.00
1980 Solange et Enfant	19,500	35.00
1980 Colette	19,500	35.00
1980 Jean et Jeanette	19,500	35.00
The Four Faces of Love		
1980 Romeo & Juliet	17,500	55.00
1980 Young Galahad	17,500	55.00
1980 At Locksley Hall	17,500	55.00
1980 St. Agnes Eve	17,500	55.00
Royal Worcester		
Currier & Ives		
1974 Road-Winter	10,000	59.50
1975 Old Grist Mill	10,000	59.50
1976 Winter Pastime	10,000	59.50
American History		
1977 Washington's Inauguration	1,250	65.00
Annual		
1977 Home to Thanksgiving	500	59.50
Royalwood		
(Single issue)		
1977 Doctor and Doll	Year	21.50
Leyendecker		
1978 Cornflake Boy	10,000	25.00
1978 Cornflake Girl	10,000	25.00
E. Ward Russel (Imperial)		
America the Beautiful		
1969 U.S.Capitol	500	17.50
1970 Mount Rushmore	500	17.50
1971 Statue of Liberty	500	17.50
1972 Monument Valley Arizona	500	17.50
1973 Liberty Bell	500	17.50
1974 Golden Gate	500	19.95
1975 Mt. Vernon	500	19.95
John A. Ruthven		
Moments of Nature		
1977 Screech Owls	5,000	37.50
1979 Chickadees	5,000	39.50
1980 California Quail	5,000	39.50
Schmid (Pewter)		
Christmas		
1977 Santa	5,000	30.00
1978 Beautiful Snow	5,000	45.00
1979 I Hear America Singing	6,000	50.00
Beatrix Potter (Pewter)		
1978 Peter Rabbit	5,000	50.00
1979 Jemima-Puddle Duck	5,000	50.00
Sebastian		
America's Favorite Scenes		
1978 Motif #1	10,000	75.00
1979 Grand Canyon	10,000	75.00
Seeley's Ceramic Services		
Antique French Dolls		
1979 Bru	5,000	39.00
1979 E.J.	5,000	39.00
Seven Seas		
Historical Event		
1969 Moon Landing, No Flag	2,000	13.50
1969 Moon Landing With Flag	25,000	13.50
1970 Year of Crisis	4,000	15.00
1971 First Vehicular Travel	3,000	15.00
1972 Last Moon Journey	2,000	15.00
1973 Peace	3,000	15.00
Mother's Day		
1970 Girl of All Nations	5,000	15.00
1971 Sharing Confidence	1,400	15.00
1972 Scandinavian Girl	1,600	15.00
1973 All American Girl	1,500	15.00
Christmas Carols		
1970 I Heard Bells	4,000	15.00
1971 Oh Tannenbaum	4,000	15.00
1972 Deck Halls	1,500	18.00
1973 O Holy Night	2,000	18.00
1974 Jingle Bells	1,200	25.00
1975 Winter Wonderland	1,500	25.00

	EDITION LIMIT	ISSUE PRICE (US)
1976 Twelve Days of Christmas	1,200	$ 25.00
1977 Up on the Housetop	1,500	25.00
1978 Little Town of Bethlehem	1,500	25.00
1979 Santa Claus is Coming to Town	1,500	25.00
1980 Frosty the Snowman	1,500	25.00
New World		
1970 Holy Family	3,500	15.00
1971 Three Wise Men	1,500	15.00
1972 Shepherds Watched	1,500	18.00
Passion Play (Single issue)		
1970 Oberammergau	2,500	18.00
Silver Creations		
Churchillian Heritage		
1972 Hour of Decision	N/A	150.00
1973 Yalta Conference	N/A	150.00
1973 Clydesdales	N/A	150.00
Smith Glass		
Americana		
1971 Morgan Silver Dollar	5,000	10.00
Christmas		
1971 Family at Christmas	N/A	10.00
1972 Flying Angel	N/A	10.00
1973 St. Mary's in Mountains	N/A	10.00
Famous Americans		
1971 Kennedy	2,500	10.00
1971 Lincoln	2,500	10.00
1972 Davis, Jefferson	5,000	11.00
1972 Lee, Robert E.	5,000	11.00
Sterling America		
Christmas Customs		
1970 England	2,500	18.00
1971 Holland	2,500	18.00
1972 Norway	2,500	18.00
1973 Germany	2,500	20.00
1974 Mexico	2,500	24.00
Twelve Days of Christmas		
1970 Partridge	2,500	18.00
1971 Turtle Doves	2,500	18.00
1972 French Hens	2,500	18.00
1973 Colly Birds	2,500	18.00
1974 Five Rings	2,500	24.00
1975 Six Geese	2,500	24.00
1976 Seven Swans	2,500	24.00
1977 Eight Maids	2,500	28.00
Mother's Day		
1971 Mare & Foal	2,500	18.00
1972 Horned Owl	2,500	18.00
1973 Raccoons	2,500	20.00
1974 Deer	2,500	24.00
1975 Quail	2,500	24.00
Stieff		
Bicentennial		
1972 Declaration of Independence	10,000	50.00
1974 Betsy Ross	10,000	50.00
1975 Crossing Delaware	10,000	50.00
1976 Serapio & Bon Homme	10,000	50.00
Stuart Devlin Silver		
Americana Series		
1972 Gaspee Incident	1,000	130.00
Syracuse China		
Grandma Moses (Sets of four)		
1972 Old Checkered House in Winter Mary and Little Lamb In Harvest Time Sugaring Off	N/A	80.00
1972 Hoosick Valley from Window Taking in Laundry It Snows, Oh it Snows Joy Ride	N/A	80.00
Towle Silversmiths		
Valentines		
1972 Single Heart	Year	
1973 Entwined Hearts	Year	10.00
Christmas		
1972 Three Wise Men	2,500	250.00
Trester (Ridgewood)		
Little Women		
1976 Sweet Long Ago	5,000	45.00
1976 Song of Spring	5,000	45.00
Little Men		
1977 Come Ride With Me	9,500	50.00
Trester (Gorham)		
Little Women		
1977 Joy in Morning	5,000	45.00
Trester (Kaiser)		
Little Men		
1978 Magical Moment	9,500	60.00
U.S. Historical Society		
Annual Historical		
1977 Great Events	5,000	60.00
1978 Great Events	10,000	75.00

	EDITION LIMIT	ISSUE PRICE (US)
Stained Glass Cathedral Christmas		
1978 Canterbury Cathedral	Year	$ 87.00
1979 Flight Into Egypt (St. John the Divine)	10,000	97.00
Vague Shadows		
The Plainsmen		
1979 Buffalo Hunt	2,500	300.00
1979 Proud One	2,500	300.00
The Great Chieftains		
1979 Chief Sitting Bull	7,500	65.00
1979 Chief Joseph	7,500	65.00
1980 Chief Red Cloud	7,500	65.00
The Professionals		
1979 Big Leaguer	15,000	29.95
1980 Ballerina's Dilemma	15,000	32.50
Masterwords of Impressionism		
1980 Woman With a Parasol	17,500	35.00
Masterworks of the West		
1980 Texas Night Herder	17,500	35.00
Masterworks of Rockwell		
1980 After Prom	17,500	35.00
Vernonware (Metlox)		
Songs of Christmas		
1971 Twelve Days	9,000	15.00
1972 Jingle Bells	8,000	17.50
1973 First Noel	9,000	20.00
1974 Upon A Midnight Clear	9.000	20.00
1975 O Holy Night	10,000	20.00
1976 Hark! Herald Angels	10,000	20.00
1977 Away In Manger	10,000	30.00
1978 White Christmas	10,000	30.00
1979 Little Drummer Boy	10,000	30.00
Viletta		
Disneyland		
1976 Betsy Ross	3,000	15.00
1976 Crossing Delaware	3,000	15.00
1976 Signing the Declaration	3,000	15.00
1976 Spirit of '76	3,000	15.00
Bicentennial		
1977 Patriots	15,000	37.00
In Tribute to America's Great Artists		
1978 DeGrazia by Don Marco	5,000	65.00
Viletta		
Days of The West		
1978 Cowboy Christmas	5,000	55.00
Viletta (Homan)		
Seasons of the Oak		
1979 Lazy Days	5,000	55.00
1980 Come Fly with Me	5,000	55.00
Viletta (McCalla Enterprises)		
Making Friends		
1978 Feeding Neighbor's Pony	5,000	45.00
1979 Cowboys 'n' Indians	5,000	47.50
1980 Surprise for Christy	5,000	47.50
Love Letters		
1980 Mail Order Bride	5,000	60.00
Viletta (Westbury)		
Tender Moments		
1978 Old Fashioned Persuasion	7,500	40.00
1979 Dandelions	7,500	45.00
Viletta (Weston)		
Unicorn Fantasies		
1979 Follower of Dreams	5,000	55.00
1980 Twice Upon a Time	5,000	55.00
Weddings Around the World		
1979 Hawaiian Wedding	5,000	75.00
1980 Dutch Wedding	5,000	75.00
Volair (Gorham)		
Audubon American Wildlife Heritage		
1977 House Mouse	2,500	90.00
1977 Royal Louisiana Heron	2,500	90.00
1977 Virginia Deer	2,500	90.00
1977 Snowy Owl	2,500	90.00
Warwick (Viletta)		
Great Comedians		
1978 Little Tramp	7,500	35.00
1978 Outrageous Groucho	7,500	35.00
Wendell August Forge		
Great Americans		
1971 J.F.K. (Pewter)	5,000	40.00
1971 J.F.K. (Silver)	500	200.00
1972 Lincoln (Pewter)	5,000	40.00
1972 Lincoln (Silver)	500	200.00
Great Moments		
1971 Columbus (Pewter)	5,000	40.00
1971 Columbus (Silver)	500	200.00
1972 Landing of Pilgrims (Pewter)	5,000	40.00
1972 Landing of Pilgrims (Silver)	500	200.00
1973 First Thanksgiving (Pewter)	5,000	40.00
1973 First Thanksgiving (Silver)	500	200.00

	EDITION LIMIT	ISSUE PRICE (US)
1974 Patrick Henry (Pewter)	5,000	$ 40.00
1974 Patrick Henry (Silver)	500	200.00
1975 Paul Revere (Pewter)	5,000	45.00
1975 Paul Revere (Silver)	500	200.00
1976 Signing of Declaration (Pewter)	5,000	50.00
1976 Signing of Declaration (Silver)	500	200.00

Wings of Man

1971 Columbus' Ships (Pewter)	5,000	40.00
1971 Columbus' Ships (Silver)	500	200.00
1972 Conestoga Wagon (Pewter)	5,000	40.00
1972 Conestoga Wagon (Silver)	500	200.00

Peace (Single issue)

1973 Facing Doves (Silver)	2,500	250.00

Christmas

1974 Caroler (Bronze)	2,500	25.00
1974 Caroler (Pewter)	2,500	30.00
1975 Christmas in Country (Bronze)	2,500	30.00
1975 Christmas in Country (Pewter)	2,500	35.00
1976 Lamplighter (Bronze)	2,500	35.00
1976 Lamplighter (Pewter)	2,500	40.00
1977 Covered Bridge (Bronze)	2,500	40.00
1977 Covered Bridge (Pewter)	2,500	45.00

Wildlife

1977 On Guard (Aluminum)	1,900	35.00
1977 On Guard (Bronze)	1,500	45.00
1977 On Guard (Pewter)	1,500	55.00
1977 On Guard (Silver)	100	250.00
1978 Thunderbird (Aluminum)	1,900	40.00
1978 Thunderbird (Bronze)	1,500	50.00
1978 Thunderbird (Pewter)	1,500	60.00
1978 Thunderbird (Silver)	100	250.00

Westminster Collectibles

Holidays

1976 All Hallows Eve	5,000	38.50
1977 Christmas	5,000	38.50

Westmoreland

Christmas

1972 Holy Birth	2,500	35.00
1973 Manger Scene	3,500	35.00
1974 Gethsemane	1,500	35.00
1975 Christ is Risen	N/A	45.00

Wheaton

Presidential

1971 Adams	9,648	5.00
1971 Eisenhower	8,856	5.00
1971 Hoover	10,152	5.00
1971 Kennedy	11,160	5.00
1971 Lincoln	9,648	5.00
1971 Madison	9,504	5.00
1971 Monroe	9,792	5.00
1971 F.D. Roosevelt	9,432	5.00
1971 Taft	9,648	5.00
1971 Van Buren	9,576	5.00
1971 Washington	10,800	5.00
1971 Wilson	8,712	5.00

Whitehall China

Raphael Soyer

1979 Model on Bed	10,000	39.95

White House of The Confederacy (Lenox)

Confederacy Collection

1972 (Set of ten)	1,000	900.00

GLOSSARY OF COMMONLY USED TERMS

A

AFTERMARKET See MARKET.

ALABASTER A dense, fine-grained form of gypsum (calcium sulfate) stone, usually white to pink and slightly translucent. Alabaster stone can be carved in fine detail for ornamental objects and hardened by intense heat. Italian alabaster is also called Florentine marble. Ivory alabaster is composed of alabaster but is non-translucent and acquires a patina with age like that of old ivory.

ALLOTMENT A number of plates, all alike and usually at issue, allocated by a maker to a distributor or dealer. See LOT.

ALLOY Two or more metals combined while molten. Alloying is done to achieve hardness, toughness, or luster. See PEWTER.

ANNUAL A plate issued once each year as part of a series. The term is most often used when a plate does not commemorate a specific holiday.

ANNULAR KILN A round oven made from brick used to fire ceramic plates.

ART DECO, ART DECORATIF A style of decoration popular in Europe and America from 1920 to 1945. The Art Deco movement sought to glorify progress and the future by using as motifs such shapes as the cylinder, circle, rectangle, and cone.

ART NOUVEAU A style of decoration in Europe and America from 1890 to 1920. The Art Nouveau movement used twisting vegetable forms as its primary decorative motifs.

ASKED PRICE The price posted for a plate by a seller on the exchange.

AT ISSUE A plate being offered for sale at the time of its manufacture and at the original price set by the maker.

B

BACKSTAMP The information on the back of a plate, usually including the maker's signature or name (logo-type). It may also record serial number, title, artist's signature, explanation of the plate, sponsor, production techniques, awards, or release initials. It may be stamped, incised (cut or pressed), or applied as a decalcomania.

BAROQUE An elaborate style of decoration developed in Europe in the seventeenth and eighteenth centuries and noted for exaggerated gesture and line. Example: Dresden plates **(22-D.68-0.0)**.

BAS-RELIEF See RELIEF SCULPTURE.

BAVARIA A province in the southwest corner of Germany long known as a center for porcelain factories. The region contains large deposits of kaolin, the key porcelain component.

BEDROOM DEALER A trade term for a small dealer who usually operates from his home, buys discounted plates and resells them for a small profit.

BID PRICE The amount a prospective buyer offers to pay for a plate on the exchange.

BISQUE, BISCUIT A plate that has been fired but not glazed, leaving it with a matte texture. So called because of the biscuit-like appearance. Example: Lladró plates **(72-L.41-0.0)**.

BLUE CHIP An established series by a well-known maker in which nearly every issue shows a steady sequence of price rises above issue price.

BODY 1. The formula or combination of substances that make up potter's clay, generally referring to stoneware and earthenware. 2. The basic plate form to which ornamentation is applied.

BONE ASH Calcium phosphate, a component of bone china, added to give whiteness and translucency. It is obtained by calcinating (reducing to powder by heat) animal bones, usually those of oxen.

BONE CHINA (BONE PORCELAIN) A type of china developed by Josiah Spode in England in the 1790s. By replacing part of the kaolin in the china formula with bone ash, greater translucency and whiteness is obtained at lower firing temperatures. The finest bone china contains up to 50% bone ash. It is the most commonly made china in England. Examples: Royal Doulton **(26-R.62-0.0)**, Royal Worcester, England **(26-R.76-0.0)** plates.

BULLISH Marked by rising prices, either actual or expected, and optimistic atmosphere. A *bull market* is one of rising prices.

BUY ORDER A bid offered by an individual or dealer to purchase one or more plates of the same edition on the secondary market. See EXCHANGE.

C

CAMEO EFFECT Ornamentation in relief on a background of contrasting color to resemble a cameo. Examples: Wedgwood Jasperware plates **(26-W.90-0.0)** and Incolay Studios **(84-I.57-0.0)**.

CELSIUS, CENTIGRADE The thermometric scale in which 0° represents the freezing point of water and 100° the boiling point. Celsius temperature is denoted by "C" after the number.

CERAMIC A general term applying to all of the various plates made from clay and hardened by firing.

CERTIFICATE An attestation of authenticity which may accompany each plate in an edition. A certificate authenticates a plate as being part of an issue and usually confirms the plate's individual number within the edition.

CHINA, CHINAWARE A hard, vitreous ceramic whose main components are kaolin and china stone fired at high temperature. Originally the term was used for these

ceramics which only came from China. Later it was applied to all "hard" and "soft" *porcelain*. China is often used as a generic term which includes *porcelain*, but is properly distinguished from it by a high bisque firing temperature and a low glaze firing temperature. The main firing (bisque) of china is approximately 7% lower than the main firing (glaze) of *porcelain*. In china production, the glaze is applied after the main firing and fixed with a second lower-temperature firing. A typical china formula is 40% kaolin, 10% ball clay, and varying proportions of china stone, feldspar and flint. See PORCELAIN.

CHINA CLAY See KAOLIN.

CHINA STONE, PETUNTSE A feldspathic material in china formulas. China stone acts as a flux which helps dissolve and fuse the other components into a vitreous mass.

CHRISTMAS PLATES, CHRISTMAS SERIES Annual plates issued to commemorate Christmas, usually as part of a series. Plate names for Christmas include Noel (French), Weinachten (German), Jul (Danish), Navidad (Spanish and Portugese), and Natale (Italian). The oldest Christmas series is that of Bing & Grøndahl, produced continuously since 1895 **(14-B.36-1.0)**.

CLAY Any of various plastic, viscous earths used to make plates. It is formed by the decomposition, due to weathering, of igneous rocks such as granite, feldspar, and pegmatite.

CLOSED-END SERIES A series of plates with a predetermined number of issues. Example: Haviland *Twelve Days of Christmas* series **(18-H.6-1.0)**. See OPEN-END SERIES.

COBALT BLUE Cobalt oxide in the form of a dark black powder which, when fired, turns a deep blue. It was the first known and is still the most commonly used ceramic underglaze color because of its ability to withstand high firing temperatures. It can produce a variety of shades. Examples: Kaiser cobalt blue **(22-K.4-0.0)**, Bing & Grøndahl Copenhagen blue **(14-B.36-0.0)**, Royal Copenhagen Danish blue **(14-R.59-0.0)**, Rorstrand Scandia blue **(76-R.54-0.0)**.

COLLECTOR'S PLATE A decorative plate produced in a limited edition for the purpose of being collected. Although the earliest plates were not produced with this objective, they have since acquired the name by virtue of being collected and are now produced for this purpose.

COMMEMORATIVE PLATE A plate produced in remembrance of an event. Example: D'Arceau-Limoges *Lafayette Legacy* **(18-D.15-1.0)**.

COTERIE PLATE A collector's plate with a limited following whose trading is too infrequent to be listed on the Exchange but which may be traded over the counter.

CRYSTAL See LEAD CRYSTAL.

CUT GLASS Glass decorated by the cutting of grooves and facets, usually done with a copper engraver's wheel.

D

DAMASCENE An electroplating effect created and patented by Reed & Barton **(84-R.18-0.0)** of etching and then depositing layers of gold, copper and silver on bronze. Originally the term referred to the art, developed in Damascus, of ornamenting iron or steel with inlaid precious metals.

DEALER A marketer of plates who buys primarily from makers or distributors and sells primarily to the public.

DELFTWARE Earthenware covered with an opaque white glaze made of stannic oxide, an oxide of tin. Originally developed in Delft, Holland in the sixteenth century, Delft-

ware has the appearance of being covered with a thick white paint. Similar ware is the *Majolica* of Italy and *Faience* of France and Germany. See FAIENCE, MAJOLICA, TIN GLAZE.

DISTRIBUTOR A marketer of plates who buys from manufacturers and sells to dealers. Some distributors also act as makers and as dealers.

DRESDEN, MEISSEN Nearby cities in eastern Germany where the first hard-paste porcelain outside of China was produced by Johann Fredrich Bottger in 1798.

E

EARTHENWARE A term for any ceramics which are not vitrified. Typical components of earthenware are 43% ball clay, 24% kaolin, 23% flint and 10% pegmatite. Fired earthenware is normally covered with either a transparent or opaque glaze. *High-fired earthenware* is fired at a higher temperature to produce a harder ware. Example: Royal Doulton Christmas plates **(26-R.62-1.0)**.

EDITION The total number of plates, all with the same decoration, produced by a maker. Editions of collector's plates are normally limited to a fixed number and are not repeated.

ELECTROPLATING A process by which metal plates are coated with another metal by electrical charges.

EMBOSSED DESIGN Raised ornamentation produced by the plate mold or by stamping a design into the body of the plate. Example: BELLEEK plates **(26-B.18-0.0)**.

ENAMEL A glaze material colored with suspended mineral oxides for decorating plates.

ENGRAVED DESIGN Decoration produced by cutting into the surface of metal, glass or china plates with either a tool or acid, as in etching. Example: Veneto Flair plates **(38-V.22-0.0)** See INTAGLIO.

ETCHED DESIGN Decoration produced by cutting into the surface of a plate with acid. The plate is first covered with an acid-resistant paint or wax, and the design is carved through this coating. When the plate is immersed in acid, the acid "bites" into the plate surface in the shape of the design. Example: Franklin Mint silver plates **(84-F.64-0.0)** See INTAGLIO.

EXCHANGE A place where plates are traded, most commonly the Bradford Exchange, the world's largest trading center. Incorporated in 1962, it was formerly known as Bradford Galleries Exchange. See BUY-ORDER.

F

FAIENCE Tin-enameled earthenware from France, Germany, or Spain developed in the seventeenth century and named for the Italian town of Faenza, a center for *Majolica*, another name for this ware. See DELFTWARE.

FELDSPAR A mineral composed of aluminum silicates with either potassium, sodium, calcium, or barium. Feldspar decomposes to form kaolin, the key ingredient of china and porcelain. The addition of undecomposed feldspar to china formulas gives the ware greater hardness.

FIRE The heating process which hardens ceramic plates in a kiln. Ceramic clay begins to undergo chemical change at 500°C and vitrifies around 1300°C.

FIRST EDITION The first, and presumably the only, edition of a collector's plate. The term (or its abbreviation "FE") is sometimes used for the edition which is the *first issue* in a series of collector's plates. However, since no edition is nor-

mally ever reopened and therefore no "second edition" is possible, all issues of collector's plates are properly termed first editions.

FIRST ISSUE Chronologically, the first plate in a series, i.e., the plates issued in the first year of an annual series.

FLUX Finely ground material added to porcelain formulas which lowers the vitrification temperature and helps fuse the components. Example: Feldspar.

G

GLAZE Glassy, hard surface coating on plates made of silicates (glass-forming compounds) and mineral oxides. Glaze is put on ceramic ware to make it wear-resistant, waterproof, decorative, and to seal the pores. Glaze material suspended in water is applied after the first firing and is heated to the glaze's vitrification point when it fuses to the plate body. Glaze is applied by dipping, spraying, or painting. Decorating is added under, over, or with the glaze layer. See UNDERGLAZE.

I

INCISED DESIGN Ornamentation cut into the body of the plate.

INCOLAY STONE The material from which the cameo-like plates produced by Incolay Studios are made. Incolay stone contains, among other minerals, both semi-precious carnelian and crystal quartz. See INCOLAY STUDIOS, **(84-I.57-0.0)**.

INLAID Decoration on a plate created by etching, incising or engraving a design on the surface and filling with another material.

INTAGLIO Decoration created by cutting beneath the surface of the plate. See ENGRAVED DESIGN, ETCHED DESIGN.

IRIDESCENCE A rainbow effect on a plate's surface caused by the diffraction of light. True iridescent color effects are readily distinguished from a plate's inherent color because the pattern will change as the plate is moved. Example: BELLEEK plates **(26-B.18-0.0)**.

ISSUE 1. The release for sale of an edition of plates by a maker. 2. A plate in an edition. 3. An edition within a series.

ISSUE PRICE Original or first price of plate established by the maker at the time the plate is released for sale.

J

JASPER WARE Hard, fine-grained, unglazed stoneware made by adding barium sulfate to clay, developed by Josiah Wedgwood in the 1770s. The term "jasper" does not indicate the presence of jasper stone but most likely denotes the varieties of colors in which Jasper ware can be produced. Though white in its original form, Jasper ware can be stained in blue, green, lilac, yellow, maroon, or black to serve as a background for embossments of white Jasper relief for a cameo effect. When stained throughout the body of it is

called *solid Jasper ware*. Example: Wedgwood plates **(26-W.90-0.0)**.

K

KAOLIN The only clay which yields a white material when fired and the indispensable element of porcelain and china plates. Also called *true clay* or *china clay*, it is formed by the complete decomposition by weathering of feldspar. Kaolin is a refractory clay which can be fired at high temperatures without deforming. It produces a vitreous, translucent ceramic when fired with fluxes (fusible rocks) such as feldspar. The components of kaolin clay are 50% silica, 33% alumina, 2% oxides, 1% magnesia, 2% alkali, and 12% water. See CHINA CLAY, TRUE CLAY.

KPM The trademark on plates from Konigliche Porzellan Manufaktur, Meissen, Germany. Plates made by this manufacturer date from as early as 1723.

L

LEAD CRYSTAL Extremely transparent fine quality glass, also called *flint glass* and *lead glass*, which contains a high proportion of lead oxide to give extra weight, better refractiveness, and a clear ringing tone when tapped. *Full lead crystal* identifies glass with a 24% or greater lead content. Example: Lalique **(18-L.3-0.0)** plates. See CRYSTAL.

LIMITED-EDITION PLATES Plates produced in a fixed quantity, either predetermined or determined by a specific period of production. All true collector's plates are in limited editions.

LIMOGES A town in south central France famous for its porcelain production because of the discovering of nearby kaolin deposits in 1768. Limoges porcelain manufacturers have joined together to enforce quality standards. Examples: D'Arceau-Limoges **(18-D.15-0.0)**, Haviland **(18-H.6-0.0)**, Haviland Parlon **(18-H.8-0.0)**, and Limoges-Turgot **(18-L.52-0.0)**.

LISTED PLATE A plate listed and regularly quoted on the Bradford Exchange. See OVER-THE-COUNTER PLATE.

LOT A number of plates, all in the same edition and represented by a self order on the exchange, usually on the secondary market and not at issue. See ALLOTMENT.

LUSTER Decoration applied to a plate surface by application of metallic oxides such as gold, silver, platinum, or copper over the glaze. When gently fired, this leaves a thin metallic film.

M

MAJOLICA, MAIOLICA Earthenware finished with opaque white enamel, similar to *Faience* and *Delftware*, but first made in the Spanish island of Majorca. See DELFTWARE.

MAKER The name by which a plate is known or under which it is issued, e.g., manufacturer, distributor or sponsor. In most cases the "maker" is the actual manufacturer, i.e., Bing and Grøndahl **(14-B.36-0.0)**. However, it can also be a commissioner or distributor, e.g., Schmid **(22-S.12-0.0)**, using a trade name, while the physical production is in fact done by a sub-contractor.

MARKET The structure within which plates are bought and sold. The *primary market* consists of new issues which are sold by the makers or their sales representatives to dealers and distributors. Dealers and distributors in turn normally sell the new issues to the public at issue price. The *secondary market* or *after-market* is the buying and selling of plates previously sold, and usually sold out, on the primary market. In many cases secondary market prices are higher than those of the primary market. See SECONDARY MARKET.

MARKET BRADEX A kind of "Dow Jones" index of the overall collector's plate market expressed as a percentage, determined by the current price/issue ratio of 12 key series.

MARKET PRICE The price at which a plate is currently traded regardless of its issue price. See ISSUE PRICE.

MARKET PRICE ORDER An open bid posted on the exchange to purchase a top advancing issue at the price the market demands.

MEISSEN See DRESDEN.

MINT CONDITION A plate in new or like-new condition accompanied by any original certificates and packing materials included at issue.

MODELING The process of making the original pattern from which the master mold is made for a sculptured plate.

MOLD A general term for the form which gives a plate its shape. Clay, metal or glass is pressed into a mold to form a *blank* (without ornamentation). Intaglio decoration or rasied ornamentation may also be formed in the mold. China or porcelain *slip-casting* is done in plaster of paris molds. Slip (diluted clay formula) is poured into the mold, and the excess water is absorbed into the plaster of paris. See SLIP.

O

OPEN-END SERIES A continuing series of annual plates with no established termination. Example: Royal Copenhagen Christmas series **(14-R.59-1.0)**. See CLOSED-END SERIES.

OPEN STOCK Plates available in or produced in unlimited numbers or for an unlimited time period (and therefore not considered collector's plates).

OVER-THE-COUNTER PLATE A collector's plate occasionally traded directly between specialized dealers but not listed on the exchange and not normally traded through it. See LISTED PLATE.

P

PARIAN CHINA A highly vitrified, translucent china characterized by an iridescent luster and rich, creamy tint much like that of parian marble for which it is named. The process for parian ware was invented by the Copeland and Garrett firm in England in the mid-nineteenth century. See BELLEEK, **(26-B.18-0.0)**.

PASTE The combination of substances that make up potter's clay, generally that for porcelain or china.

PEWTER An alloy of tin with copper and antimony as hardeners. The greater the amount of copper and antimony, the harder the ware. *Fine pewter* is composed of 80% tin and 20% antimony and brass or copper. Examples: International **(84-I.61-0.0)** and Royal Worcester (U.S.A.) **(84-R.76-0.0)** plates. See ALLOY.

POINT, BRADEX POINT One percentage point of the Market Bradex.

PORCELAIN The hardest vitreous ceramic fired at the highest temperatures. Although the term *porcelain* is often interchanged with *china*, true porcelain as the term is used in the field is distinguished from china by its very high glaze firing and low bisque firing temperature compared with the high bisque firing and low glaze firing of china. The main firing (glaze) of porcelain is approximately 7% higher than the main firing (bisque) of china. The glaze fuses with the porcelain plate body and produces an extremely hard surface. *Hard-paste* or *true porcelain* is made from a formula whose primary components are kaolin and china stone (petuntse). When fired, the china stone vitrifies, producing a hard, glassy ceramic. True porcelain is translucent when thin, white unless colored, impervious to scratching, and transmits a ringing tone when struck. A typical porcelain formula is 50% kaolin, 25% quartz, and 25% feldspar. *Soft-paste porcelain* was developed in Renaissance Europe in an attempt to imitate the true porcelain of China. Soft-paste porcelain was a mixture of white sand, gypsum, soda, alum, salt, and niter, fired until it vitrified. It had a soft texture, great sensitivity to sudden temperature changes, was warmer to the touch than true porcelain, and could be scratched with a file. The terms "hard" and "soft" porcelain refer to the "hard" firing temperature (around 1450°C) required for true porcelain and the "soft" firing temperatures (around 1150°C) used for soft-paste porcelain. See CHINA.

POTTERY 1. A general term used for all ceramic ware but strictly speaking for earthenware and non-vitrified ceramics. 2. The place or kilns where ceramic objects are fired.

Q

QUEEN'S WARE An earthenware of ivory or cream color developed by Josiah Wedgwood. The name "Queen's Ware" was adopted by other potters for similar stoneware; also often referred to as "white ware."

QUOTE The current market value and selling price of a collector's plate on the exchange.

R

RELIEF SCULPTURE Sculpture in which the design or figure is not free-standing but is raised from a background. There are three degrees of relief sculpture: *Alto-relievo* or high relief, where the design is almost detached from the background; *Basso-relievo* or bas-relief, where the design is raised somewhat; and *Relievo-stiacciato*, where the design is scarcely more than scratched. Relief designs on plates may be formed in the plate mold or formed separately and applied to the plate body.

S

SECOND, SECOND SORTING A plate judged to be a grade below first quality, usually indicated by a scratch or gouge through the glaze over the backstamp on the back.

SECONDARY MARKET See MARKET.

SELL ORDER An offer at an asked price given by an individual or dealer to sell one or more plates of the same edition on the secondary market, usually on the exchange. See LOT.

SLIP Ceramic paste or body diluted with water to a smooth, creamy consistency used for *slip-casting*. See MOLD.

STEATITE, SOAPSTONE A natural rock whose primary component is talc. Steatite is used in porcelain formulas as a flux.

STERLING SILVER An alloy which, by United States law, must have the minimum fineness of 92.5% by weight of pure silver and a maximum of 7.5% by weight of a base metal, usually copper. Example: Franklin Mint plates (84-F.64-0.0).

STONEWARE A hard ceramic fired to vitrification but not to translucency. Typical components of stoneware are 30% ball clay, 32% kaolin, 15% flint, and 23% cornish stone. Example: Wedgwood's Jasper ware plates (26-W.90-0.0).

SUPERMARKET PLATE Common term for a plate edition of dubious limitations, cheaply produced, and not considered a true collector's plate.

T

TERRA COTTA A general term for any kind of fired clay. Strictly speaking, terra cotta is an earthenware produced from a clay which fires to a dull ochre or red color. The ware, left unglazed, is coarse and porous. Example: Veneto Flair plates (38-V.22-0.0).

TIN GLAZE A glaze colored white by oxide of tin which produces a heavy opaque surface when fired. See DELFT-WARE.

TORIART The process by which wood shavings and resin are combined forming a wood material which is then molded and carved into three-dimensional forms. Example: Anri (38-A.54-0.0).

TRANSLUCENT The quality of transmitting light without transparence. In a plate, translucency depends on the quality of the china or porcelain, thickness of the plate, and firing temperature. Underfired porcelain is not translucent.

TRIPTYCH A set of three panels hinged side by side, bearing paintings or carvings usually on a religious theme; used as a portable altarpiece.

TRUE CLAY See KAOLIN.

U

UNDERGLAZE DECORATION Decoration applied after a plate has been fired once (bisque fired) but before it is glazed and fired a second time. Underglaze painting is most commonly done in cobalt blue pigment (although other colors can be used) because this is the most stable color and can withstand high firing temperatures. *"True underglaze technique"* means such painting was done by hand.

V

VITRIFICATION A fusion of potters clay at temperatures between 1250°C and 1450°C, to form a glassy, nonporous substance. With continued heating, the substance will become translucent.

INDEX OF BRADEX-LISTED
PLATE MAKERS AND SPONSORS

NOTE: "Maker" is a general term for the name under which a plate is issued which is not necessarily the actual "manufacturer." A Maker can be a distributor, manufacturer, or occasionally a "sponsor." See GLOSSARY OF COMMONLY USED TERMS.

Alboth . . . . See Kaiser
Alvarez . . . . See Santa Clara
Anri 38-A.54-0.0
Anna-Perenna 22-A.3-0.0
Arabia 16-A.69-0.0
Artists of the World 84-A.72-0.0
L'Association l'Esprit
 de Lafayette . . . . See D'Arceau-Limoges

B & G . . . . See Bing & Grondahl
Bareuther 22-B.7-0.0
 See also Danish Church
Belleek 26-B.18-0.0
Berlin Design 22-B.20-0.0
Beswick, John Potteries . . . . See Royal Doulton
Bing & Grøndahl 14-B.36-0.0

Giuseppe Cappe . . . . See King's
Carborundum Company . . . . See Spode
Chambre Syndicale de la
 Couture Parisienne . . . . See D'Arceau-Limoges
W. T. Copeland & Sons, Ltd. . . . See Spode
Creative World . . . . See Veneto Flair

Danish Church 22-D.5-0.0
D'Arceau-Limoges 18-D.15-0.0
Désirée . . . . See Svend Jensen
Dresden 22-D.68-0.0

Eslau . . . . See Grande Copenhagen

Fairmont 84-F.4-0.0
Franklin Mint 84-F.64-0.0
Fukagawa 42-F.78-0.0
Fürstenberg 22-F.82-0.0

Goebel 22-G.54-0.0
Gorham 84-G.58-0.0
 See also Royal Devon
Grande Copenhagen 14-G.65-0.0
Dave Grossman Designs 42-G.74-0.0

Haviland 18-H.6-0.0
Haviland Parlon 18-H.8-0.0
Hibel Studio 22-H.31-0.0
Hummelwerk . . . . See Goebel
Hutschenreuther . . . . See Schmid (Germany)

Incolay Studios 84-I.31-0.0
International 84-I.61-0.0

Jasper ware . . . . See Wedgwood
Svend Jensen 14-J.21-0.0

Kaiser 22-K.4-0.0
Kern Collectibles 84-K.20-0.0

King's 38-K.32-0.0
Kirke Platten . . . . See Danish Church
Edwin M. Knowles 84-K.41-0.0
 See also Rockwell Society
Königszelt Bavaria 22-K.46-0.0

Lafayette Society . . . . See D'Arceau-Limoges
Lalique 18-L.3-0.0
Lenox 84-L.18-0.0
Lihs-Lindner 22-L.31-0.0
Limoges-Turgot 18-L.52-0.0
Lladró 72-L.41-0.0

Lotus Ware . . . . See Edwin M. Knowles

Museo Teatrale alla Scala . . . . See di Volteradici

Orrefors 76-O.74-0.0

Pickard 84-P.29-0.0
 See also Kern Collectibles
Porcelana Granada 4-P.61-0.0
Porcellanas Verbano . . . . See Porcelana Granada
Porcellanzfabrik Tirschenreuth . . See Dresden
Porsgrund 54-P.62-0.0

R.C. . . . . See Royal Copenhagen
Reco International 84-R.17-0.0
Reed & Barton 84-R.18-0.0
RiverShore Ltd. 84-R.69-0.0
Rockwell Society of America 84-R.70-0.0
Rogers Brothers . . . . See International
Rorstrand 76-R.54-0.0
Rosenthal 22-R.55-0.0
Roskilde Church . . . . See Danish Church
Royal Bayreuth 22-R.58-0.0
Royal Copenhagen 14-R.59-0.0
Royal Devon 84-R.60-0.0
Royal Doulton 26-R.62-0.0
Royal Tettau . . . . See Royal Bayreuth
Royal Worcester . . . . (G.B.) 26-R.76-0.0
 (U.S.) 84-R.76-0.0

Santa Clara 72-S.6-0.0
La Scala . . . . See di Volteradici
Schmid . . . . (Ger.) 22-S.12-0.0
 (Jap.) 42-S.12-0.0
Silbermann Brothers . . . . See Kaiser
Spode 26-S.63-0.0

Veneto Flair 38-V.22-0.0
Verbano . . . . See Porcelana Granada
Viletta 84-V.36-0.0
di Volteradici, Studio Dante 38-V.90-0.0

Wedgwood 26-W.90-0.0

INDEX OF PLATE TITLES AND SERIES BY TYPE

NOTE: Plate titles are listed in alphabetical order and enclosed in quotation marks:
"Aabenraa Marketplace" . . . . **14-R.59-1.14.**

Types of series are listed in bold face with individual makers indented and listed below:
Anniversary
Goebel *(Hummel)* . . . . . . **22-G.54-3.1.**

A-10

INDEX OF PLATE ARTISTS

The editors acknowledge with gratitude the invaluable supplementary information supplied by:

Anna-Perenna, Inc.
Klaus Vogt

Arabia of Finland
Kurt Pousar

Armstrong's
Dave Armstrong

Artists of the World
James LaFond

Bing & Grøndahl Copenhagen Porcelain, Inc.
Joan Doyle
Jorgen Sannung

Creative World, Ltd.
Richard Gabbe

D'Arceau-Limoges
Gerard Boyer

Downs
Deborah Magnuson
Joan Russo

Ebeling & Reuss
A. L. Goeldner

Fairmont China
Thomas W. Hogan

Fisher, Bruce & Co.
Thomas Moleski

Fukagawa Porcelain Manufacturing Ltd.
K. Nishiyama

Gorham Division of Textron, Inc.
Roy Moffett

Dave Grossman Designs
Steven B. Weinreich

Hackett American Collectors Co.
James Hackett

The Hamilton Mint
Melanie Hart

Haviland & Co., Inc.
Richard Coyle

Hibel Studios
William Hibel

Hummelwerk
James P. Kelly

Helmut H. Lihs Imports
Helmut H. Lihs

International Silver Co.
Cindy Haskins

Jacques Jugeat, Inc.
Lloyd Glasgow

J.A.R. Publishers
William Hibel

Joy's Limited
Helene Dunn
Susan Jones

Kaiser Porcelain Co.
Hubert E. W. Kaiser

Kern Collectibles
Matthew P. Brummer

Kosta Boda U.S.A. Ltd.
Raymond Zrike

Lenox China Co.
Karen Cohen

Nielsen Import Co.
Jon Nielsen

Pemberton & Oakes
John Hugunin

Pickard China Co.
Henry Pickard
Suzanne Quigley
Larry D. Smith

Porcelana Granada
Trudy Fennell

Rasmussen Import Co.
R. D. Rasmussen

Reco International Corp.
Brigetta Moore
Heio Reich

Reed & Barton
Patrice Johnson

RiverShore Ltd.
Richard Spiegel

Rosenthal U.S.A. Limited
Lilie Mahlab

Royal Copenhagen Porcelain Corp.
Ivar Ipsen
Hans W. Harbou

Royal Doulton & Co.
Christopher McGillivary

Royal Worcester/Spode
Joyce Hendlewich

Schmid
Richard Acton
JoAnne Kennedy

Svend Jensen
Per Jensen
Erik Larsen

Trein's
Gordon Brantley

Viking Import House, Inc.
Pat Owen

Viletta China Co.
Tom O'Meara

Wara Intercontinental Co.
Walter A. Rautenberg

Waterford Glass Inc.
Dick Oster

Wedgwood, Incorporated
Ann Bierbower
Harvey Dondero

Weil Ceramics & Glass, Inc.
Charles Morgan